Performance Coaching

Performance Coaching

A complete guide to best practice coaching and training

Carol Wilson

KoganPage

LONDON PHILADELPHIA NEW DELHI

First published in Great Britain and the United States in 2007 by Kogan Page Limited as Best Practice in Performance Coaching
Paperback edition, 2011
Second edition, 2014, as Performance Coaching

2nd Floor, 45 Gee Street	1518 Walnut Street, Suite 1100	4737/23 Ansari Road
London EC1V 3RS	Philadelphia PA 19102	Daryaganj
United Kingdom	USA	New Delhi 110002
		India

www.koganpage.com

© Carol Wilson, 2014

The right of Carol Wilson to be identified as the author of this work has been asserted by her in accordance with the Copyright, Designs and Patents Act 1988.

ISBN: 978 0 7494 7031 9
E-ISBN: 978 0 7494 7032 6

British Library Cataloguing-in-Publication Data

A CIP record for this book is available from the British Library.

Library of Congress Cataloging-in-Publication Data

Wilson, Carol.
 [Best practice in performance coaching]
 Performance coaching : a complete guide to best practice coaching and training / Carol Wilson.
  pages cm
 Earlier edition published as: Best practice in performance coaching : a handbook for leaders, coaches, HR professionals and organizations.
  ISBN 978-0-7494-7031-9 — ISBN 978-0-7494-7032-6 (ebk) 1. Employees—Coaching of. 2. Performance. 3. Mentoring in business. I. Title.
  HF5549.5.C53W55 2014
  658.3'124—dc3
                                                                            2013033898

Typeset by Amnet
Printed and bound in India by Replika Press Pvt Ltd

CONTENTS

About the author xvi
Foreword by Sir John Whitmore xviii
Foreword by Sir Richard Branson xx
Acknowledgements xxii

PART ONE The fundamentals of performance coaching 1

Introduction 1

01   **What is coaching?** 3
      Origins of the term 'coaching' 3
      The principles of coaching 6
      Types of coaching 8

02   **The differences between coaching, therapy, counselling, mentoring and consultancy** 10
      Coaching 11
      Therapy: psychiatry, psychology and psychotherapy 12
      Counselling 13
      Mentoring 13
      Consultancy 14
      Comparisons 14

03   **The directive–non-directive continuum** 16
      Resisting the urge to offer solutions 16
      The differences between coaching and mentoring 17
      Clean coaching 17
      The client's demands 18
      Advice from Association for Coaching members 22
      The coaching–mentoring–management continuum 23

04   Self-limiting beliefs 25

Formation of self-limiting beliefs 25
Challenging self-limiting beliefs 26

05   Coaching and neuroscience 28

Neuroscience and bullying 28
Goal-setting 29
Positive feedback and learning 29
Self-directed learning 30
Insights 30
Multi-tasking 31

PART TWO Creating a coaching culture in organizations 33

Introduction 33

06   The meaning of a coaching culture 35

The coaching culture at Virgin 35
The pillars of a coaching culture 37
Other examples of coaching cultures 40

07   Ten steps to creating a coaching culture 42

The ten-step plan 42
Kent County Council's South East Coaching and
    Mentoring Network 46

08   Coaching in the workplace 47

Uses for coaching in the workplace 47
Internal coaching 49
External coaching 49
Coachable moments 50
Speed coaching in industry 51

09   Coach training in the workplace 52

How to choose a coach training supplier 52
The length and depth of coach training 53

Training coaches at the BBC 54
Training the coach trainer at IKEA 55

10   Coaching in leadership 57

Identifying the traits of leadership 57
Coaching skills vs behaviour and attitude 59
Transformational Leadership Programme at CLM 2012 Olympic
    Delivery Partner 60
Leadership and coaching in the arts sector 61
Coaching a senior team leader in a multinational organization 63

11   Cross-cultural coaching 65

What are cultural differences? 65
Cultural differences in team roles 67
Coach training for sales leaders at a global business services
    organization 69
Creating a global coaching culture 71
Insights in Finland 72
Cross-cultural differences across roles 72

12   Coaching in schools 74

The alignment of coaching with learning 74
A coaching programme for North Somerset schools 76
Coach training for teachers in Hong Kong 79
Coaching adolescents 81

13   Coaching for Crisis at Christmas 83

**14   Corporate social responsibility and shared value:
        bringing business and society back together** 86

What is corporate social responsibility? 86
Organizations who care 88
Shared value 89
The emergence of the 'social enterprise' 91

15   Bullying in the workplace 95

Bullying: nature or nurture? The neural perspective 95
Reforming the bully 98

Coaching the accidental bully 99
How to cope with being bullied 100

16   Resilience in leadership 103

What is resilience? 103
Resilience in leaders 104
What makes a resilient organization? 105
Developing resilience 106

**17   Coaching supervision: a workplace
perspective** 108

Differences between traditional and coaching
    supervision 108
Supervision in therapy 109
Coaching supervision in the workplace 110
What to do in a coaching supervision session 113
Types and frequency of supervision 115
Credentials of the coaching supervisor 116

**18   ROI: Measuring the return on investment
in coaching** 117

Planning 118
How to get quantifiable results from surveys 119
Leveraging feedback 121
Leveraging research 122
Measuring the value of coaching at OFGEM 122
Conclusion 126

PART THREE Skills for coaches and managers 127

Introduction 127

19   Listening 129

The five levels of listening 129
The power of listening 131
Non-verbal signals 132

20   Reflecting, summarizing and clarifying 134

Reflecting 135
Summarizing 135
Clarifying 136
Benefits 136

21   Questioning 138

Open and closed questions 139
Beware of judgemental questions 139
Beware of leading questions 140
Beware of multiple questions 142
The significance of silence 142

22   Permission protocol 144

Permission as a tool 144
Permission protocol 145
When is permission not permission? 147
Permission and the need for control 147

23   The GROW coaching model 149

The history of GROW 149
Practical application 150
Flexibility of GROW 154

**24   The EXACT model: a coaching approach
to goal setting** 155

The EXACT goal-setting model 155
Comparison between EXACT and SMART goals 156
How to set a goal 158
Goal setting with teams 161
Conclusion 162

25   Coaching feedback 163

Why feedback models don't work 163
Eliciting self-feedback 164

Relationship to the GROW model 165
General feedback guidelines 169

26   **The structure of coaching** 173

The coaching contract 173
Structure of a coaching session 174
Structure for a series of coaching sessions 175

27   **Setting and reviewing actions** 178

Exploring the 'Will' part of GROW 178
Setting actions 178
Reviewing actions 181

PART FOUR Tools of the trade: continuing
professional development 185

Introduction 185

28   **David Grove's Clean Language** 187

History and principles of Clean Language 187
Metaphor 188
Traumatic memory 189
Clean Language questions 190
Reflecting words back 191
Clean conversations 193
Clean Language in coaching 194
Clean Language at the BBC 197
Grovian techniques in industry 198
Research into Clean Language 200

29   **David Grove's Emergent Knowledge** 201

Clean Space 202
Principles of Emergent Knowledge 203
Science of Emergence 204
Small world networks 205
Emergent Knowledge processes 206

Clean Language and Emergent Knowledge for BBC
    internal coaches 209
Emergent Knowledge in one-to-one coaching 213

30   Transpersonal Coaching 216

Origins of transpersonal psychology 216
Sub-personalities 216
Transcript of a coaching session by
    Sir John Whitmore 217
Commentary by Sir John Whitmore 225

31   An introduction to neuro-linguistic programming 228

The origins of NLP 228
NLP processes 229
NLP at work 239
Conclusion 240

32   Systemic Coaching 241

Systems in families, teams and communities 241
Knock-on effect of change 241
Repetition of childhood behaviour 242
Coaching the organization 243
Systems theory, cybernetics, family systems theory, complexity
    theory and chaos theory 244
Systemic Coaching in the public sector 244

33   Transactional Analysis and the OK Corral 248

Social transactions 248
The states of parent, child and adult 248
Changing behaviour 249
Franklyn Ernst's OK Corral 250

34   360-degree feedback 253

The process 253
Pitfalls 255
Coaching the results 255
Alternatives 257

35   The Reuven Bar-On Emotional Quotient inventory (BarOn EQ-i) 258

History 258
The five elements 259
Validity safeguards 259
Emotional intelligence in the IT department 261

36   Thomas-Kilmann Conflict Mode Instrument 264

Dealing with conflict 264
Using the TKI 266
Pitfalls of using the TKI 267
The conflict continuum 268
The TKI at work 269

37   Marshall Rosenberg's 'Non-Violent Communication' 272

Exploring conflict 272
Finding the compromise 273

38   Situational Leadership 275

Origination by Blanchard and Hersey: the original
    quadrants 275
Blanchard's revised quadrants 276
Delivering all types of leadership in a coaching style 277
Situational Leadership and Japanese hierarchy 278

39   Kouzes and Posner: The Leadership Challenge 282

Development by Kouzes and Posner 282
The five elements 283

40   Cultural Transformation Tools 286

Origination by Richard Barratt 286
The Seven Levels of Consciousness 286
Identifying values 287
Building a values-driven organization in IT services 291

41   The Inner Game 294

Timothy Gallwey's background 294
The inner opponent 294
The Work Triangle 296
Non-judgemental awareness 297
Self-directed learning 297
The Inner Game in team building 298

42   Nancy Kline's Thinking Environment 302

Origins of the Thinking Environment 302
The 10 components of a Thinking
    Environment 303
The Thinking Session 304
The Incisive Question 305
The power of listening 306
The Thinking Partnership in action 307

43   Appreciative Inquiry 310

Origins of Appreciative Inquiry 310
The four stages of Discovery, Dream, Design and
    Destiny 311
Appreciative Inquiry in the United Arab Emirates 314

44   Mindfulness 318

History of mindfulness 318
Relaxation exercises 319
Mindfulness in yoga and other practices 319
Mindfulness in conflict 320
Mindfulness questions 320
Mindfulness at work 321

**45   Elizabeth Kubler Ross's Change Curve six
    stage model** 325

The six stages of the Change Curve 325

46   Bruce Tuckman's 'forming, storming, norming and performing' team development model 327

The four elements of team development 327
Addition of 'adjourning' 328
Additions of 'mourning' and 'dorming' 328
Recommendations for teams and team leaders 329

47   The Myers-Briggs Type Indicator (MBTI®) 332

Jung's archetypes 332
Development by Isabel Myers and Katherine Briggs 333
The 16 personality types 333
The difference between extraversion and introversion 334
MBTI in team development 336

48   The Enneagram 338

Ancient history 338
The nine types 338
Differentiating core values from personality traits 339
Manifestation of types 341

49   Kolb's learning styles 342

Background 342
The learning styles quadrants 342
The four preferences 343
Learning styles at work 344

50   DISC 347

The four types 347
William Moulton Marston's instigation of behavioural science 347
Comparison with Jung's archetypes and MBTI personality types 349
DISC in team building 350

51   Johari Window 354

Development by Joseph Luft and Harry Ingham 354
The four quadrants 355

Dangers of public feedback 355
Team development with the Johari Window 358

52   More team role models 363

Belbin's Team Role Inventory 363
FIRO-B (Fundamental Interpersonal Relations Orientation) 364
Nigel Risner's animal types 364
Conclusion about team models 365
The case against learning styles 366

Conclusion 369
References 371
Index 376

ABOUT THE AUTHOR

International speaker, writer and broadcaster Carol Wilson is Managing Director of Performance Coach Training, which she founded with Sir John Whitmore, a Member of the Global Advisory Panel to the Association for Coaching, a Fellow of the Professional Speaking Association, a Member of the Global Speakers Federation and a Trustee of the MOE Foundation for youth leadership.

She experienced the value of a coaching culture at first hand while working at board level with Sir Richard Branson during the first decade of Virgin. After founding Virgin Music Publishers and elevating it to the position of the third most successful music publishing company in the United Kingdom, Carol became the first woman in the world to found her own chart-topping record label. Called Dindisc, this label today generates over one million pages on Google. Subsequently, Carol held corporate board-level positions at PolyGram, Island, WEA and Pinnacle. While discovering and working with many artists such as Sting, Martha & The Muffins, The Human League, Tom Petty and Orchestral Manoeuvres in The Dark, Carol found her greatest satisfaction was in developing staff and artists to reach their full potential.

Carol designs and, through her team of international trainers, delivers coaching and leadership programmes all over the world and in all languages for corporate, public sector and charitable organizations. She is a cross-cultural specialist with multicultural groups and won the 'Change Leader of Tomorrow' award from Thought Leaders in Mumbai, and was nominated for 'Influence in Coaching' and 'Impact in Coaching' by the Association for Coaching. Her article 'Developing a Coaching Culture' was chosen as a Highly Commended Award Winner at the Literati Network Awards for Excellence 2012. She is a contributing author to *Excellence in Coaching: The Industry Guide*, *The Handbook of Knowledge Based Coaching*, *Essential Life Coaching Skills* and *The Handbook of Coaching and Feedback*, an internal publication at IKEA. She has published over 50 articles in a wide range of publications, including a monthly column for *Training Journal*.

Carol partnered David Grove, the founder of Clean Language, in defining his therapeutic Emergent Knowledge techniques into methods suitable for coaches and similar practitioners. She is currently completing a doctorate in Grovian techniques at Middlesex University and a book on Grove's life and work.

At The Ministry of Entrepreneurship (MOE Foundation) Carol designs and delivers coach training programmes for young people who have had challenging lives.

www.coachingcultureatwork.com
www.performancecoachtraining.com
www.cleancoaching.com
www.associationforcoaching.com
www.moefoundation.com

Carol Wilson holds positions in the following organizations:

FOREWORD BY
SIR JOHN WHITMORE

I must begin by acknowledging my bias. I know Carol well, have experienced her delivery of coaching, and I admire her track record with Richard Branson at Virgin, with the Association for Coaching, and elsewhere. Furthermore it is largely because of all this that she now works with me at Performance Consultants International. It is therefore fairly obvious that I am going to be upbeat about her contribution to the growing coaching library. However, those that know me are aware that I am not inclined to hold back if I don't like something. To make that more credible I have been looking for something to criticize about this book, but after several readings I have failed.

Starting to read another book is always a bit of a struggle because I am goal oriented and the beginning is always too far from the end. The first few pages are always accompanied by the thought, 'Do I really need to read this?' coursing round another part of my brain, before I get into it. This did not occur this time and I found myself in Chapter 3 before I knew it.

Ah! here is the error. In that chapter, she attributes the GROW model coaching sequence to me. However I was just the first person to publish it, in my book *Coaching for Performance*. It originally emerged in a discussion between several coaches with whom I was working at the time, including Graham Alexander, in the McKinsey office in London, and it has been in the public domain ever since. This is worth mentioning because unlike so many coaches who get fixated by GROW, Carol rightly places awareness, responsibility and self-belief at the top of her seven principles of coaching. GROW is no more or less than an easy to remember and useful sequence for a coaching conversation to follow.

Carol gives us another such model, EXACT, which she prefers, as do I, to the overused and incomplete SMART for goal setting. She goes on to explore the structure of a coaching relationship, the training of coaches and the pleasures and pitfalls of setting up a coaching practice. She ends the main text with a chapter on coaching in organizations. All of this essential information to a new or practising coach, or to a potential client, is very easy to absorb largely because she provides numerous coaching dialogue examples, plenty of headings and quotations to break it up visually, some exercises at the end of each chapter, and it ends with 18 pages of seriously useful appendices.

This is the best coaching starter kit I have come across to date, but it goes beyond mere starting to provide a real understanding of the depth of coaching in a very practical readable way. Thank you, Carol. I am glad to have you on board, and I hope this book will attract more to join us, as well as enriching existing fellow travellers on the coaching express that is charging through the world of work.

Sir John Whitmore

Sir John Whitmore is executive chairman of Performance Consultants International Ltd. A pre-eminent thinker in leadership and organizational change, John has personally trained some of the leading organizations in the world, such as McKinsey, Deloitte, Pricewaterhouse Coopers, Barclays, Lloyds, Rolls-Royce, British Airways, Novo Nordisk and Roche. He has produced and directed a feature film, and performed in many guises on radio and television and on conference platforms.

One of John's greatest achievements is to have founded the groundbreaking 'Be The Change' conferences that are held in London each May, to bring together the top minds in the world to discuss sustainability, environmental and social issues, and geo-political change.

John has written five books on sports, leadership and coaching, of which Coaching for Performance *is the best known, having been translated into 19 languages.*

Sir John Whitmore
Executive Chairman
Performance Consultants International
Tel: +44 (0)20 7373 6431
Email: johnwhitmore@performanceconsultants.com

FOREWORD BY SIR RICHARD BRANSON

When I started Virgin, none of us had worked anywhere else so we didn't know how managers were 'supposed' to behave. We approached it like everything in our lives at the time; it had to be lots of fun and we chose our staff the way we chose our friends – on gut instinct. It was like a family and we partied and went on holiday together all the time.

Not much has changed in that respect – it has just got bigger, and the great thing about owning an airline is that you can ship 300 people across the world to a party. In Carol's day, it was more like eight of us in a ski chalet where the hot water ran out before everyone had showered. But the main thing was that work had to be fun.

Carol fitted in because her approach was quite similar to mine in a lot of ways; she would always 'come up to the plate' and do whatever needed to be done, whether it meant staying in a studio half the night and attending an 8 am meeting the next morning, or flying to Los Angeles and back on the same day for a breakfast meeting. She was not afraid of trying new things or taking risks. One of the reasons her divisions worked well was because she built strong teams and looked after them. She made a great role model because she was completely passionate about everything she did and I think that, to this day, no other woman in the world has matched her achievement of founding a successful record company.

The way we hired people in the early days was that if their faces fitted, we would find them something to do; qualifications and experience were pretty irrelevant. I think I gave Carol the publishing company to run because she said she didn't want to be a secretary, which was what most women were doing in 1974, and because it was the only job going in Virgin at the time. As far as we knew, it mainly involved filling out copyright forms, but before long she was signing chart-topping acts like Sting and the company was showing up as Top Three in the *Music Week* trade press chart, alongside Warners and CBS. So I suggested we start a record label together and within six months the acts she signed to that were topping the charts as well. That record label pioneered the 'small label within a big label' format that proliferates throughout the record industry today.

Carol shared my view on mistakes being part of the learning curve. Whenever I experience any kind of setbacks, I always pick myself up and try again. I prepare myself to have another stab at things with the knowledge I've gained from the previous failure. My mother always taught me never to look back in regret, but to move on to the next thing. The amount of time that people waste on failures, rather than putting that energy into another project, always amazes me. At Virgin, we allow people freedom to be themselves and we trust them to make the right decisions, and the odd mistake is tolerated. Our people know we value them.

When I see Carol now, writing books and at the top of another profession altogether, it doesn't surprise me at all and I sometimes wonder what we might have achieved if she had stayed at Virgin instead of wanting to spread her wings all those years ago; I used to call her a 'golden girl' because of the people, business and opportunities she attracted to Virgin, and it seems she has not changed at all.

Sir Richard Branson

ACKNOWLEDGEMENTS

For his Foreword I thank Sir John Whitmore, who lit the first beacon at the start of my own journey into coaching, and who, I was delighted to discover as I got to know him, remains an original and maverick thinker. I followed from a distance in the early days, and as I moved closer, the trail led me along some fascinating, powerful and moving pathways.

I am grateful to Sir Richard Branson, without whom I would almost certainly never have run a record company at a time when most working women were chained to typewriters, and whose management skills have been the blueprint for my own and the foundation for this book.

I owe a lot to all of the following people for their contribution to my professional and personal journey over the last 13 years:

- James Wright has been a true friend and trusted colleague, providing support, insight, talent and general all-round brilliance.
- Tracey Woodcock's astonishing efficiency keeps our business wheels turning, coupled with her loyalty and caring approach to all the people we deal with.
- I thank Wendy Oliver for her friendship and exceptional skill as a coach and facilitator, as well as Paul Tabley, Clara Seeger, Liz Macann, Liz Hall, Allard de Jong, David Brown and Les Ronaldson, for their support and contributions, plus all the coaches who have taught me through teaching them and all the coachees who have coached me through coaching them.
- Thanks also to Katherine Tulpa and Alex Szabo, two extraordinary women who created the Association for Coaching, and the mega-talented Darren Robson for the AC and MOE.

I am grateful to the editorial team who have knocked this book into shape through all of its stages:

- Michelle Drapeau at www.thewritingshop.co.uk for her brilliant and creative suggestions while expertly editing this edition, and as a co-writer on the chapters about 'Corporate social responsibility' and 'Resilience in leadership'.
- Steve Breibart (slbreibart@tsocommunication.com), consultant, coach, coach trainer and co-founder of the Coaching Foundation, edited the original version.

- Dr Christopher Tilley, who has proofed, edited and contributed to much of my work over the past six years.
- Elizabeth Eyre (Editor, Training Journal: elizabeth.eyre@training.journal.com) for contributing to the editing of most of Section 4.

Writers who have given their ideas and case studies:

- Dr Clara Seeger (clara@claraseeger.com) for contributions to 'Coaching and neuroscience'.
- Sir John Whitmore and Hetty Einzig for 'Transpersonal Coaching'.
- Nancy Kline (www.timetothink.com) for permission to use the 'Thinking Environment' diagram, and for teaching me more than I knew there was to learn about listening; also Ruth McCarthy, Emily Havers and Stephanie Archer from her team.
- Jonathan Passmore for help with the Harvard-referenced book list.

For case histories (in alphabetical order):

- Alex Feher (alex.feher@bigpond.com) on 'Cultural Transformation Tools'.
- Allard de Jong (allard@allarddejong.com) on 'Coaching a senior team leader in a multinational organization' and 'Coaching the accidental bully'.
- Amanda Bouch (www.amandabouchconsulting.co.uk) on 'Kolb's learning styles'.
- Angela Dunbar (coach@angeladunbar.co.uk) on 'David Grove's Emergent Knowledge'.
- Barry Rogers (Dir.Inspire Mankind Ltd) on 'Cross-cultural coaching'.
- Bev Morton (www.theartofpossibility.co.uk) on 'Coaching and leadership in the arts sector'.
- Caitlin Walker (caitlin@trainingattention.co.uk, www.trainingattention.co.uk) on 'David Grove's Clean Language'.
- Carolyn Pickin (Carolyn@motiv8development.co.uk) on the 'Myers-Briggs Type Indicator (MBTI®)'.
- Coral Ingleton (coral.ingleton@kent.gov.uk) and Serena Cunningham (serena.cunningham@kent.gov.uk) from Kent County Council's South East Coaching & Mentoring Network.
- Darren Robson (www.moefoundation.com, darren@moefoundation.com) on the 'Ministry of Entrepreneurship (MOE)' and the 'Reuven Bar-On EQi'.

- David Fitzgerald (School Development Adviser, English Schools Foundation, Hong Kong, david.fitzgerald@esfcentre.edu.hk) on 'Coaching in schools'.

- Deb Barnard (Deb Barnard MBE (www.relationaldynamics1st.co.uk) on 'Coaching and leadership in the arts sector'.

- Deni Lyall (MD Winning Performance Associates Ltd, deni@ winningperformance.co.uk) on 'NLP'.

- Denise Taylor (Career Psychologist with www.amazingpeople.co.uk) on the 'Thomas-Kilmann Conflict Mode Instrument (TKI)'.

- Fiona Kerr (kerr4u@btinternet.com) on 'DISC'.

- James Wright (www.kidproquo.co.uk)

- Graham Silverthorne (graham.silverthorne@gmail.com) and David Fitzgerald on 'Coaching in schools'.

- John Newton (Head of Learning and Development, State of Flux Limited, john.newton@stateofflux.co.uk) on 'NCR'.

- Lindsay Levin (Managing Partner at Leaders' Quest, www. leadersquest.org), Melanie George and Anna Finn at Leaders Quest (www.leadersquest.org).

- Liz Hall (Coach, mindfulness trainer and editor of *Coaching at Work*, www.mindfulcoaches.org) on 'mindfulness'.

- Liz Macann (liz.macann@gmail.com) for 'Training coaches at the BBC'.

- Lynne Cooper (Managing Partner, www.changeperspectives.co.uk) on 'NLP'.

- Mandy Gutsell (www.knowlimitscoach.com) on 'Systemic Coaching'.

- Matt Somers (www.mattsomers.com) on 'Tim Gallwey's Inner Game'.

- Michael Daly (info@ecam.nu) on 'Appreciative Inquiry'.

- Niran Jiang (MD Institute of Human Excellence, niran@ihexcellence. org) on 'Cultural Transformation Tools'.

- Dr Paul Howard-Jones, Senior Lecturer in Education at the University of Bristol for his quote in 'The case against Learning styles'.

- Paula Sugawara (MD Coaching Services, info@tokyocoach.com, www.tokyoexecutivecoaching.com) on 'Situational leadership'.

- Ruth McCarthy (Think it Through, ruthmccarthy@thinkitthrough. co.uk) on Nancy Kline's 'Thinking Environment'.
- Steve Higgins, Professor of Education at Durham University for his quote in 'The Case against learning styles'.
- Baroness Susan Greenfield for her quote in 'The Case against learning styles'.
- Wendy Oliver (MD Oliver Purnell, wendy@oliverpurnell.co.uk) on 'Measuring the value of coaching at OFGEM'

And my thanks for a long and rewarding relationship go to past and present employees and associates of Kogan Page including my current editor Liz Gooster, Martina O'Sullivan, Viki Williams, Charlotte Atyeo, Martha Fumagalli, Joanne Glover, Kerrisue Morrey, Peter Gill, Susan Curran, Caroline Carr, Sara Marchington, Fiona Dempsey and supreme supremo Helen Kogan.

PART ONE
The fundamentals of performance coaching

Introduction

Coaching is a relatively new profession yet arguably as old as human communication itself. Socrates is sometimes said to be the first coach, because many of the quotes attributed to him display a coaching approach of asking questions instead of giving instructions, for example: 'I cannot teach anybody anything; I can only make them think.'

So how did the skills that we now term 'coaching', which are widely used in management training in organizations across the world, become recognized as an effective method of communication? How does it differ from sports coaching or teaching, the more well-known applications of the word? How did the coaching we teach to managers to motivate their staff become known as 'performance coaching'?

My first chapter explores the broad range of trends, professions and academic disciplines from which the framework of performance coaching has been extracted.

What is coaching?

SUMMARY

- Origins of the term 'coaching'
- The principles of coaching
- Types of coaching

Origins of the term 'coaching'

In the free Western world of the 1950s, a post-war zeitgeist embraced a new sense of optimism, self-responsibility and focus on the future. Over the next three decades, these trends showed up in psychology, business, sport, culture, politics and parenting.

The twentieth century saw rapid developments in the field of psychology. Until the 1940s, psychology focused on identifying problems and fixing what was wrong, notably through the work of Freud and Jung. A major shift then occurred through the work of psychologists such as Abraham Maslow and Fritz Perlz.

Maslow's widely publicized 'hierarchy of needs' (1968), shown on the next page, depicted the stages through which people have to pass in order to reach what Maslow called 'self-actualization', meaning the fulfilment of the best that a person could be in terms of his or her own unique potential (Maslow, 1998).

Maslow chose to study exemplary people such as Albert Einstein rather than mentally ill or neurotic people, writing that: 'The study of crippled, stunted, immature, and unhealthy specimens can yield only a cripple psychology and a cripple philosophy.'

The difference between this approach and what went before is that Maslow looked at what was right about human beings rather than what was wrong. In this lies one of the key principles of coaching: focus on the solution, not the problem.

Maslow's hierarchy of needs

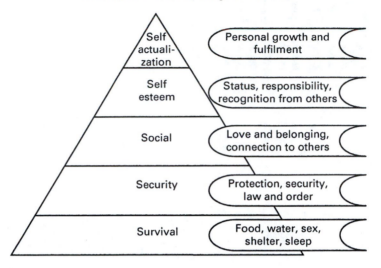

Perls' Gestalt therapy (1951) focused on creating awareness in people. Its principles were:

'Live now, stay in the present
Live here, be with the present
Stop imagining, experience reality
Stop unnecessary thinking
Express, rather than manipulating, explaining, justifying, or judging
Give in to unpleasantness; do not restrict your awareness
Accept no 'should' or 'ought' other than your own
Take full responsibility for your own actions, feelings and thoughts
Surrender to being who you are right now.'

Therein lie the two principles of 'awareness' and 'responsibility', later identified by Sir John Whitmore as the essence of good coaching (Whitmore, 2009).

During the 1980s, solution focused brief therapy (SFBT) (Shazer, 1988) was developed through the collaboration of a number of psychologists including Steve de Shazer and Milton Erickson. As its name infers, SFBT encouraged people to look to the future and take action, rather than analyzing and therefore remaining limited by the past. SFBT's methodology is illustrated by its 'miracle question', of which there exist many variations:

'Suppose our meeting is over, you go home, do whatever you planned to do for the rest of the day. And then, sometime in the evening, you get tired and go to sleep. And in the middle of the night, when you are fast asleep, a miracle happens and all the problems that brought you here today are solved just like that. But since the miracle happened overnight nobody is telling you that the miracle happened. When you wake up the next morning, how are you going to start discovering that the miracle happened? … What else are you going to notice? … What else?'

At the same time as these later developments in psychology, there were extraordinary changes taking place in the field of commerce. Ricardo Semler, for example, turned control of his multi-national organization Semco over to its employees, even allowing people to set their own salaries (Semler, 2001). Andy Law practised a similar style of management when he formed St Luke's Advertising Agency (Law, 1999).

In education, responsibility for learning started to be handed over to the pupils, sometimes at the expense of a formal curriculum.

Meanwhile, whole new areas of personal self-development emerged, encouraging people to create their own solutions for their physical, mental and spiritual health. This trend occurred both in the field of fitness, with the proliferation of gyms and the spread of practices such as yoga, Tai Chi and aerobics, and in personal wellbeing, which spawned a multitude of books starting with Dale Carnegie's 1956 best-seller, *How to Win Friends and Influence People*, and including *Zen and the Art of Motorcycle Maintenance*, *The Female Eunuch*, *The Games that People Play*, *Men are from Mars, Women are from Venus* and numerous guides on how to be happy, including one by the Dalai Lama.

The principles now identified as coaching (which are explored later in this chapter) were evident to some extent in many of these areas and have been particularly identified in the writings of psychologists, especially organizational, over the last 30 years. However, the only direct link between these principles and the word 'coaching' that I have been able to find came from the sports arena, and offers an answer to the question of why the term, with its inappropriate implication of instruction, has been applied at all.

Timothy Gallwey was a Harvard graduate of the 1970s who became captain of the tennis team while on sabbatical. Gallwey noticed that when he left the court, his students tended to improve their game more quickly than when he was there to instruct them. Already a disciple of spirituality and psychology, Gallwey explored this paradox and developed a series of questions, statements and exercises to support the self-teaching process. One of his key actions was to apply 'directionality' – identifying one's goal before starting out (Gallwey, 1986).

During the 1980s, Gallwey's work was embraced by English baronet, Sir John Whitmore, who in 1992 published *Coaching for Performance*, a book now regarded as the 'bible' of coaching and available in 19 languages. Whitmore, the son of a baronet, entered his twenties in the 1960s as a member of the elite British aristocracy and a racing driver who moved in international circles and counted Steve McQueen among his friends. Then he discovered the Esalen Institute in California and his life changed profoundly and acquired a deeper direction. Esalen was founded in 1962 as a series of encounter groups and an extraordinary number of influential thinkers, psychotherapists, spiritual leaders and writers became involved, including Fritz Perls, Carl Rogers, Abraham Maslow, Virginia Satir, Aldous Huxley, Timothy Leary, Arnold Toynbee, Deepak Chopra, RD Laing, Susan Sontag, Joan Baez and Ken Kesey (Wildflower, 2013). Whitmore is quoted as recently saying that Esalen was vital to the development of coaching: 'That time and Esalen were crucial [to the coaching profession] and that is where, in a way, it all started' (Wildflower, 2013).

Whitmore combined this personal development journey with Gallwey's techniques and brought the package to Europe by founding schools for skiing and tennis that used the new approach of self-directed learning. At one point, his team was asked to provide a day of tennis coaching by a large organization that wanted its managers to incorporate the 'Inner Game' approach into their leadership styles. Whitmore termed this 'performance coaching' to differentiate it from conventional sports coaching, and gave his book a similar title.

And this, it seems, is how the term 'coaching', to which the fields of psychology, business and self-development have all contributed so much, originated.

The principles of coaching

There has been some confusion over the application of a word that conventionally means 'instructing' to an area whose guiding principle has been described as 'self-directed learning'. The overall principles of coaching may be summed up as shown in the diagram below.

> *Awareness:* Awareness of self and others is a key aspect of coaching and gives rise to many other benefits. The coach provides a space where clients can uncover knowledge that already lies within, but that may have been obscured by the turmoil of fear, confusion or limitations imposed by other people's agendas.

The principles of coaching

Responsibility: A core principle of coaching is self-responsibility, or taking ownership of our decisions; most people enjoy creating their own solutions rather than being told what to do. In terms of leadership, this means treating people with respect and providing opportunities for development where possible.

Self-belief: There are two components involved in building confidence in people: firstly, allowing them the space to practise, stretch themselves and make mistakes; secondly, giving them recognition for their achievements.

Confidence that we can do something is a key factor in achieving it. Giving people praise builds their belief that they can achieve more and raises the energy required to do that. It is important to remember that all praise must be authentic, specific and deserved, and this will be covered in Chapter 25, 'Coaching feedback'.

Blame free: Children cannot learn to walk without falling over. Imagine what would happen if the child was scolded every time it fell – it would stop trying, and all the potential that might have grown out of that ability to walk (or run or play sport) would be lost. Now apply this to the workplace, schoolroom or family: imagine the potential that might be sacrificed if people are feeling too discouraged to take risks. When mistakes are treated as opportunities for learning, individuals are motivated to try again and profit from experience.

Solution focus: When we dwell on a problem, it seems to get bigger and drains our energy. When we focus on the solution, the problem shrinks and we find we have more energy to deal with it. This is why solution focus works in coaching – and other areas of life.

Challenge: Most people enjoy being challenged and stretched within a supportive and encouraging environment. When they overcome a frightening hurdle like public speaking, or winning a new job, they walk away from the experience with renewed energy and an urge to take action. Coaches and coaching managers know how to provide exactly such an environment.

Action: Coaching uncovers new perspectives and insights for its clients. Coachees who were previously stuck start to see a way forward and are able to delineate a plan of action which was hitherto not apparent.

Trust: Without trust between coach and coachee, no real coaching can take place. Trust is pivotal to the coaching relationship and is one of the most common reasons why some managers can successfully coach their reports and others cannot. While techniques exist which can enhance a sense of rapport in the moment, there are no quick fixes in an ongoing relationship. Managers have to earn the trust of their reports over a period of time. However, if the intention is there, then coaching skills can enable this to happen quite quickly.

Self-directed learning: This is the core principle of coaching and behaving in a coaching style. Coaches believe that people already have the answers they need, but these answers may be hidden, as described in 'Awareness' above. The coach's function is to provide a space where people can think more clearly, look at situations from new perspectives, and uncover inner resources that may have become obscured over time.

Types of coaching

Adding to the confusion around the term 'coaching' is a proliferation of categories, such as executive, business, career or personal coaching. However, these are all based on the above principles. The term 'life coaching' is less in favour now as it has been used to describe forms of personal help (not necessarily any less valuable than coaching) which do not apply these principles.

The process of coaching remains the same regardless of the context. Some coaches tend to emerge from a psychology background and others from business or education; all benefit by being on a continual learning path during which they can learn new models, skills and tools from other disciplines that will enhance their practices.

Happily coaching is no longer limited to the company managers and middle class professionals who can afford to pay for it. Many charities are now hosting coaching programmes, having realized how effective the process can be in helping people to save themselves, and a new type of 'social' business is appearing, where profits are made for the owners while the business is benefiting others. This is explored in Chapter 14 'Corporate social responsibility'.

Coaching programmes are also becoming widespread in education, with many teachers being trained in how to use the skills not only in the classroom but for interpersonal relationships and leadership issues as well. An account of the coaching programme run by the English Schools Foundation in Hong Kong is included in Chapter 12 'Coaching in schools'.

Other specialities have grown from the movements and zeitgeist I mentioned at the beginning of this chapter, such as positive psychology, neurolinguistic programming (itself a collection of tools and models derived from other theories), Appreciative Inquiry, Clean Language (described in Chapter 15 and in Chapter 21, 'Questioning'), Systemic Coaching, cognitive behavioural therapy and mindfulness (described in Chapter 44), which draws on ancient spiritual practices.

Overall, it is easier on the brain to accept and rejoice in the proliferation of ways of helping human beings to be happier, more fulfilled and more productive, than to try to identify a hierarchy of who discovered what first. The field continues to grow, reshaping and redefining itself all the time.

Confusion continues to arise in terms of the semantics used to describe coaching, counselling, mentoring and some similar fields, so I am exploring these in depth in the next chapter.

02

The differences between coaching, therapy, counselling, mentoring and consultancy

SUMMARY

- Coaching
- Therapy: psychiatry, psychology and psychotherapy
- Counselling
- Mentoring
- Consultancy
- Comparisons

Coaching draws on influences from, or the same influences as, a wide range of fields including counselling, leadership skills, sports coaching, personal development and psychology. The history and principles of coaching are explored in depth in Chapter 1, 'What is coaching?'

There are a number of core differences that distinguish coaching from similar areas, such as therapy, counselling, mentoring and consultancy.

Coaching

Coaches work on improving the performance and wellbeing of an individual or group through setting goals, exploring values and beliefs, and facilitating their clients in creating plans of action. This is achieved not by advising or telling, but largely by questioning to enhance awareness and self-directed learning.

Coaching is sometimes split into categories, such as life, executive, team, group and career coaching, but the underlying process is much the same and is sometimes termed 'performance coaching'. Just as the more successful an athlete may be, the more likely he or she is to work with a sports coach, performance coaching is not necessarily about fixing problems but sometimes helps successful individuals and teams to improve further.

The roots of communicating in a coaching style are ancient and, indeed, Socrates is recognized as an early coach, because his philosophy was to question people rather than instruct them:

> 'I am so far like the midwife, that I cannot myself give birth to wisdom; and the common approach is true that, although I question others, I can myself bring nothing to light because there is no wisdom in me. Those who frequent my company at first appear, some of them, quite unintelligent; but, as we go further with our discussions, all who are favoured by heaven make progress at a rate that seems surprising to others as well as to themselves, although it is clear that they have never learned anything from me; the many admirable truths they bring to birth have been discovered by themselves from within.' (Socrates' comment in *Theaetetus* by Plato 360BC)

A more accurate description of coaching would be hard to find. Some people are lucky enough to have been raised in a family where the principals of coaching are habitual, with parents who listen to, encourage and challenge their children to think for themselves. Fortunately, it is also possible to learn these skills later in life. In terms of organizations, good leadership is arguably synonymous with coaching, for the most part because the process of coaching and being coached feels better than telling or being told what to do. It enables people to approach the holy grail of enjoying going to work.

The coaching profession is currently self-regulated, but most coaches undergo some form of training and accreditation, particularly those working with executives in organizations. These training options are explored in Chapter 9 'Coach training in the workplace'. Coaching can be practised either one to one or with groups of any size and is particularly effective in team building. Coaches are expected to work with a coaching supervisor at all times (see Chapter 17, 'Coaching supervision: a workplace perspective') and to update their learning continually with further study and training. University degrees in coaching now proliferate and there are growing numbers of coaches exploring at doctorate level.

Occasionally, emotional baggage may surface during a session and the coach may feel it appropriate to refer the coachee to a counsellor or psychotherapist. However, sometimes the process of coaching is found to be the most effective because of its solution-focused approach. While it is important that boundaries are recognized, it is not necessarily appropriate for the coaching to be replaced by another intervention. My rule of thumb is to have an open discussion with the coachee about whether coaching is the best and safest way forward, and what other options might be available. The final decision is up to the coachee.

Although the control of the process lies with the coach, the content always lies with the client, making the coaching experience an empowering, productive and enjoyable one. It is possible for the coach to introduce suggestions, opinions or information into the process according to the guidelines in Chapter 3, 'The directive–non-directive continuum'.

Coaching can be practised either one to one or with groups of any size and is used with teams to achieve a unified and supportive force. The roots of communicating in a coaching style are ancient and inherent in all people; some are natural coaches who were raised in a coaching atmosphere. For others, it is possible to learn the skills and change their style of communication, hence the growing popularity of coaching in corporate and public organizations.

Whereas 40 years ago a leader's job was to tell subordinates what to do and make sure that they complied, workers today expect more autonomy and thrive on self-responsibility. An effective leader is able to move smoothly between directive and non-directive management, serving his or her subordinates sometimes as a coach, sometimes as a mentor, and where necessary giving orders.

Coaching is a process, like accountancy, and the process remains much the same regardless of which type of coaching is taking place.

Therapy: psychiatry, psychology and psychotherapy

A psychiatrist is a qualified medical doctor with additional training in psychiatry but not necessarily in psychology. A psychiatrist is the only practitioner who can prescribe drugs to treat a mental health condition.

A psychologist will have general training, usually to degree level, plus further training in a specialist field.

A psychotherapist works with deep-seated emotional difficulties and must undergo rigorous training and ongoing supervision.

All of the three categories above usually involve some form of judgement, diagnosis, prescription or advice on the part of the practitioner, whereas such concepts are not part of the coaching philosophy, although occasionally suggestions may be made.

In recent times, basic coaching skills are often included in any kind of psychotherapy training.

Counselling

Counsellors often provide the simple service of 'someone to talk to', particularly in situations of grief, shock or anxiety. There are various levels of training, ranging from short courses to full certification programmes. Sessions can be on a one-off basis, or occurring regularly over months or years.

There are times when people need to come to terms with, say, a recent bereavement, by talking it through, and this is where counselling is more appropriate than any other intervention. Solution-focused techniques are sometimes used in counselling but its function is not necessarily to move the client forward.

Mentoring

A great deal of confusion arises from the various uses of this term. In some organizations 'mentoring' means coaching, as described in this book, whereas a more commonly accepted definition is that mentors are people who impart their own experience, learning and advice to those who are newer to a particular field. In modern business, the practice of delivering mentoring in a coaching style is on the increase and it is regarded as acceptable for coaches to impart advice and share experience, although by observing certain guidelines that maintain the principles of coaching. These are explored in Chapter 3, 'The directive–non-directive continuum'.

Consultancy

'Consultant' is a broad term commonly used to describe anyone who works for an organization at executive level from time to time, but is not actually employed by it, so this category can include external coaches. A consultant is someone who brings outside expertise into the organization in any field, whether setting up computer systems or knowing how to conduct coaching sessions.

Comparisons

A simple analogy with driving a car helps to define the differences between all of the above fields.

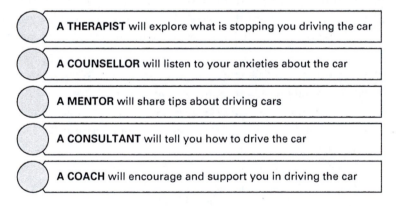

Differences between coaching and other disciplines

A **THERAPIST** will explore what is stopping you driving the car

A **COUNSELLOR** will listen to your anxieties about the car

A **MENTOR** will share tips about driving cars

A **CONSULTANT** will tell you how to drive the car

A **COACH** will encourage and support you in driving the car

As well as coach training courses I am occasionally asked to deliver training in mentoring skills as well, and recently provided programmes for mentors in Russia. I have found the workplace culture there and in Eastern Europe to be fairly directive, but people are showing signs of wanting to move towards a more peer-to-peer coaching style of management.

There was a highly developed mentoring programme in place at the Russian organization, but mentees were falling away from the programme and clearly were not finding the process as useful as had been hoped. My guess was that the mentors were doing too much telling and advice-giving, rather than drawing out the inner knowledge of their mentees. It is much more exhilarating to come up with one's own insights than to assimilate someone else's, and I felt that the Russian managers needed to learn how to ignite creative thinking in their mentees.

The training I designed centred around coaching skills and particularly focused on how to move smoothly between mining for a mentee's knowledge more than delivering the mentor's own. So we began with the usual foundation coaching skills exercises on listening, questioning and the GROW model, all described in Part 3 of this book, 'Skills'. Another key element of the training was the use of 'permission', described in Chapter 22, 'Permission protocol'.

Throughout all of the practice sessions, the participants were asked to mentor each other about real situations. Then they went away to work in pairs for six weeks, a regular format of our training style. During the classroom exercises they came to understand the benefits of the coaching style of 'asking' rather than 'telling', and during the six-week practice period they taught themselves how to do it in the way that would suit them best, in terms of their circumstances, personalities and management styles.

The training was delivered by my colleague James Wright, and when the group met with him again six weeks later, we were pleased to hear that the sessions the mentors were now delivering had become not only more effective and meaningful, but were more enjoyable for both mentors and mentees.

One of the issues that managers often wrestle with, after training in coaching or mentoring, is whether they are allowed to direct their staff, or give their mentees advice, and still be a coaching manager. Similarly, coaches question whether it is permissible to offer advice when they know something that might be useful to their coachees. Some ways of achieving both of these without breaking the coaching ethos are explored in the Chapter 3.

03 The directive–non-directive continuum

SUMMARY

- Resisting the urge to offer solutions
- The differences between coaching and mentoring
- Advice from Association for Coaching members
- Clean coaching
- The client's demands
- Guidelines for suggestions
- The coaching–mentoring–management continuum
- The cross-cultural approach

Resisting the urge to offer solutions

A question frequently asked by managers on coaching skills courses is, 'When should I coach and when should I be directive?' A short coaching course may create a conflict that can reduce a manager to silence when faced with a perceived obligation to ask instead of tell.

Coaches in training to deliver formal sessions sometimes experience a similar conflict, experiencing an overwhelming urge to 'help' by providing a solution instead of asking the type of questions that will facilitate the coachee's own ideas.

A debate on this topic on the e-mail forum of the Association for Coaching (AC) demonstrated that there are many different opinions and approaches to this issue, not least what exactly is meant by 'directive coaching' and whether the two words together constitute an oxymoron.

The differences between coaching and mentoring

I have noticed, while acting as an assessor for both newly trained and experienced coaches that people who describe themselves as coaches are sometimes actually delivering what might be defined as 'mentoring' in the last chapter – sharing their experience and advice with their clients. This is not to say that it is any less valuable than coaching, but it does not comply with the principles defined by the leading coaching bodies.

Some of my most productive moments as a coach have occurred when simply reflecting back a coachee's words, perhaps asking an open question, and then getting out of the way while my coachee explores the fascinating realm of the self. The insights (and consequent change) that can evolve during this process are more powerful than any advice I could offer.

This is eloquently expressed by AC member David Finney, who prompted the AC Forum debate:

> 'I got into coaching for many reasons, two of which were Tim Gallwey and Sir John Whitmore. For me they were the pioneers of something very new and very powerful. To "learn without being taught" called out to me. It radiated energy and empowerment.' (David Finney, www.theenergyofconversation.co.uk)

Clean coaching

The work of Gallwey and Whitmore in developing performance coaching is described in Chapter 1 'What is coaching?' People have different reasons for coming to coaching, and there are many who still do not understand what it is. In the corporate sector a coachee may be there simply because all managers at that level have been ordered to work with a coach, whether they want to or not. Therefore, a manager may be less willing to explore the 'inner self' or to accept any tips the coach can offer. In the quote below, AC member Jenny Gould uses the term 'clean' in the sense of being non-directive:

> 'I think it depends so much on what the client wants from the coaching. If it's life coaching then I generally use a more "clean" style, but I tend to include more directive coaching with corporate clients, because in my experience the clients feel it adds a great deal of value to the work I do with them. It's horses for courses.' (Jenny Gould, jenm.gould@virgin.net)

The client's demands

Some managers might choose to work with me because of my experience as a corporate MD and in particular my work with Sir Richard Branson; the possibility of picking up tips about Branson's management style may attract a client more than coaching itself. However, I am a coach and I do not believe that solely offering solutions from my own experience matches my job description, however beneficial it may be to the manager, and it is not what I want to do, which relates to my point below, about the coach's own values.

AC member William Barron puts it like this:

'I tell my clients that I am sitting on a three legged milking stool, switching from one leg to another at any one moment in time:

One leg is called coaching, which is when I haven't a clue what the answer is and am dancing with the client in the moment hoping to be as clean as possible with my language.

The second leg is called mentoring, when I have some experience of the situation and am able to bring all of that to enrich and support the conversation.

The final leg is called co-consulting, which is where the client and I pool our resources to investigate and brainstorm the situation to come up with an action plan.' (William Barron, william@creatinginsight.co.uk)

Three issues arise here:

1 Satisfying the client – should he who pays the piper call the tune?

2 Satisfying one's own wishes as a coach about how to spend one's time – I think that most coaches choose the profession because the satisfaction factor in asking rather than telling is high.

3 Being as useful to the client as possible.

First of all, let us look at 'satisfying the client'. It is crucial to be clear at the contracting stage about what the client requires and what you as the coach can deliver. The challenge is that it can be difficult for a new client to understand what coaching does without having experienced it.

I was once asked to coach a top-level leader in a large organization whose directive style was on the brink of causing resignations among the team of directors he led. During our first meeting he enthusiastically welcomed coaching by telling me: 'When I was a child I didn't do what my father told me but I obeyed my teacher. Now my team won't listen to me, so you can be the teacher – I'll tell you what I want them to do and they will listen to you.'

My instinct was to get straight into the coaching so that he could experience the benefits rather than hearing me try to explain them, but I knew it was essential for us both to be clear on expectations in advance. What I chose to say was: 'How about if I could help YOU become the person they listen to?'

This conveyed the possibility that coaching, while not in line with his expectations, might offer something even more valuable. The challenge for this manager was that he believed he could give his staff the best solution in a fraction of the time it would take them to reach it during a meeting and, therefore, he was acting in their best interests as well as the organization's by saving their time and effort. And this may have been true, because he possessed a brilliant intellect matched with a long and glitteringly successful track record. However, times have changed and people do not like to be managed in this way, and this is where the problem lay.

This contrasts with my experience of working with Sir Richard Branson, who probably developed his coaching style because, not only did he have no knowledge or experience of the record industry, but he was also dyslexic. Either way, the coaching style of management motivates staff while a directive style tends to have the opposite effect.

During my sessions with the directive manager, I spent roughly half the time asking non-directive questions, during which time he came to understand the impact that his current style had on the business and his own position, and the other half teaching him skills that would enable him to manage in a coaching style. Once he had grasped the coaching concept intellectually, he was able to deliver the coaching style of management with ease, with the result that energy levels at meetings soared and people began to enjoy working with him.

Organizations today tend not only to require their managers to have a coach, where affordable, but that those managers also incorporate the skills into their day-to-day leadership styles. The most efficient way of achieving this is by group training courses, but I find that during one-to-one coaching sessions I am often asked for advice on a situation where some coaching skills could help, and I impart them where useful.

This touches on the third element above: 'Being as useful to the client as possible'. The coach's advice may relate to coaching skills, banking processes, marketing or wherever one's area of excellence lies, or it may simply be that the coach's intuition offers a way forward which the client may have missed.

It seems to be expected in corporate coaching that some advice will be offered – and when one has a useful tip to give, where is the benefit in withholding it? So I suggest three guidelines that apply both to formal coaching and to managers-as-coach:

1 Offer suggestions only after the coachee has run dry.

2 Ask permission before giving advice, for example: 'Could I offer something from my experience/intuition here?' This marks a boundary where the coach is stepping out of coaching and into consulting. It also gives the client permission to reject the coach's suggestion without fear of causing offence. (This is expanded in Chapter 22, 'Permission protocol'.)

3 Aim for suggesting no more than 10 per cent of the time.

It is assumed here that 'suggesting' is as far as 'directive' coaching will go, and I think that advice is usually offered in this way in all schools of coaching today. Coaches never tell their clients what to do.

For coaching managers the situation is different. Sometimes people need a straight instruction and, at other times, the manager's responsibilities towards the organization require him or her to be directive or corrective. Once a manager has integrated coaching skills, they can be drawn on and mixed with other styles at will. The managers we train have to practise delivering pure coaching sessions to each other, even if their intention is only to integrate the skills into their own leadership styles rather than become internal coaches. This ensures that they will be able to manage in a coaching style smoothly and that when an instruction has to be given, it can be done without jarring the coaching relationship.

There is a misconception that coaching is a set of skills. However, I believe that it is the intention behind the words that matters. Coaching leaders treat people with respect, trust their teams to take responsibility, and earn trust through consistency and being good role models. Without these intentions, no amount of coaching skills will make a good leader.

It is even possible to fire people in a coaching style and you cannot get any more directive than that. A manager I was training once reported back to me:

'I had to fire someone. I coached him for ten minutes and he fired himself, having come to the conclusion that it was in his best interests to leave. And then he thanked me for it!'

Alan Sugar is famous for the firing techniques he displays on his television show *The Apprentice*, where contestants are regularly reduced to tears.

However, it is not so well known that Sir Richard Branson made a similar series in the United States called *The Rebel Billionaire: Branson's Quest for the Best*. The show was considered a ratings failure, probably because Branson was nice to the participants. Each week, like Sugar, he had to fire someone. However, in contrast to *The Apprentice*, Branson's rejects tended to react with inspired enthusiasm, thanking Branson for the best experience of their lives. The difference was that where Sugar told people what was wrong with them, Branson summarized their strengths and expressed how much he regretted having to let them go. Sugar's approach often leaves participants looking dejected, demotivated and bereft of self-esteem. The people fired by Branson, on the other hand, seemed to feel that they had gained from the experience and felt positive about the future. It is not hard to imagine the differences in the long-term effects of each approach upon the participants.

Translating this back to the company's reputation and ability to attract the best talent, it is equally easy to imagine the negative comments that Sugar's contestants might make about working for his organization, and the positive recommendations that Branson's might take away.

Both asking and telling can be done in a coaching style as long as they are grounded in emotional intelligence rather than, say, bullying, or a desire to appear clever. There is also the question of what we mean by 'directive coaching', raised by AC coach Angela Dunbar:

> 'Any question is going to be at least partially directive, isn't it? We shine a light on a particular aspect of a coachee's experience and, by doing so, we are directing their attention on some aspect that we have decided to focus on.' (Angela Dunbar, www.cleancoaching.com)

Coaching is indeed directive in terms of the *process*, and that is where coaches have the right to challenge and lead. As illustrated below, the coach

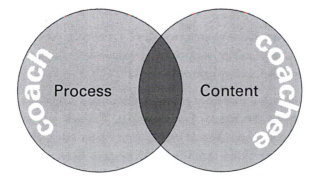

is responsible for the process and the coachee for the content. However, if coaches stray over the line into content, without recognizing the boundary by asking permission first, then they are no longer coaching but colluding with or leading their clients.

The least directive form of coaching is arguably David Grove's 'Emergent Knowledge', described in Chapter 29. Initially Grove evolved a set of questions that would least influence the coachee's thoughts, which he called Clean Language; this evolved into Emergent Knowledge and converted the whole coaching process into spatial exercises which require no verbal content at all from the client, and only the sparsest of questions from the coach. Angela Dunbar, quoted above, worked with myself and David on these techniques and now trains practitioners in the skills through www. cleancoaching.com.

Advice from Association for Coaching members

AC member Edna Murdoch describes the subtle influences that occur in and empower the coaching relationship, and the pitfalls that lie therein:

> 'There is a living, energetic, embodied connection between us which quietly – or not so quietly – influences every intervention, pause, powerful question, comment and shrug of the shoulders! That connection also influences the coachee's perception of us and their capacity for learning in coaching sessions. If we are not mindful of the power of relationship, we may be blind to its influence which might then "muddy" the clean spaces that we seek to create and affect the coaching much more than we had originally intended.' (Edna Murdoch, www.coachingsupervisionacademy.com)

AC member Stephen Burt describes the difference as a continuum rather than opposing processes:

> 'Directive and non-directive are two ends of a spectrum, not two discreet options. We can tell, advise, suggest, offer, speculate, feedback or ask.' (Stephen Burt, stephen@thefaradaypartnership.co.uk)

This is not a question that only arises in the United Kingdom. Management styles vary across the world. For example, Western cultures are said to exhibit more open aggression at work than Asian ones. My experience of delivering coaching skills training to managers from all over the world (including America, Malaysia, China, India, Australia, Europe and Eastern Europe) is that different cultures experience cultural challenges in introducing a coaching style, but that once the managers successfully assimilate the skills, they find the coaching style works better both for themselves and for their staff, providing a bridge not only across cultural differences, but differences of personality as well.

In his 'Global Coaching Survey 2008/2009', AC member Frank Bresser finds:

> 'There is an overall balance of directive and non-directive coaching approaches in the world. The predominant coaching style is directive in 28 countries, non-directive in 24 countries. In 110 countries, this is undecided.' (Frank Bresser, www.frank-bresser-consulting.com)

The coaching–mentoring–management continuum

Ideally a manager will be able to move smoothly between being directive, guiding as a mentor and eliciting self-directed learning by asking questions.

The coaching–mentoring–management continuum

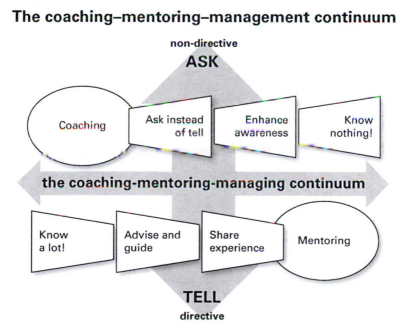

At times managers must tell people what to do or what not to do; it is part of their role. A coach, whether internal or external, will never be directive in the same way. When a coach talks of being directive, it is in the sense of imparting information ideas or advice rather than purely asking questions.

Coaching is a fledgling profession and I am struck by how often a trainee coach will come up with an observation that adds a new perspective to my own knowledge. The real learning takes place out in the field when putting the skills into practice. I believe that once the foundation principles have been absorbed, every new coach and coaching manager has the potential to contribute new wisdom of their own.

A coaching approach provides an excellent way of helping people to think clearly and move past immediate barriers. Sometimes, however, there are blocks more deeply embedded and it is useful for both coaches and coaching managers to be aware of some common ones and how to move past them. My next chapter is about the type of obstacles that we throw in our own path without even realizing that it is happening.

Self-limiting beliefs

SUMMARY

- Formation of self-limiting beliefs
- Challenging self-limiting beliefs

Formation of self-limiting beliefs

We sometimes limit ourselves by our own lack of belief, often without even being aware of it. The limits arise from our past, through experience, failure, baggage and being told that we are not good enough to achieve something. These beliefs are often expressed using fixed words like 'can't', 'should', 'never', 'always'. These words have the effect of predicting and creating the future: as we speak so it will be.

Self-limiting beliefs

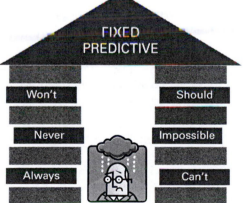

Limiting beliefs are often formed early in life, when we hear judgemental comments such as:

- 'You're hopeless at sport.'
- 'You'll never amount to anything.'
- 'Women can't read maps.'

These pronouncements can have the effect of providing a label that we stick upon ourselves and then behave accordingly.

Other ways of developing limiting beliefs are:

- failing at something once and not trying again, eg 'I'm terrified of public speaking', 'I'm afraid of horses';
- having a poor teacher, leading us to label ourselves at being useless at, say, maths or science; and
- being influenced by generalizations, such as 'women can't reach board level'.

Challenging self-limiting beliefs

Sometimes we unconsciously cling to a limiting belief because it is easier than stepping out of our comfort zone. The question 'How does this belief serve you?' is a way of investigating that possibility.

If coaches hear coachees express what might be a limiting belief, it is important not to assume that the belief is false. The way to challenge the belief is to look for evidence, eg:

- How do you know?
- How often does that happen?
- Has there been a time when it didn't happen?

When asked these exploratory questions, coachees often recognize that the situation is not as fixed as they thought. On the other hand, the belief may be true and the coach can help the coachee work around it and come up with strategies to compensate.

The following questions can help the coachee discover whether the belief is true or not:

- What would you like instead of your belief?
- How do you know your belief is true?

- What evidence is there to support it?
- Can you counter the evidence?
- Has there been a time when...?
- Where might your belief have come from?
- Is it still relevant to you?
- How does the belief serve you?
- What do you notice about your language?
- Can you change the language?
- Can your belief change?

'Whether you think you can, or you think you can't – you're right.'
(Henry Ford)

This approach starts to blur the edges between coaching and psychology. As long as the coaching principles of following one's coachee rather than diagnosing or directing are complied with, there is no risk of the coach straying into therapeutic areas that he or she may not be qualified to manage.

In recent years advances in neuroscience have provided some interesting discoveries that explain the effectiveness of coaching and psychology, and these are explored in Chapter 5.

05 Coaching and neuroscience

SUMMARY

- Neuroscience and bullying
- Goal setting
- Positive feedback and learning
- Self-directed learning
- Insights
- Multi-tasking

One interesting outcome of the rapid progression in the understanding of how our brains work in recent years is the discovery of how the effectiveness of coaching techniques has been explained by neurological processes. There are a number of other areas where neuroscience has provided new insights and a physical reason as to why coaching works:

Neuroscience and bullying

In Chapter 15 'Bullying in the workplace', I describe how Professor James Fallon (2012) identified distinctive patterns in the brains of psychopaths, and that these patterns exist in other individuals who exhibit personality traits that might be regarded as callous, but who do not go as far as murdering people. He concluded that extreme psychopathic behaviour requires a trigger, such as the experience of brutality in childhood.

Goal-setting

Many sports coaches use the technique of asking their players to envisage making a winning shot: to see in their mind's eye the ball moving, the roar of the crowd, the sensation of winning and so on. It is thought that this technique is effective because it is creating new neural pathways in the brain. In terms of these neural pathways, the brain is now said to be unable to distinguish between fact and fiction, which is why we cry during sad movies or feel fear during thrillers. Imagining an experience will create new pathways in the same way as if the event had actually taken place. To do something a second time is easier than it was the first time, hence the success of the winning shot exercise, and if physical activity accompanies the imagined shot, the effect will be even stronger (Roche and Commins, 2009).

This resonates with one of the most effective sets of questions I know, not only during goal-setting but in coaching in general, which is to ask coachees to imagine that they have achieved their goal, not as some distant desire in the future, but that they are actually there. I ask them to take a look around and tell me what they see (notice that this is in the present tense, not 'what would you see?' or 'what will you see?'). Then I offer further prompts, such as 'What are people saying? How are you feeling?'

The effect is to create energy and clarity as the ideal future is explored in all its glory and the process helps the coachee to find the way forward and past any obstacles that may have been blocking success. I suggest that this is because setting oneself in what might be described as the 'future present' creates neural pathways that establish the goal as a reality, and from this stance the coachee can simply look back and see how he or she arrived at this point. The variation on questions about seeing, hearing, feeling etc, is employed because the more senses that are involved in such a visualization, the deeper the neural pathways become embedded, and the easier it is for the coachee to access the reality that he or she has conjured up. This in turn makes it more likely that the goal will be achieved.

Positive feedback and learning

This is a way of countering the bias of the brain towards negativity. We have five times as many negative circuits as positive ones in our brains, because we are naturally geared towards detecting threat rather than reward (Gordon, 2000).

It has been shown that learning is embedded more effectively when emotions are aroused. People are shown to become more engaged when placed in a threatening environment (Kohlrieser, 2006) or even shown angry faces (Ohman, Flykt and Lundquist, 2000). However, negative emotional triggers carry the disadvantages of dampening enthusiasm and innovation, and are unlikely to secure the managers' buy-in to attend workshops.

A positive stimulus is more effective and can be attained through praise and a sense of achievement around having learned new skills. It increases the dopamine neurotransmission, which is the key to embedding learning (Shultz, 1997).

Self-directed learning

It has been proved that when we generate our own answers, we are more likely to remember and sustain what has been learned.

Insights

Coaching is a way of eliciting insight through specific techniques that encourage the coachee to make connections across different areas of the brain, rather than linear or analytic processing. At the moment of insight, brain scans have shown that a burst of gamma waves occurs. This helps to create the energy and motivation needed to put ideas and plans into practice, provided that the 'aha' moment is followed up with the action setting which I refer to in Chapter 27.

In her book *Investing in Meaning* (Seeger, 2012), neuro-leadership coach Dr Clara Seeger describes how insights arise from a neurological point of view. Research has shown that people approach problem-solving in one of two ways: either through insight or analytical reasoning. Mark Jung-Beeman (Subramaniam *et al.*, 2009) has proved that insight involves activity in different areas of the brain from analytical reasoning: during insight fMRI (functional Magnetic Resonance Imaging) studies have shown high activation in an area called the Anterior Cingulate Cortex, but this is not nearly as active during analytical problem-solving. Insight also appears to involve more spread-out neural activity as it creates connections across different areas of the brain, whereas greater visual tension can be detected during analytical problem-solving.

In addition, insight seems to occur in the right hemisphere of the brain, which is traditionally associated with creativity, as opposed to the left hemisphere, which is thought to deal with language and logic. However, neuroscientists have successfully demonstrated through EEG and fMRI studies that insight follows a structured neurological process rather than constituting completely random mental events. Dr Seeger recommends mindfulness (described in Chapter 44) as a way of triggering the restful alpha waves that create the conditions for insight to happen, and insight is of fundamental significance in coaching, whether in the personal development environment of a one-to-one session, or for triggering great ideas among teams at work.

Multi-tasking

In 2012 an exciting experiment was demonstrated in a Horizon documentary on UK television called *Out of Control*. The neuro-scientist in charge was fascinated by the amount of activity that people are able to carry out by habit, without even being aware of it. One example is when we drive a car at a level so automatic that we find ourselves driving, say, home, instead of to a venue we do not normally visit.

By using the latest brain-scanning technology the scientist wanted to evaluate what habitual actions people could undertake and to what extent it was possible to do non-habitual actions, ones that require thinking, at the same time. The experiment was limited by the size of the scanner until he noticed that women in a knitting circle chatted to each other as they knitted. The knitting was clearly an automatic activity and it seemed that they did not even have to look at what they were doing. So he persuaded one of the women to lie in the brain scanner and knit with a customary stitch, measuring the activity in her brain all the while. Then, from time to time, she had to undertake something out of the ordinary by using a stitch she was not familiar with.

While doing the standard knitting, the basal ganglia part of her brain lit up. However, the new stitch fired her pre-frontal cortex, because she had to think consciously about what she did. He discovered that while people are able to undertake a number of different automatic activities at the same time, they struggle to complete more than one cognitive (non-automatic) task.

This is significant to me in terms of training managers in coaching skills. During the training sessions they are usually able to understand and use the skills effectively straight away. However, a significant amount of concentration is required to avoid falling back into old habits such as offering solutions too soon. So I prescribe a series of coaching assignments to be practised regularly until we meet again, say six weeks later. If they complete all the assignments I notice that they are coaching fluently to some extent, although it requires still more practice before the process becomes second nature. But it is vital for this to happen, because while they are concentrating on nothing but coaching the managers will do it well. However, they are there to manage people and, as soon as that has to happen, say in a crisis, then that activity will take over the non-automatic function in their brains, and their coaching style will only be able to persist if it has become an ingrained habit. This is why some short coaching courses fail to have any long-term effects in the workplace.

There is a distinction here between formal one-to-one coaching and 'manager as coach'. It is possible for people to create a new habit that will enable them to move automatically into what might be termed the 'coaching space', where they will listen before giving solutions and find that useful questions pop into their heads unbidden. This I would put on a par with the automatic knitting, and is what should be happening, ideally, while managers are consciously focusing on handling a crisis.

Conversely, in a one-to-one session, a much higher level of concentration is required, with the specific need for the coach to be making conscious decisions on how to facilitate new insights in the coachee, in terms of what questions are asked and other skills used. Correspondingly, the coachee in a formal session is encouraged to think differently and to view situations from new perspectives.

So for a manager, it is possible to develop an ability to be a coach without having to be consciously aware of it, whereas in a coach's role it could be said that the opposite is desirable.

We are now going to explore more fully the role of manager as coach in Part 2.

PART TWO
Creating a coaching culture in organizations

Introduction

Many organizations across the world today are putting coaching programmes in place, either by hiring external coaches or training their own managers. The word is out that a 'coaching culture' is the way to go, although there is some confusion about what the term actually means and even more about how to achieve it. This part of the book explores practical examples of how organizations all over the world have approached this problem, the challenges they have faced, and the cultures some have managed to create.

It is not an exaggeration to say that in terms of supporting a coaching culture, people who work in organizations are divided into two groups: those who want it and those who have not yet had any experience of coaching. This may sound like bias from someone who is part of the first group, but after training hundreds of managers, some of whom volunteered to be there and some who had been conscripted into the training room, I have not yet met a manager who did not agree that coaching would save time and stress, the two mammoths with which today's managers must grapple. And this revelation happens within the first morning of the programme.

In the chapter on 'cross-cultural coaching', I describe how some managers witnessed me coach a volunteer through the review of a four-page form that had to be painstakingly filled out by sales reps every time they encountered a new prospect. At the end, amid several (literally) open mouths, one said, 'You have just done in 20 minutes what normally takes me four hours.' Equally surprising to them was the moment at the start of the demonstration when, after being handed the form by the volunteer who had just completed it, I gave it back saying I did not need to look at it. Within 20 minutes, using the GROW model described in Chapter 23, I had extracted the most useful information contained in the form and worked out how to proceed with it. These managers had been forced to attend the training when they would have preferred to have been managing their clients or chasing new prospects. However, the same sentiments applied to the time they had to spend reviewing the forms filled in by their teams. From that moment on I had their attention.

On an earlier training session at a different organization I worked with a group of managers who reported to a woman forced to attend the training with them. After witnessing the first demonstration, she crossed her arms and informed us frostily that coaching would not work for her; she was the manager, she told people what to do and that was what they wanted from her. Without reacting, I asked the participants to pair up and practice what I had just demonstrated. Fortunately she had to comply as her own boss, a champion of coaching, was also in attendance and had commissioned the event. Within 10 minutes she had grasped the value of the coaching approach – it not only felt better to the person she was coaching, she found it an easier way of having a conversation as well. From that moment on, her resistance dissolved and she eventually became the most vociferous supporter of coaching throughout the whole organization.

In a management coaching situation, the report is the one who has to come up with the answers, taking pressure off the boss to feel he or she should know everything, and giving the report a chance both to shine and exercise creative thinking. How could this not be an advantage to both? Of course, the manager must be in possession of a sound coaching style, so that the report does not feel 'put on the spot'.

In the first chapter of this part, the coaching culture during the first 10 years of the Virgin Empire is described: an exemplary case of coaching in action, with all of its scope for innovation, excitement, passion and healthy conflict, leading to the creation of the worldwide brand that is Virgin today. In the next I lay out a 10-step plan on how to build such a culture, including the ever present question of how to gain buy-in from the managers and secure their attendance.

The meaning of a coaching culture

SUMMARY

- The coaching culture at Virgin
- The pillars of a coaching culture
- Other examples of coaching cultures

The coaching culture at Virgin

I joined the fledgling Virgin Records during the 1970s after dropping out of my degree course followed by a fruitless search for work that might be challenging and interesting. In those days women at work in business were almost all secretaries, expected to support male business leaders and eventually marry one. So I taught myself to type and started to look for a career. It did not take long to decide that the only job that really interested me in all these organizations was to be the managing director, but in terms of role models I never encountered any women managers at all, let alone senior ones. There were some gaps to cross and, at first, I would watch the male bosses whose letters I typed and wonder how they knew what decisions to make and where they got the answers from because, as women, we had been raised to ask a man when we needed an answer, or a plug fitted (electrical appliances came without plugs in those days) or a mortgage to buy a house. I remember the epiphany of realizing that the men did not actually have the answers – they simply chose an option and then implemented it with confidence and not a small amount of bluff. From then on there was no turning back, and by the age of 24 I had signed up for and resigned from 29 jobs, sometimes staying no longer than a couple of weeks. Times were different and jobs were plentiful. Nevertheless I was unable to find anything that gave me an opportunity to make decisions or stretch myself. I did, however, learn how to fit a plug during that period. Mortgages came later.

I had met Eve Branson during a sort of gap year spent living in Menorca. She owned property there and was part of the ex-pat community. She told us that her son Richard had started a record company. It had never occurred to me that record companies needed employees, just like banks and shops, and, naively assuming my musical background might be of some use, I applied for a job as head of marketing which Virgin advertised. At that time there were 20 or so employees and all the interviewing was done by Richard and his partner Nik Powell. I sensed an excitement and energy among people the first time I walked through the doors, and by the time I got through to the shortlist of three out of 50 applicants (without any experience or ever having to fill out a job application), I was beginning to understand that things were run differently around here.

As no-one else in Virgin knew anything at all about the record business, Branson had decided that in this case they needed someone with an experience of marketing (this was later reversed and for the whole decade I worked there, most senior roles were filled with people who had no experience at least in that particular field at all). However, Branson explained that he could not offer me the marketing job as I did not actually know anything about marketing (and I had to agree) but asked me what job I would like. It was simple: anything but a secretary. By the mid-1970s this was still the most common role for women, but women were beginning to show up in service roles such as public relations and international client liaison. I knew I wanted to be at the 'sharp' end – making decisions – but would happily have accepted any of these roles.

Yet the job Branson eventually offered me was to run the publishing company. To this day I am convinced I got the offer because the job involved filling out copyright forms, which was seen as women's work in those days. However, hearing the words 'run' and 'company' in the same sentence was enough for me and I said a very definite 'yes'.

Looking back at this situation I can see a number of reasons why all of this happened. One was that Branson had been raised by the redoubtable Eve, a woman who had trained glider pilots in the war, and believed in raising her son in an environment that was challenging but fun. So he was possibly more comfortable with the idea of working, decision-making women than most men of his time. I, on the other hand, had been raised by extraordinary parents (although I didn't see it at the time) to not even notice social barriers of gender, race, or any other kind. This was during a time when women in many organizations (including my aunt in 1963) had to resign on marrying, and London landlords displayed notices on their doors saying 'no blacks or Irish'. My father had a catch phrase 'There's no such word as can't', which used to irritate me a lot because he said it so often, but it must have stuck. My mother had read a book on positive psychology in 1953 and resolved, after her own upbringing with a highly critical father, that she would only ever tell her children what was good about them. This created a resilient form of confidence, that did not banish fear but enabled me to work alongside it. I enjoyed nothing more than a challenge and was able simply to shrug away failure.

In spite of our very different backgrounds – Branson's father was a judge and he went to top public school Stowe, mine was a lowly personnel officer and I attended the local grammar – we shared a positive and determined attitude that was unusual for its time. And this was at the root of the coaching culture at Virgin, and the coaching culture in my parents' home.

In those days of course, the expression did not exist but, having studied and trained in every leadership and coaching technique during the passing years, I now recognize how extraordinarily closely the culture at Virgin matched what we now define as a coaching culture. And I am informed by Virgin employees from time to time, that it still holds true.

The pillars of a coaching culture

The ways that this positivity and determination showed itself in the company can be distilled down into three areas.

Responsibility

Because no-one had previous experience at Virgin, we made it up as we went along and often invented new and better ways of doing things. Branson valued innovative thinking and encouraged people to take risks. In fact, I was more likely to find myself arguing with him not to invest in a risky proposition than trying to persuade him to make one. I once refused to sign an artiste he was keen to acquire because I did not see any potential there. He joked that he would put up a big sign over my desk saying 'I turned down [xxx]'. Fortunately for me the artiste, who was signed by another organization for a huge amount of money, disappeared without trace. This illustrates how Branson would never, under any circumstances, tell his staff what to do. He knew nothing about record companies, probably knows little about trains and planes and certainly nothing about spaceships. And he tried not to acquire any knowledge along the way that would get in the way of the people he employed who actually had to do the job. He believed that the best person to make a decision about a work area is the one who is there, at the coal face. That person will know more about the current state of the coal, the conditions and the context of the decision to be made than anyone further up the line who has experience of a *different* context at a *different* time and in *different* conditions.

Being given such a high level of responsibility made us super careful to investigate, research and hone our decisions. There was no-one to pick up on errors or suggest another route. The buck stopped here. The more that managers control and check up on their employees, the less effort the employees will put in themselves. Why bother to exert oneself when someone else is going to correct the mistakes and change it all anyway?

> 'Here is the good news: the more you free your people to think for
> themselves, the more they can help you. You don't have to do this all on
> your own.' (Sir Richard Branson)

Self-belief

24-year-olds are not normally brimming with confidence in their abilities and I was no exception. However, I was armed with my parents' optimism and their belief that I could achieve anything. At Virgin this was reinforced by Branson, who bore a similar legacy from Eve, imbuing him with a belief that his 'tribe' of employees could do anything too.

In many organizations, there is a culture of caution – not without reason, people are simply doing their best to protect the interests of the organization – but it results in a situation where when someone comes up with a new idea, the boss shouts it down: 'We tried something similar five years ago and it didn't work then, so it won't work now'; 'That will never happen'; 'You'll never get them to agree to this'; 'That could go wrong'; 'This could happen', etc.

There was none of that at Virgin. Branson thrived on new, untested ideas and the riskier the better. So a new plan would be greeted by enthusiasm, admiration and an unshakeable (and looking back unwarranted!) belief that whoever came up with the idea would make it work.

That provided the confidence, almost inevitably lacking in most under-25s, that propelled us towards success. If someone as powerful as our boss believed we could achieve this, then he must be right. He believed we could do it, so we believed we could do it, so we did it. The more people are believed in, the easier it is for them to believe in themselves. Praise and recognition constitute half the battle in building self-confidence. In addition, people must be allowed to take risks in order to succeed by trial and error. This is the other half of the pathway to confidence.

Learning not blame

Of course there were times when our grand schemes failed; we did not know anything and things can go wrong even when people know a lot. Looking back, now that I have seen and experienced the pervasive scapegoat culture we have, particularly in the United Kingdom, it seems extraordinary that when we failed our first port of call was Branson. I never remember it even crossing my mind to hide my mistakes. In most organizations people will go to great lengths to hide mistakes. Whole teams can put all their creative energy over an extended period of time into hiding their errors, when the situation might have an easy solution, but one that would entail informing the boss. This never happened at Virgin. Branson's attitude was as if he was standing at the start of a maze, at the end of which was his target. Every false trail identified in that maze brought us one step closer to the target. Branson wrote:

> 'Right across the business we have a philosophy of encouragement. Our people are rarely criticised. If someone makes a howling mistake, usually they don't need to be told. They know.' (Sir Richard Branson, 2009)

As Branson says, when people know they have made a mistake they do not need to be told. Who is your own worst critic? The beating we may receive from the boss is rarely as severe as the one we give ourselves. How many times have you walked away from a successful event replaying only the parts that went wrong, however insignificant? If we are aware of our errors, it is actually more useful to be told what we are doing well than dwelling on failures. Praise raises energy and reinforces confidence. It is a great motivator to do better next time.

I once coached a woman who set herself a gruelling list of actions in every session, maybe 25 to be achieved in a week. She usually not only completed them but exceeded what she had set out to achieve. One week she said she had failed to complete two of the actions. I was astonished to hear her confess 'That's the sort of person I am; I never get anything done'. I played back to her the contradiction between her view of herself and the reality I had observed. It was quite a surprise to her and she reassessed herself more generously from then on.

If people are punished for failure they will limit themselves only to taking actions in which they have succeeded before, and growth will come to a halt. How then will the organization be able to keep up in our fast-changing times? This applies outside of work as well. Imagine a child learning to walk who was hit every time it fell down: how long would it take for the child to give up altogether? Consider the potential that would be forfeited, both for the child and the world around it and then translate that into the workplace and imagine the potential that is being lost every day through the blame culture that pervades our workplaces, particularly in Britain.

Other examples of coaching cultures

Some leaders who seem to be natural coaching managers are:

Warren Buffet: one of the world's richest men, Buffet built his empire by buying chunks of other people's organizations. According to interviews with owners of the organizations he acquired, he leaves managers alone to run their businesses but is always available at the end of the phone. In a coaching culture, there is no need to check up on staff because they will come to the boss when the need presents itself. Just imagine how much time that would save a manager who feels the need to supervise staff through meetings and reports!

Ricardo Semler: In the 1980s, Semler inherited the global industry of Semco from his father. He felt there had to be a better way of managing the business than telling his workers what to do (Semler, 2001). Respecting their talent and innate intelligence, he handed them control of the organization, eventually even having people set their own salaries. There were no coaching books or courses for Semler to follow – he had to make it up as he went along and, although he faced a few pitfalls on the way, the new system thrived.

Andy Law: Law founded St Luke's Advertising and turned the entire organization over to its employees, right down to the shareholding (Law, 1999).

Ralph Stayer: In 1980, Stayer commenced a tortuous but rewarding experimental process of enabling his workers to lead his organization, Johnsonville Sausage (Stayer, 1990).

One of the most frequent questions I am asked by organizations is where to start in terms of creating a coaching culture and what pitfalls might they meet along the way. Do not think I am suggesting that anyone should turn their business culture around overnight. Most of the leaders mentioned above were the outright owners of their companies, had personally recruited the entire workforce in the early years and were each solely responsible for the financial risk. It would not be fair or right to expose someone else's organization to this level of experimentation, particularly in the public sector. Another issue is that in a corporation there is often a hierarchy to worry about – people may be expected to shoulder the blame for the mistakes of their subordinates. However, throughout this book I will demonstrate how these three pillars can bring about a gradual improvement in the culture of any organization, reducing stress and creating as sense of enjoyment among the workers, which results in higher profits for shareholders. In fact one of Branson's sayings is:

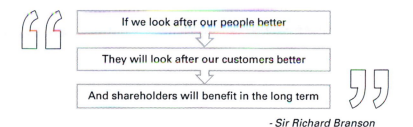

If we look after our people better

They will look after our customers better

And shareholders will benefit in the long term

- Sir Richard Branson

In the next chapter I provide a framework that can be applied to any organization to underpin the transformation into a coaching culture, and I highlight some of the challenges to look out for.

07 Ten steps to creating a coaching culture

SUMMARY

- The ten-step plan
- Kent County Council's South East Coaching and Mentoring Network

The ten-step plan

Below is a framework designed to support any organization in creating a coaching culture.

1 *Vision and purpose*: A coaching approach to any situation is to start by looking ahead to the desired outcome. This makes the pathway clearer, unifies people and aligns purpose. It enables progress to be measured and confirms whether the project is heading in the right direction.

2 *Organizational health check*: Once the goals of the programme are defined, it is time to explore the current situation. What resources are already in place? What else is required? What needs to be changed? What has been achieved so far? Who needs to be involved?

3 *Stakeholder mapping*: The stakeholders are the people who are affected by, or have an interest in, the coaching programme and the diagram on page 44 shows how the stakeholder map might look in a typical organization.

   There are people who will influence the programme and those who will give approval for it. Also there are the ones who will attend the programme, and those who will shape and plan it. The approvers

The ten-step plan

1	Vision & purpose
2	Organizational health check
3	Stakeholder mapping
4	Getting buy in
5	Where to start
6	What to measure
7	Implement pilots
8	Evaluation and forward planning
9	Implement next phase
10	Maintain the momentum

are essential, or the programme will never happen. The shapers are also necessary in terms of putting it together and driving the process. However, when designing the programme, it is productive to take in the views of everyone who will be touched by it, not only the essential players. The actual job roles in each section may vary from organization to organization and some may fit into several categories.

4 *Getting buy-in*: If the visioning and health check has been meticulously undertaken with all the stakeholders, then buy-in will be in place by now. Each of the parties will have a sense of ownership of the programme and how it will meet their needs. Visioning also tends to raise enthusiasm and energy, so the programme will already be building momentum.

5 *Where to start*: Notice how far down the list this comes. A lot of foundations need to be laid even before planning, never mind executing the programme. It is like decorating a house: if the filling and sanding is not done properly, the final effect will suffer.

The stakeholder map

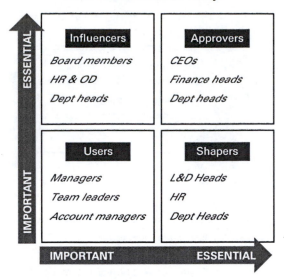

6 *What to measure*: Notice also that measurement starts here, before the programme has even been designed. In order to estimate the ROI (Return On Investment) it is necessary to have identified what can be measured, and this is explored more fully in Chapter 18, 'ROI: Measuring the Return of Investment in Coaching'. There are many ways of doing this, through new surveys or existing ones. Key elements to ask are:

- What benefits are solely due to the coaching programme, and to what extent (as an estimated percentage)?
- What tangible benefits have accrued to the organization because of the coaching programme?

If qualitative or 'soft' benefits are offered, try to pin them down to quantitative or 'hard' ones. Take this conversation, for example, with a reviewer who wishes to evaluate a coaching programme attended by the participant:

ROI reviewer: How has the coaching programme benefitted the organization?

Participant: Our customers are happier.

ROI reviewer: What difference does that make to the organization?

Participant: We are selling more products.

ROI reviewer: By what percentage do you estimate that raises profits?

Participant: 10 per cent.

Although this is not a precise statistic in itself, if questions like this are conducted across a substantial number of participants, certain trends will emerge.

People tend to be more specific about benefits when asked during the coaching programme than when filling in feedback forms later on. On training days I sometimes ask people to write down on sticky notes what benefits they have produced for the organization through coaching. I type up both the comments on the sticky notes and the verbal ones, to deliver to the organization in the form of a report. If I want to identify the contributors, I ask their permission first.

7 *Implement pilots*: It is advisable to:
   - start with one or more pilot programmes to ensure everything is on the right track;
   - meet the suppliers before deciding who will run the programme; and
   - contact referees for whom the suppliers have delivered similar programmes.

8 *Evaluation and forward planning*: Once the pilots have taken place, the programme can be re-evaluated to identify any adjustments that need to be made to suit a particular organization. All the relevant stakeholders should be canvassed for their opinions. Not only will valuable information surface but it will reaffirm their sense of ownership of the programme.

9 *Implement next phase*: After adjustments have been made, you can roll out the whole programme.

10 *Maintain the momentum*: Coaching programmes tend to have a momentum of their own because of the enthusiasm they generate and because the effects are immediately noticeable throughout the workforce. People see that the newly trained managers are communicating more effectively, delivering better results and are altogether nicer to be with. A good way of increasing the effect is to set up co-coaching groups, and train the internal coaches to supervise each other. It is also a good idea to have refresher days, perhaps one every six months.

Kent County Council's South East Coaching and Mentoring Network

One organization that took an innovative approach to creating a coaching culture is Kent County Council. In 2005, faced with the challenge of budgetary restrictions, but also passionate about the benefits of coaching, Head of Learning and Development Coral Ingleton devised a plan to spread coaching throughout the organization at minimal cost. Starting with Kent Fire and Police, she partnered other local organizations and provided coaching training courses for them. At the last count the network, now known as the South East Coaching and Mentoring Network, comprised 16 organizations, over 200 members and is still expanding.

My company provides the training courses and Kent County Council charge a mark-up to the partner organizations. The profits generated enable the internal coaches to receive continuing professional development and an even bigger benefit is that the organizations can provide external coaches to each other without paying expensive consultancies to deliver it. Naturally the skills proliferate throughout the leadership styles of the management. We have trained some internal coaching supervisors as well so the whole network can be self-supporting. Some strategies for the training of internal coaching supervisors are provided in Chapter 17, 'Coaching supervision: a workplace perspective'.

Having explored the broader meaning of a coaching culture and how to achieve it, the remainder of this part breaks down precisely how coaching can be used in the workplace, the challenges and the results that can be achieved.

Coaching in the workplace

SUMMARY

- Uses for coaching in the workplace
- Internal coaching
- External coaching
- Coachable moments
- Speed coaching in industry

Uses for coaching in the workplace

Coaching can play a variety of roles throughout an organization:

Coaching relationships

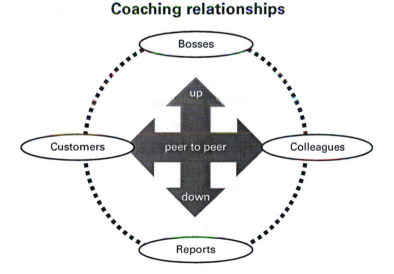

- Internal or external coaches can provide formal sessions.

- Managers can incorporate a coaching approach into their leadership style.

- Coaching is useful in peer-to-peer relationships, with colleagues and of course customers. Coaching creates empathy and rapport; it oils the wheels.

- It is also possible to deliver 'coaching up'. Using coaching skills with one's bosses, such as listening, questioning and giving some praise when deserved will promote a healthy relationship and reduce the stress of mismanagement.

In addition, many of the managers I have trained relate stories of how their newly acquired skills have improved their relationships with family, offspring and friends: An Indian manager I trained told me he had used GROW (the fundamental coaching model described in Chapter 23) to resolve a feud that had split his extended family for 20 years. He said it took 20 minutes of coaching to start the process and come up with an action plan.

An American described his relief at having rescued his son from a prolonged period of depression and inaction after failing to win his expected place at one of America's top universities. After one session the boy started researching and applying for places at other colleges; he was back on track with planning his future.

We have had many laughs in the training room when people describe their attempts at coaching their partners and children. Coaching close family members is an excellent way to gauge how you are really doing with your coaching skills; one hard pressed, over-worked European mother said her young children responded with a mortifying 'Mummy, why are you talking funny? Why aren't you telling us off like you usually do?' Others have received a short reaction from husbands and wives while some have seen an all-round improvement in home communication. And there are some lucky spouses who have discovered the joys of being listened to, perhaps for the first time in the entire marriage.

Nancy Kline, the renowned author of *Time to Think* (Kline, 1999), relates that she and her husband of over 20 years consistently provide each other with an informal 'thinking session' every day: one listens to the other without interrupting for 15 minutes, then they swap over. If they are in different places they do it by phone. The value of listening is fundamental to coaching, and to building trust and healthy relationships. It is explored further in Chapter 19.

Before managers started to become coaches themselves they experienced the value of having a coach. The greater the athlete, the more likely he or she is to have a personal sports coach. That coach will probably not ever have achieved anywhere near the performance level of the athlete, but knows how to bring out the very best in performance. Performance coaches in life and business use different techniques to conventional sports coaches (for the differences see Chapter 1 'What is coaching?') but the principle holds true.

Over recent years it has become common for organizations to require their managers to be trained in coaching skills, in order to build a force of internal coaches, which happened at the BBC, and to create a coaching culture where managers lead in a coaching style. In this chapter I will explore the nuts and bolts of how this works, the benefits and the pitfalls to avoid.

Internal coaching

There is an inherent conflict of interest when managers coach their direct reports, but this does not mean that the process will fail to deliver benefits. There are two agendas in a coaching relationship: the agenda of the coach and that of the coachee. If a coach has a relationship with a coachee that exists outside of the coaching, this will always act like a third agenda but does not have to be a disadvantage. Clearly, reports may hold back on voicing fears and failures if their coaches are also the bosses who can influence their chances of promotion; there may be an element of competition between team co-workers. And bosses being reverse-mentored or coached by their subordinates will be bound to confidentiality on certain company issues. As long as both parties realize that the third agenda exists, and respect it, and accept that no-one is at fault, this type of coaching relationship can be as fruitful as any other.

External coaching

Where the coach is an independent consultant hired by the organization to coach its managers, the question of the third agenda does not arise and the coachees are more likely to open up during sessions and explore their issues at a deeper level.

The criteria for choosing coaches may include a mixture of recommendation, prior working relationship, accreditation, experience and testimonials. The process can be informal, involving no more than a CV and interview, while some organizations have designed stringent application processes involving live panels of assessors.

Whether internal or external, the most important aspect of any coaching relationship is that the level of trust must be high. It is essential that coachees are allowed to choose their own coaches and that the coach guards the coachee's confidentiality. If a coachee's manager wishes to keep track of what is happening in the coaching relationship, then a three-way meeting between the coach, coachee and organizational representative can take place from time to time. In such meetings, the broad scope of the coaching can be determined, but the coachee's goals and all other aspects of the sessions must remain confidential. The coachee may disclose as much as he or she wishes, but must never be coerced into doing so. The coach, whether internal or external, is bound by the ethics of the profession not to disclose anything at all.

Coachable moments

Coaching does not require long periods of time. An insightful question offered during a two-minute conversation at the water cooler can be as effective in setting someone on the path towards a solution as a two-hour coaching session.

These 'coachable moments' are one of the most valuable results of training managers in coaching skills. They cannot happen unless the manager has learned and practised formal coaching skills to a degree where the techniques have become automatic and unthinking. Some people already have this ability because they have been exposed to coaching cultures previously, either at home, school or work. However, anyone can acquire the knack through effective training and assiduous practice.

I regularly coach volunteers in front of groups at conferences and workshops to demonstrate the techniques before asking participants to pair up and try it out for themselves. At one event, the time was cut short so the audience had only two minutes each way for their own practice. Steve Briebart, one of the editors of this book, was present and took part in the two-minute practice. Afterwards he shared that both he and his practice partner had reached new insights in spite of the short time given, and that he realized that when he had two hours available to deliver a coaching session, it tended to take that amount of time to reach significant new insights; given ten minutes, the same result would be achieved in that much shorter time. And now, having only two minutes, the insights had duly arrived within the deadline.

Of course this is not a hard and fast rule and it is quite possible to spend two hours coaching with not very much that is new and startling emerging from the session. However, it does seem that the unconscious mind is somehow programmed by being given a stated deadline, and will do whatever has to be done within the required time. This supports the recommended professional practice among coaches of agreeing how much time is available at the beginning of the session and sticking to it.

Speed coaching in industry

Even formal coaching sessions do not require long periods of time. I know of one pharmaceutical company that introduced a daily telephone coaching programme for its key account team, in order to promote the launch of a new product. Over a six-week period, a group of external coaches delivered 15 sessions, focused on objectives and achievement of specific goals, through daily phone calls lasting only 10 minutes per call. These were supported by five calls focused on personal development, which lasted for a longer period of 20 minutes each.

The programme provided a cost-effective way of ensuring that all the team members received coaching. Some 88 per cent of participants reported that they would recommend it to a colleague. It broke the mould of two-hour executive coaching sessions and proved that results can be obtained in short, sharp interventions. Reports were received that sales increased, leadership skills were enhanced and that team relationships were strengthened. There was a sense of pride and excitement about the programme, which has remained in operation at the organization and will continue in the future.

Clearly there are many areas where coaching and coaching skills are proliferating. The first question that will come to many readers is how to manage all of this and how to make sure that everyone is coaching within the generally accepted guidelines. This is addressed in Chapter 9.

09 Coach training in the workplace

SUMMARY

- How to choose a coach training supplier
- The length and depth of coach training
- Training coaches at the BBC
- Training the coach trainer at IKEA

How to choose a coach training supplier

At the time of writing, the coaching profession is unregulated save for self-appointed coaching bodies. Coaching incorporates methodologies taken from psychology, philosophy, business and sport and all have something to offer. I think it is more critical that the training provider has a high level of rapport with the organization and, preferably, that the trainers have all previously held organizational positions themselves, so that they are better able to understand the challenges and needs of today's managers.

The key is to work out what is required, through the programme described in Chapter 7, 'Ten steps to creating a coaching culture', and then select a coaching organization which has achieved similar results before, or which can demonstrate sufficient understanding of the requirements to be able to meet them.

Glossy marketing materials do not always represent the best quality in any business, and coaching is no exception. A thorough investigation should be undertaken in terms of understanding the components of the training provider's programme, meeting the key personnel who will deliver the programme and looking at testimonials from their previous clients.

The length and depth of coach training

Managers can be trained to various levels and it is important that the requirements are investigated and understood before designing a programme. In my experience the depth of training will produce varying results:

- One day of training can provide participants with the fundamentals of coaching. It is a relatively simple process and the theory is not difficult to grasp. However, although the participants are likely to absorb one or two useful takeaways to put into practice in the future, probably 80 per cent of what they have seen during the day will be forgotten and will not be put into practice once they are back in the workplace. This lack of translation of skills to workplace will apply to any length of course; it happens because human beings are programmed to learn through making mistakes, but managers with new skills cannot risk making these mistakes with their reports, peers and customers. So most of the skills remain dormant and are then forgotten. A remedy for this is to deliver all forms of training in at least two sections, with around six weeks in between, during which participants are paired up to practise in a safe place where they are allowed to make mistakes and can receive some feedback from their practice partner.

    Another reason for extending the learning in this way is that studies in neuroscience have proved that learning in small doses is more likely to be assimilated than large chunks of information (Crowder, 1976). The prefrontal cortex can process only three to seven pieces of information at any one time (Linden *et al*, 2003).

- Two/three days of training over a period of time as specified above will provide managers with useful tools and skills that will enhance their style of management. The pitfall is that they may try to adhere too much to process without having achieved the mastery to adjust it according to the context of the situation and their own personalities. When this happens an awkward and inauthentic-feeling situation can be created. It is not sufficient to qualify the candidate to act as an internal or external coach over a series of formal sessions. However, the organization is likely to see a substantial improvement in leadership, team building, motivation and customer service.

- Five or more days of training, with practice periods in between, will provide managers with skills and tools that are integrated into their own authentic leadership style. Candidates will be ready to become accredited as internal or external coaches (subject to a series of examination criteria) and true culture change can happen.

Even if internal coaches are not required, training managers to a certified standard of coaching will embed the coaching to the extent that they are able to use coaching skills fluently during day-to-day leadership situations, whether between managers, reports or colleagues, and to move smoothly along the coaching–mentoring–managing continuum described in Chapter 3 from directive management, through mentoring, to coaching.

I have witnessed whole teams transformed, after a relatively short of amount of coach training, into energetic units where people feel safe to take risks, challenge and support each other, generate healthy conflict, and function as a united and creative entity.

Training coaches at the BBC

One of the many organizations that have invested in coach training is the BBC, under the leadership of former Head of Coaching Liz Macann. By the end of the 1990s, coaching was beginning to be experienced by the very top team but was largely unknown throughout the rest of the organization.

Liz felt inspired to approach the challenge of introducing the concept to the wider BBC, and created a robust structure for training internal coaches and maintaining standards by co-founding the BBC's in-house Executive, Leadership and Management Coaching Network and the BBC Coach Foundation Course. She selected and trained around 250 coaches over a 12-year period; set up systems for allocations, evaluation, supervision and continuing professional development; and oversaw the service provided by the coaches. The team decided that a healthy approach would be for coaches to come from all over the business and the result was that, once the programme became known throughout the organization, applications came in from all areas including senior leaders and managers, programme makers, engineers, technical staff and professional services.

None of the coaches receives any financial reward for the extra work and all must undertake to coach three internal clients, at any one time, from divisions other than their own. All of this has to be accommodated into their existing work schedules.

The course comprises three modules totalling nine days, interspersed with six weeks' fieldwork supported by a coach mentor, including one day for assessment and internal individual certification. The graduates go on to coach internal clients on one of four coaching programmes: the Executive Coaching Programme, the Leadership Coaching Programme, the First One Hundred Days and Career Management Coaching. In addition, the Network provides training in Coaching Skills for Managers for anyone who requests it, via monthly two-day courses.

The BBC Coaching Network has won several national and international awards for its professionalism and impact, including the ICF's Prism Award, and Liz Macann was voted Coach of the Year by *Coaching at Work* readers in 2009. The programme has won accreditation by the European Mentoring and Coaching Council and the International Coach Federation.

A number of evaluation studies have been run on the programme and have delivered significant findings:

- Somewhat surprisingly, staff reported that they were completely comfortable with the notion of internal coaches (provided they are rigorously trained) and thought that external coaching was preferable only for those in particularly high-profile, outward facing roles.

- Challenges considered to have been significantly helped by coaching included confidence building, transitioning, dealing with uncertainty and change, career issues, performance management, building relationships, managing upwards, creating strategies and resolving business issues. The least successful areas were generating creative thinking and managing resources. Interestingly, established and senior leaders reported largely the same level of impact for the same topics.

- People reported raised levels of awareness in terms of their personal leadership capability, their strengths and weaknesses, how their behaviour impacts on others, their ability to find alternative approaches and their relationships in general.

Training the coach trainer at IKEA

Another organization that champions a coaching approach is international retailer IKEA. The company has always nurtured a thriving coaching culture, embedded by its founder from its inception, but is challenged by the nature of the business, which involves a great deal of change, many temporary staff, a diverse cultural mix and the continuing movement of managers into different positions, something which is encouraged in all coaching cultures.

In 2006 I was asked by Performance Consultants International to create a substantial coaching and train the trainer programme at IKEA. Working with Sir John Whitmore and James Wright, our Head of Training, I designed a programme comprising fast, simple methods to help new and temporary staff assimilate the coaching culture, to improve the skills of existing managers in providing feedback and to build a team of in-house coach trainers to sustain the new techniques.

We delivered a two-day foundation skills course to 80+ managers over a period of six months. During this time, a team of 30 or so potential trainers emerged, and we trained these individuals to deliver the two-day programme by working as apprentices on the courses our own trainers were delivering. Altogether the trainee trainers undertook an eight-day programme over the six-month period, enabling them to deliver the two-day course at regular intervals. In addition, I wrote a short book called *The Coaching and Feedback Handbook* for internal use at IKEA.

Three years later IKEA reported back that 140–160 managers a year are receiving the two-day training. Their internal management evaluation tool, VOICE, showed an increase from 67 per cent to 72 per cent and they were expecting it to rise the following year. The IKEA trainers created a lively coaching intranet hub with videos, podcasts, people and coaching materials, which supports the coaching programme today.

A common assumption in training managers as coaches is that the training must start at the top, so that the style of management can filter down the organization like a type of osmosis. A difficulty here is that many senior managers want their staff to be trained but do not accept the need for training themselves. In fact I have found that the reverse is the case, because younger managers are more likely to have been exposed to a coaching style of management than their older bosses, who may have started their working lives in the seventies or eighties when the workplace was more dictatorial than it is today.

I am not infrequently asked by a senior leader to 'fix my team', only to hear from the team that it is their boss who needs to be 'fixed'. However, if the training starts in the middle of the organization rather than at the top, all is not lost, because as soon as someone at any level adopts a coaching style of management, it is likely that the difference will be noticed. The filtering effect can work sideways or upwards as well as downwards, so it will not be long before senior managers who refused to attend the initial round of training are asking for a course themselves. They will have started to become aware of some of the benefits of a coaching approach in leadership, which is described in Chapter 10.

Coaching in leadership

10

SUMMARY

- Identifying the traits of leadership
- Coaching skills vs behaviour and attitude
- Transformational leadership programme at CLM 2012 Olympic Delivery Partner
- Leadership and coaching in the arts sector
- Coaching a senior team leader in a multinational organization

Identifying the traits of leadership

Coaching in leadership existed for many years before the term acquired its meaning in the workplace today, and there are widespread misconceptions about it. To enable people to understand the principles of coaching in leadership, I use an exercise developed by Sir John Whitmore, which I suggest you try out now:

Think of someone in your life who was in a position of leadership to you and who inspired you – someone you had a personal relationship with, not a leader viewed from afar. It might be a relative, a teacher, a youth leader, or, later, a business manager. It will be someone you were always pleased to see, and who, you felt, helped you to develop as a person.
Now ask yourself:

- What did that leader do that worked for you? What skills did your leader use? How did he or she behave?

- How did you feel when you were with your leader? What impact did he or she have on you?

Write down a list in each category. Take five or ten minutes to do this before turning the page to look at the lists below, so that you are not influenced by my list.

When you have finished your list, consider how the lists below compare with what you have written:

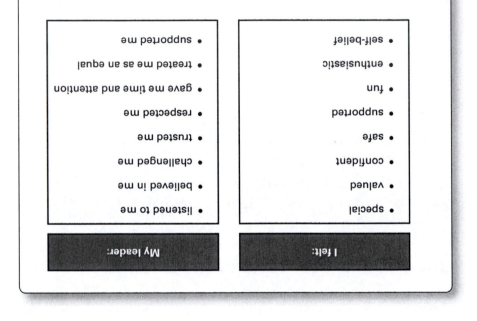

I felt:	My leader:
• self-belief	• supported me
• enthusiastic	• treated me as an equal
• fun	• gave me time and attention
• supported	• respected me
• safe	• trusted me
• confident	• challenged me
• valued	• believed in me
• special	• listened to me

I have undertaken this exercise with managers who were American, Arabian, Indian, Malaysian, Australian, East or West Europeans, male or female, old or young. Extraordinarily, the answers are always the same, often not just in the sentiments but also in the use of the exact words.

The factors on this list represent common values that underlie inspiring leadership across all cultures, age groups and sexes. Yet when describing leadership in the abstract, people tend to talk about charisma, knowledge, experience and flag-waving at the front of the crowd, larger-than-life aspects rarely mentioned when people describe the leader who meant the most to them personally.

Take another look at the list. Who can own these skills of listening, showing belief in others, giving time and so on? Anyone can! Therefore, *anyone* can be a great leader!

Coaching skills vs behaviour and attitude

There is a misconception that coaching is about learning particular techniques, such as active listening, open questioning and clarifying. These are indeed coaching skills, but for me what turns someone into a coaching manager is the underlying intention behind the words – treating people with respect, focusing on their development, believing in them and raising their awareness and self-belief:

Coaching skills vs intention

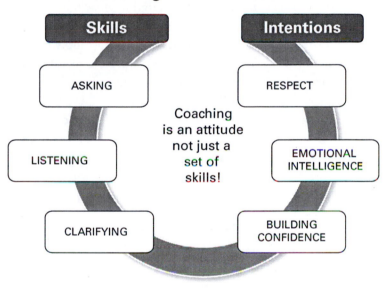

If managers display emotional intelligence, as described by Daniel Goleman (Goleman, 1996), they will be leading in a coaching style, whether or not they have been trained on coaching courses. Further training will enhance these skills and help them to realize why their style of leadership is so effective. However, if managers complete the training but the intention to serve their reports is not in place, they may well find themselves saying, 'I'm using open questions but my staff still hate me!'

I have found that the most effective way of becoming a coaching manager – if one is not, due to culture and upbringing, a natural coach – is to learn and copy the skills as taught on courses, integrate them through practice, and then throw the rule book away. In this way, it is possible to manage in a coaching style but with authenticity in terms of one's own personality and values. Coaching skills should always be the tool, not the master.

Transformational Leadership Programme at CLM 2012 Olympic Delivery Partner

In 2005 I met Tom Dalton, then Chairman of Laing O'Rourke, at a presentation I delivered in Dubai. He was fascinated by coaching and two years later invited me to create a transformational leadership and team building programme for the newly formed construction consortium which had won the bid to build the 2012 stadium, including planning, integration with public services and legacy. The three partners in the Consortium were Laing O'Rourke, Mace and CH2M Hill.

I worked closely with the Head of Organizational Development Caroline Blackman to design a leadership programme that would help the consortium to unite into a cohesive team. The group was led by a CEO, COO and eight senior directors, all of whom had excellent track records in leading teams and successfully completing large construction projects. However, each organization had its own distinct culture and way of communicating, so the challenge was to align the three cultures so that they would be able to work towards common goals.

The situation was made more complicated by the fact that the construction consortium reported to the Olympic Development Authority, a public sector organization with very different values from the construction industry in terms of risk and decision-making, and that all the teams who worked for the new leaders had to be created from scratch.

I started by having an informal chat with each member of the team and observing some of their board meetings. Then, over a period of six months, I coached each individual member of the leadership team, but only at their request. When, after a few months had passed, one who had not agreed to meet with me stopped me in the corridor one day and asked 'And when am I going to get one of your sessions?' I felt that the coaching programme must be making an impact.

I believe that the ability to coach is essential for any successful leader in today's work environment. Indeed, I have found myself spending a fair proportion of the time in corporate coaching sessions teaching skills that would be better learned in a training room, with other participants to practise with.

So I put together a two-day course in coaching skills for this group of leaders to experience together. It was more or less the same programme I offer any other group, from CEOs to shop floor team leaders. Coaching skills are no respecter of rank – everyone needs first of all to understand the basic principles of how to listen, ask questions that make people think, and focusing someone else's agenda. In fact it is often the more senior leaders who need the most practice, because they are less likely to have been exposed to coaching role models than younger workers.

The Chairman awarded this session ten out of ten, and as I facilitated my last board meeting there, it was satisfying to see the amount of energy, laughter and fast decision-making that was happening across the team, to a much greater extent than when we had started the programme. No doubt there were more challenging times for the group ahead, but several years later, after the stadiums had been built and the legacy protected, I was not at all surprised that throughout the usual backbiting that the British press directed at the Olympics, no one was able to criticize the buildings. The consortium had completed the job on time, within budget and to the usual high standards of excellence that each of the organizations was accustomed to delivering.

Leadership and coaching in the arts sector

In 2007 the Cultural Leadership Programme (CLP), an Arts Council England initiative to improve leadership in the arts sector, commissioned Deb Barnard MBE, of Relational Dynamics 1st, to provide a pilot course in coaching skills. The project started with a series of standalone days led by a variety of invited trainers, following which Deb invited me to develop with her a 'Coaching skills for leadership' course which launched in 2008.

Coaching was relatively new within the arts sector and, where it was being used, coaches were usually sourced from the business sector at business sector fees. The aim was to redress the balance and to begin to 'grow' coaches from and working within the creative industries.

CLP subsidized the cost, making it possible for people to attend who would not normally have had access to coaching skills training, and the project pioneered the first accredited coaching course from and for the cultural sector. Not everyone wanted to practice as a one-to-one coach – at least 50 per cent of participants wanted to acquire skills for leadership, management of others or facilitation, and every course was over-subscribed.

Bev Morton, Director of The Art of Possibility, was commissioned by CLP to study the impacts of the Coaching Skills for Leadership programme for CLP and I have drawn on her report for the information which follows.

Participants were recruited through the CLP's networks and mirrored the diversity of the creative sector in their occupations, which included researchers, facilitators, theatre producers, mentors, freelance consultants, artists, development workers, project coordinators, artistic directors, writers, local authority arts officers and CEOs of small to medium organizations. They came from arts festivals, heritage organizations and included workers who were part time, full time, employed, self-employed or engaged in portfolio careers.

The course comprised five days spread over four to six weeks followed by a day for assessment and accreditation awarded by the Cultural Leadership Programme and my organization Performance Coach Training Ltd.

The main outcomes reported were:

- Leadership practice shifted, improving communication and relationships within teams and partner organizations, increased confidence and staff engagement, and improved quality of decision-making.
- Personal development, enhanced understanding of self, emotional literacy and personal thinking processes, an increased sense of an authentic self in leadership, cultivation of an internal coach and a greater understanding of others.
- For some, a crucial turning point or insight occurred during the programme leading to new career opportunities.
- Many participants noted that they connected to their leadership role more directly and began to see themselves more clearly as leaders than they had done previously.
- Some freelancers found they acquired more confidence in their own businesses, which may have been due as much to the coaching they received during the practice sessions as the skills training itself.

What began to emerge for both freelance and employed leaders was that they may have previously thought that leadership was about 'knowing what they knew'. Through the process of coaching training they now had a framework to lead in a different way by stepping back and facilitating other people's thinking, and creating opportunities for them. Bev reported that it was noted again and again that this was a change of perspective and style that would not have happened before the programme.

Eight courses were delivered from 2008 to 2010, when funding ran out and the CLP was disbanded. However, Deb Barnard went on to set up a sister coaching course, Relational Dynamics 1st, in Lancaster, bringing to it a greater emphasis on psycho-dynamics, awareness of self, transference, boundaries, group coaching, supervision and NLP, and thereby sustaining the alumni of trained coaches in the arts sector.

Coaching a senior team leader in a multinational organization

Allard de Jong, a widely experienced international leadership coach and trainer, was recently asked to help a high-performing senior team leader, who led a pan-European team of country managers, to make the most of her leadership and the way in which it was perceived throughout the company. Allard soon enabled this manager to identify the need to expand her scope of leadership behaviours, and positively shape the conversations that peers and other leaders within the organization conducted about the coachee and her department. In short, Allard helped her 'produce' (boosting perform-ance) and 'seduce' (personal profile building) by enabling the coachee to purposefully craft a professional image that was a true reflection of her abilities and aligned with her leadership objectives.

In the second phase of the assignment, it was decided to raise the bar and, in addition to a continued focus on the above topics, a) aim to stretch the coachee's comfort zone in the area of presentation skills; and b) help her to optimize the time spent with remotely located peers.

The main thrust of Allard's work with this coachee was the purposeful and strategic management of her visibility and personal leadership 'brand', which shifted from 'the coachee as a capable results-getter' to 'the coachee as a visionary leader of the business and its people'. This leadership aspiration needed to be built on the organization's quadruple foundation of 'charts the course', 'does the right thing', 'achieves great results' and 'brings out the best in people'. Different interventions (for example, presentations, one-to-one meetings, written communication, setting specific and strategic objectives, securing certain business results and optimizing resource alloca-tion) were planned and skilfully executed in each of these four areas.

Newfound gains in self-awareness and the opportunity to focus on her-self allowed this coachee to use her innate resources more effectively. Fol-lowing the coaching, her leadership began to focus more on vision and strategy, and became recognized as such. She gained a better understanding of who her key interfaces were, what her core messages were and what communication opportunities existed, both written and oral. In addition, her interventions became more impactful.

Meanwhile, she continued to strengthen existing relationships, energize others at new levels and consolidate her team's role and image as that of a versatile and truly 'leaderful' contributor to the worldwide organization. As part of this, she succeeded in building and maintaining strong relationships amidst a complex organization.

One of the greatest outcomes of the coaching was that the coachee made tremendous efforts to maximize her interactions with others and to manage her time with them more carefully. These achievements were evidenced by recent performance evaluations and through discussions with the project sponsors (her line managers) as well as other stakeholders (eg HR).

With his fluency in four languages, Allard is often called upon to work with groups of mixed nationalities. Most of our work with large corporations today requires the trainer to manage the learning of multicultural groups because, no matter which country we might be working in, if there are 12 managers in the room there are likely to be as many different nationalities. This is explored in Chapter 11.

Cross-cultural coaching

11

SUMMARY

- What are 'cultural differences'?
- Cultural differences in team roles
- Coach training for sales leaders at NCR
- Creating a global coaching culture
- Insights in Finland

What are cultural differences?

International organizations today seem to enjoy moving their staff around all over the world; to obtain a promotion managers sometimes have to uproot to another country.

This creates a number of challenges:

- Isolation from their workforce: Sometimes people are sent to countries where they do not speak the language. Most of my global corporate clients work in an environment where the common language is English, which often means that no-one in a senior team is communicating in their first language.

- Separation from friends and family: Executives are expected to work long hours and travel every week, while their spouses struggle with loneliness and their children have to fit into new schools.

- The compensation: These peripatetic executives are paid a lot of money, often including housing and other allowances. The benefits can become 'golden handcuffs' by which families condemn themselves to years of homesickness, never convinced they have made enough to retire, or start that business, or buy that vineyard:

Golden handcuffs

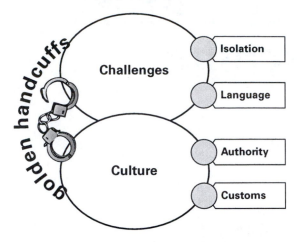

The most common challenge raised is 'cultural differences'. These are distinctions that have been reported by numerous myths and studies. For example, Americans are considered to be direct, while Asians circumspect. It is said that the American directness might be regarded as rude by people from some Asian cultures and that Americans find Asian reticence baffling. Then there are the stories of impulsive Italians, critical Germans and efficient Swiss.

Sometimes these national cultural differences turn out to be true, and if one comes across an attitude that is hard to understand, it is worth seeking out a colleague from the country concerned to see if there is a cultural tradition behind it. However, something else I have discovered through personal experience is that it is important to distinguish between culture and habits – and what is culture, after all, other than habit? Cultures must be respected, while habits can be changed.

For example, I once coached an Indian manager who was being trained in coaching skills. During the action setting stage, I was slightly surprised when he asked me to write the e-mail for him. I automatically separated the boundaries in my head, as coaches must, and suggested that I would support him in writing the e-mail himself. Later, he explained his reason for asking me to write the e-mail; his concern had been that, given the nature of his culture, he would lose authority if he used the coaching 'ask instead of tell' approach. After our session, he was now satisfied that the boundaries could be preserved, and felt that the coaching approach would reinforce his authority rather than weaken it.

Another example is a colleague who worked with a group of Chinese senior managers. She set them an exercise to go away and ask their teams instead of telling them. She met a wave of protest – the managers said they could not possibly do this in their culture, and that it would be unacceptable not only to the managers themselves, but to their reports. She stood her ground, and the managers came back full of enthusiasm and examples of how this new style worked better than the old way.

Whenever someone says, 'This wouldn't work in my culture', the statement can be tested with appropriate questions and the person encouraged to take the risk of doing something differently. Then it can be ascertained whether there is a real cultural issue, which must be respected, or simply a habit that might benefit from being changed.

An example of this might be practising listening skills in Africa. In coaching, one of the ways we show we are listening is to keep our eyes on the person, yet I am told that in parts of Africa it is considered rude to look another person in the eye. This might be a habit that needs to be respected when in Africa, but if the African manager were to move to the United Kingdom, he or she might want to work on changing this habit.

My general guidelines in such situations are:

Cultural differences in team roles

Anyone who is coaching in organizations today, whether as an external or internal coach or a coaching manager, is likely to be involved in cross-cultural coaching, even if no difference in nationality is involved. As well as perceived differences in behaviour dictated by nationality, a second set of distinctions emerges in job roles, where it is said that certain types of people are attracted to certain roles, eg sales, administration, IT or engineering. Yet more categorizations can be made through tools that divide people into types according to their learning, behavioural or working styles.

Again, the dilemma here lies in whether to encourage change or accept the inherent nature of traits that may be causing difficulties and misunderstandings. For example, I once met a successful head of department in IT whose team ran happily and efficiently until all the senior managers in the organization were forced to complete an emotional intelligence inventory. This manager's scores were low and he was thereafter subjected to all kinds of interventions, including coaching, in order to 'improve' his communication skills. However, he believed that he communicated in the manner that suited his teams, who all behaved in a similar way, being IT engineers, which did not mirror the behaviour of, say, the sales people or the HR department.

The words 'if it ain't broke' came into my mind as I saw the frustration experienced by this manager through being subjected to processes that seemed to him to be wasting his time and energy. It could be said that he had an obligation to fit into his peer team, who were from all areas of the business. However, there is a counter argument here that it takes all types to make an effective team, and that some tolerance was required from those whose behaviour styles were different from those of the IT manager – something to be addressed perhaps by the overall team leader (in this case the CEO) with support from the HR department.

The cultural gap between people drawn to various roles in an organization can be greater than that which arises between different nationalities, and needs to be respected with the same care in terms of managing diversity. Similarly, where people's individual learning styles are respected, namely when they are encouraged to approach tasks in the way that feels most natural to them, their performance will be maximized and they will feel happier and more confident about their work in general.

One aspect I have noticed while designing and delivering global coach training programmes is how coaching seems to provide a universal language, which could be described as the 'Esperanto' of communication. It is not uncommon within international corporations for every person in a team to be of a different nationality, with native tongues ranging from Czech to Chinese. As I watch individuals like these in my coaching programmes, I am always struck by the way that coaching skills provide bridges across the gulf of misinterpretation. I have noticed the same effect in uniting workers from different areas of the business, for instance the IT people might seem to speak a different language from the sales people, even though they may both be of the same nationality and from similar cultures. Coaching skills provide a bridge across such different perspectives.

Coach training for sales leaders at a global business services organization

Several years ago I was asked to design a coach training programme for the first line sales managers at a global organization. These very senior managers handled major accounts which could represent a multi-million dollar value and each might head whole teams that worked solely with one client. To support the complexity of the major account sales processes at this level the organization employed solid structures provided by a leading global sales training organization. Of necessity these structures required a fair amount of form filling and analysis and, while the managers respected the processes and understood why they were necessary, sales teams and paperwork do not always mix well together – in short, the organization was making a significant investment in sales process training, but the application of process to the job needed a lot of help from the sales managers.

Newly appointed Global Head of Sales Learning, John Newton, had the inspired idea that combining coach training with the sales process training might address the issue by equipping sales managers with the 'what' and the 'how' together and in a realistic context, as well as enhancing the ability of the managers to lead their teams. Together with the sales training organization, we devised a three-day training programme which combined the two types of training. After inspecting the resulting programme, I proposed that the managers underwent a day of foundation skills coach training followed by the usual sales training programme, during which they would focus on a coaching skill for each practice. I demonstrated how to undergo each process in a coaching style with a volunteer, then the managers paired up to practise the skills between them.

One of the biggest challenges we faced was that not all the managers had volunteered for the training and some might have preferred to be spending their time working with their accounts. I overcame any resistance by introducing a practical session within the first hour, because I find that although it is difficult to explain what coaching is and what it does, people have to experience only a few minutes of coaching to understand that it not only feels better to be on the receiving end, but it is more enjoyable to lead in a coaching style as well.

Firstly I asked for a volunteer to be coached about a detailed document (an account plan) that the managers had completed as part of their sales training. Normally this would be undertaken by a member of their team, then the manager would have to spend time analyzing the team member's view of the account and making decisions about how to move forward. The volunteer began by handing me his account plan to start this process. I said I did not need to look at it, and noticed a few jaws dropping around the room.

Naturally I used the coaching approach of asking the manager who was acting as a team member for his own thoughts, conclusions and proposals for action on the content of the account plan, supported by the GROW model described in Chapter 23. After just 20 minutes we had an action plan in place for that account and the atmosphere was charged with energy and motivation. Afterwards one of the managers said I had just done in 20 minutes what normally took him four hours. And I had not even understood a fair amount of what the volunteer had said! From then on I had their attention and the group could not wait to learn the new skills.

One innovative step was to combine the practice in between sessions, which we normally build into our programmes in order to embed the learning with the sales processes. The result of this was that the managers absorbed both sets of learning into the context of their day-to-day work, so none of the training was lost. They came together on a conference call six weeks later to review the practice, and we received feedback such as 'all training should be run this way'. I value work between sessions as highly as the learning that takes place in the training room, because it is where the participants can make mistakes in the 'safe space' of working with a buddy, stretch their capabilities, make the process their own and teach themselves to coach.

John, as the Global Head of Sales Learning, believed that the skills would be useful worldwide, so we faced the challenge of getting buy-in from other regional sales leaders who might have no idea of what coaching was or why it would be useful. I always ensure that written feedback is collected after every module of training, while the reactions are fresh in people's minds, and I take note of verbal feedback given in the training room or by phone, because this is often fresher and more spontaneous than the written kind. I collated some useful comments, obtained permission from their originators, and we were able to present recommendations from internal staff to illustrate and sell the value of the training. I think this attracted candidates from all over the world, particularly where the feedback was from senior and influential managers, and we eventually delivered the training in numerous locations to the North America and Asia Pacific first line sales leaders.

Creating a global coaching culture

In 2010 I started working with one of the growing number of corporations who are centralizing coach training for managers around the world. I was asked to create a manager-as-coach programme which could be delivered through a team of international trainers all over the world and in the main business languages. The programme has been delivered to hundreds of managers and is still being rolled out from Senegal to Kazakhstan at the time of writing.

I think the prime directive of such programmes is to embed the skills thoroughly while taking up as little of the managers' time as possible. Having spent so many years as a corporate director at the 'sharp' end of businesses, I am aware of the pressure that managers face and that, while complex theories may be fascinating, what happens in the training room must be of immediate practical use.

So I created an intensive programme lasting only five days, but – and this is the crucial element – those five days are spread over three separate modules with at least six weeks of practice in between. Again, this is where the managers take what we have taught them and then teach themselves to coach. In this way, and because in the training room we coach volunteers who choose topics closely related to their day-to-day work, every manager has the sense of undertaking a course specifically designed for his or her own work environment. It is all in the spirit of coaching, where people take ownership and responsibility for their own development.

The emphasis on practical work is backed up by course manuals which provide in-depth explanations of the theory and principles behind coaching, so that if the participants encounter any challenges further down the line they should be able to find help in the reference materials. During the courses we teach the elements of coaching supervision as well so that those who go on to deliver formal sessions will be familiar with the process and understand the benefit of having a supervisor. I believe that peer supervision is as useful as supervision from a more experienced coach, so the participants can supervise each other, and this is described more fully in Chapter 17, 'Coaching supervision: a workplace perspective'.

The purpose of the coach training in this organization is for managers to enhance their leadership styles and team building rather than to deliver coaching sessions. However, we find that taking the training to the level where managers emerge as fully certified internal or external coaches is the best way of ensuring that they can move fluently along the line described in

Chapter 3, 'The directive–non-directive continuum', between coaching, mentoring and directive management.

Insights in Finland

Barry Rogers is an Independent Consultant and Cultural Development Coach at Insights Finland, and contributed to the development of the Insights Discovery model. Today this is recognized globally as a leading psychometric instrument and is available in 30+ languages.

One occasion when Barry used this tool occurred several years ago when he was asked to facilitate a three-day team development workshop in Finland. The group comprised 18 members, predominantly Finns plus two Estonians. The overall Insights profile of the group was noticeably 'extraverted intuitive', which meant that Barry could look forward to plenty of ideas and energetic chatter.

The event started at 8.30 in the morning but by coffee break at 10.00 nobody had spoken. This triggered Barry's own extraverted side to go into overdrive and he became even more animated, to the point when his Finnish colleague stepped in and said 'Barry, you have to stop this. You're frightening people!'

Barry realized that he had been viewing the group dynamics from an Anglo-Saxon perspective. It became clear as the workshop progressed that although the individual participants were, it was true, representative of their type as defined by Insights, their cultural preferences caused them to present themselves in a totally different way to Barry's expectations.

Cross-cultural differences across roles

Another case Barry was involved with illustrates the difficulties that different types of thinkers sometimes experience in communicating with each other. He was coaching the technical manager of a US chemical company based in the UK, whom we will call John. This manager was a recent recruit and had to work with a team of eight laboratory staff from science-related backgrounds. John's own background was as a project manager in the civil engineering sector, where his *extraverted, intuitive* thinking style, identified by the Insights profile he had completed, was just right for the culture. However, within a fairly short time in his new job, it became evident that

John's 'getting down to business' approach was not appreciated by his team of research chemists, who were predominantly what the Insights model defines as *introverted sensing*.

Over a six-month coaching period, during which Barry had access both to John and his team, the profiles played an important part in resolving some of the attendant challenges. Simply through an enhanced awareness of individual and team preferences, the members began to appreciate different management styles and to develop outside of their natural and preferred work practices.

Coaching may be prevalent today in multinational commercial conglomerates because they have the profits to pay for it. However, other organizations are finding ways to make coaching work for them and the educational sector is one that might be more aligned with coaching principles than most. An exciting part of our work in recent years has been in schools, and some of this is described in Chapter 12.

12 Coaching in schools

SUMMARY

- The alignment of coaching with learning
- A coaching programme for North Somerset schools
- Coach training for teachers in Hong Kong
- Coaching adolescents

The alignment of coaching with learning

Coaching skills are naturally suited to schools and any kind of learning environment. I quoted the Socratic questioning method in Chapter 1 of this book and I think it is the experience of many teachers that students perform the best, and are most inspired, when taking responsibility for their own learning. Indeed it was this discovery that led Tim Gallwey, on his tennis court at Harvard (whose story is told in Chapter 41, 'The Inner Game') to the formation of the principles of performance coaching as we know it today.

Contemporary developments in educational philosophy are also highly congruent with a coaching approach to education. Broad access to digital media resources has seen the focus of pedagogy move away from a 'know what' towards a 'know how' approach. Students can instantly access more content than any teacher can possibly provide and a teacher is no longer the gatekeeper and judicious disseminator of knowledge. Thus, teaching in many classrooms today is much more inclined to be about guiding lines of enquiry, encouraging self-diagnostic reflection and highlighting skill-based and attitudinal approaches to learning than about instruction. The profession is on the cusp of fundamental change and an understanding of the principles of coaching can be critical in tipping the balance of a school's philosophy from a 'factory model' of command and control to a school hub of innovation, creativity and discovery. In one way, this is nothing new – ask anyone to recall their favourite teacher, and it is likely to be the one who inspired pupils to think for themselves rather than those who were the most eloquent or well informed about their subjects.

However, although the learning interface between teacher and student may be changing globally in countries with open access to e-media, it would be harder to find such differences in the developing world where 60 to a class, a blackboard and some chalk may still be the norm. Education systems vary but the demands on teachers are extensive.

In the United Kingdom, for example, in addition to their hours in the classroom, today's teachers have to deal with after-school activities, including discussions with parents, reports to the school board and close scrutiny by inspectors responsible for maintaining standards in schools. The Victorian education system was designed as a vehicle for social instruction and the establishment of order and keeping discipline remains an essential component of a teacher's required skill-set. I am told by teachers in some state schools that lessons are considered a success simply when complete uproar has been avoided; the chance of pupils learning anything is almost considered a bonus. Where children have come to understand that they have certain rights that can be exercised, an accusation against a teacher may prove a tempting distraction for a bored pupil in a frustrating school environment, regardless of whether it is true or not. Even in this setting, there is plenty of learning going on but the learning is about limiting beliefs, low expectations and fixed mindsets which polarize teacher from learner and cement adversarial relationships.

In such situations the emotional intelligence of a coaching based approach can re-empower students, relieve tension, reduce conflict and bring back the focus of the original purpose which is, after all, education. Of course, in contrast to this socially challenging picture, there exist many schools where a focus on outcomes (exam results and university entrance) is paramount, attainment is high, and both teachers and pupils feel they are spending their days in a meaningful way. In these apparently 'successful' schools, the need for an emotionally intelligent approach is equally high. In this context there are huge pressures on students – from their families, their peers and their schools – not to 'fail'. Coaching can provide a pressure release in this situation and a more realistic perspective where anything less than full marks looks like disaster.

From time to time news items are published about schools which appear to have been turned around from socially embattled stagnation to places of academic achievement, presided over by a new head teacher who has reformed attitudes throughout the establishment. Graham Silverthorne, a visionary head teacher whose story is told below, questions to what extent this is the reality, or whether the school has just learned to play by the rules to please inspectors. Graham believes that it is the values-based schools that are the outstanding ones, and that academic achievement is generally (but not always) the by-product of these strong values. The additional benefit that coaching can bring is to facilitate the discussion between all members of the community about establishing a common value set and then walking the words.

In all contexts, leadership is the key to establishing a values-based culture. School leaders, like leaders in any other organization, have to know how to develop and motivate their 'teams', which commonly comprise several dozen teachers and hundreds of pupils. Over the last five years I have been asked to create programmes for a number of educational institutions around the world, and these have been designed and delivered in conjunction with my colleague James Wright, who specializes in the field of children and learning.

A coaching programme for North Somerset schools

A series of such projects was commissioned by Graham, who at the time we met was responsible for a large comprehensive school in Portishead. After becoming intrigued by coaching he joined one of our open courses in 2007. The training ran over two parts, with practice assignments in between, and Graham returned to the second module with the tale of how he had been in the difficult position of having to fire someone. 'So I coached him using GROW, and he fired himself!' Graham recounted with surprise. 'And then he thanked me for it!'

This resonated strongly with my experiences at Virgin. For the first seven years no-one was fired, because in a coaching culture people take responsibility for their own development. If they believe themselves to be in the wrong job they will recognize the fact and take action, even if it means 'firing themselves'. Graham had discovered this for himself, by adhering to the principles of coaching.

Graham found the coaching approach useful at many levels within his role and asked us to help him create a coaching programme for his school. He was sensitive to the teachers' need to embrace the plan rather than feel it was something that was being forced upon them. He wanted to introduce the concept of coaching gently, as it was not well known at that time, and arranged for James to coach five teachers on a one-to-one basis over a ten-week period. (Incidentally, his request for five volunteers to be coached – partly within school hours but also over a weekend, on areas of their lives chosen by them and kept completely confidential to them – was met with an immediate clamour from 25 members of staff, from whom he was obliged to choose!)

Ten weeks later, this yielded a core coaching group who could speak from personal experience about the benefits of coaching, and led to a four-day course spread over two months where substantial numbers of teachers were trained. The 'pay-back' from the trained teachers was an expectation that they would coach at least one peer within the school and join a development group to look at further roll-out strategies. Requests to be coached started to come in from other members of staff and Graham found himself coaching several line reports. Despite initial reservations about how possible this would be within the hierarchical framework, these coaching sessions proved highly successful, positively transformational in a number of cases. An unexpected consequence, for Graham as a leader was the change in other people's perceptions of him, which opened up doors to emotionally literate exchanges previously denied by the glass walls of perceived authority-based behaviours.

Psychologists will tell us that perceived behaviour becomes reality. Graham told me that the biggest 'win' for him in introducing coaching to his school was the learning that it could change people's perceptions, both of their own circumstances and of himself as leader. This became a driver to change the reality in that school.

Following the one-to-one coaching series and the coach training programme, James presented the benefits of coaching to the entire staff, including 120 teachers, before rolling out the training to the next group of selected teachers. Then 11 students were trained as peer coaches, and this group went on to work within the student body, and with students from another school, to develop their own coaching model.

Graham found that coaching teenagers presented its own challenges. Contemporary neuro-science suggests that the teenage brain does not achieve its full capacity for strategic awareness until the very late teens or early 20s, so Graham advocates that when coaching teenagers, goal setting, in particular, requires a slightly different approach. Because teenagers simply do not have the hard wiring to think 'strategically' (in the manner that distinguishes adult human beings who can 'construct' future pictures, assess likely emotional responses and make 'virtual' selections from these constructed realities) it is much harder for them to set goals and create metaphorical meaning. Graham suggests that is a combination of the fact that they have not lived long enough to have very comprehensive 'reference libraries' of experiences that they might use to construct future possible scenarios, and because their brains often do not have the physical hard-wiring to develop consequential outcomes. We are all familiar with this apparent recklessness of youth, these days given the acronym YOLO on social networking, as in 'you only live once'. However, the dictum 'live fast, die young' looks a lot less attractive as the adult brain begins to identify patterns of behaviour and the likely consequences of actions. It is this ability to forward-project that allows coachees to choose preferred outcomes in a goal-setting process.

So Graham proposes that the challenge for the coach is to scaffold the goal-setting process by helping the construction of future possibilities and goals in a more directive way than is advised or desirable with adults. This can be achieved by spending more time coaching the teenager to construct images, metaphors and possibilities, in effect intervening more than would be considered 'clean' with adults (in the sense of not leading or influencing the coachee).

The teachers who took part in the coaching programme reported that as well as having learned useful new communication skills, they experienced an improvement in terms of leadership and driving forward the aims of the organization, and they were excited by the prospect of cascading the coaching approach through the school. The programme was designed to be highly practical and interactive, which mirrored the way that teachers work, and all the skills were modelled in live demonstrations, discussed, practised and thoroughly examined. The overwhelming themes that emerged from their feedback were that they felt inspired and that all the staff in their schools should have the opportunity to be trained in coaching skills, not just for the benefit of their schoolwork but for use in their everyday lives.

The success of that coaching programme was noticed by the education chiefs in the County and led to the creation of the North Somerset Coaching Partnership. Within a couple of years this became a network of local schools committed to the coaching approach, with the stated aim 'for coaching to be the preferred strategy for leadership across North Somerset Council and its schools'. The participants were mostly head teachers and deputy heads who wished to become accredited coaches and to use the skills to create a coaching culture within their schools.

Accompanied by another colleague of ours, Wendy Oliver, who is also passionate about coaching in schools, James delivered a series of training courses that resulted in the accreditation of over 60 new teacher-coaches using the skills with their departments and their students. These heads and deputy heads reported that the programme not only empowered them to influence the lives of the young people in their schools, and enhanced their relationships with parents and governors, but that their personal lives were improved as a result of the training as well. Time and again we hear from teachers that coach training has been the most accessible and practically useful that they have ever attended and that the skills will enhance every aspect of their teaching work, team leadership and their lives in general.

Coach training for teachers in Hong Kong

The next leg of this journey happened when Graham moved to Hong Kong to take up the post of Principal in one of the 17 schools governed by the English Schools Foundation (ESF) group. In a fee-paying international setting, teaching conditions are very different to those found in many state school systems, worldwide. Campuses are full of dedicated pupils eager to learn but also highly pressurized in an atmosphere of competition, high expectation and extra-curricular tutoring. In Hong Kong Graham outlined to James his vision of building a coaching culture throughout a number of closely linked schools, and within the ESF itself.

Over the next two years James trained and accredited nearly 100 teachers as coaches in Hong Kong. By this time Graham had become an accomplished coach in his own right, so we organized a Train the Trainer course for Graham and a colleague, David Fitzgerald, a graduate of the first ESF coaching courses. Graham and David are now delivering the training themselves to teachers throughout the network and have created a regular Coaching Club which meets monthly to embed and practice the coaching. Graham is also currently engaged in creating a protocol that articulates a coaching based approach to line management and the formal performance management process in his school. His experience in this area already suggests that employees set themselves 'owned' and more demanding targets in this setting than a line manager would set for them. A no-blame, aspirational development conversation that leads to goals that are congruent with the broad aims of the organization is the ideal way of embedding the practice of coaching within a professional setting.

The feedback on both the courses that James delivered and the in-house training led by Graham and David has been enthusiastic and passionate. David reports that many ESF leaders believe that a coaching culture increases focus on developing others and managing performance; promotes the sharing and utilization of knowledge; leads to more participative and transparent decision-making; and makes learning and development a top priority. He outlined the shape of the ESF coaching approach by couching it within the GROW model (the fundamental coaching model described in Chapter 23):

Goal

   ESF embracing a coaching culture.

Reality

   There are pockets of innovation in the schools and in their governing body, the English Schools Foundation Centre, where the way they do business is changing. Coaching is becoming part of everyday work and coaching strategies such as GROW are being used more commonly. At the moment this is the case in a growing number of schools and is beginning to become evident in system wide committees and groups at the Centre. An additional challenge is that there are senior leaders who have completed other coaching courses and who have shown some resistance to the new programme. They think that the one-day 'Coaching and Mentoring' course they completed 10 years ago is similar to the current model, when in reality it is vastly different: the original training was an outside-in approach rather than inside-out, meaning that coaching was something 'done to' people rather than 'done within', whereas the GROW model brings about real internal change. This needs to be kept in mind when making decisions.

Options

   Creating a coaching culture requires a new approach to change, and the leaders in a recent study identified five key strategies to achieve the desired result.

1. ***Seed the organization with leaders and managers who can role-model coaching approaches.***

   This approach is the one currently underway in ESF. Already 25 a large number of senior leaders have trained as coaches and two as coach trainers. David would like to make completion of the coaching course a priority for all principals and members of the senior management team and education advisory team.

2. ***Link coaching outcomes to success of the business. Develop a competency model with strategic coaching goals, tactics and measures around coaching behaviour.***

   David is not entirely comfortable with this strategy because once coaching outcomes are linked to business outcomes there is a risk of tainting coaching with results. He prefers the pure approach, but agrees it is an area that could be explored, especially around coaching goals and tactics.

(Continued)

3. **Coach senior leadership teams in creating culture change. Over twice as many leaders wanted team coaching as those who said they were receiving it.**

   The use of coaching strategies is growing in ESF's schools and there is real potential for this approach to be the norm in terms of the way its people approach change and the challenges that go along with that.

4. **Recognize and reward coaching-culture behaviours. Highlight role models and the positive outcomes produced by these new behaviours.**

   It would certainly be possible to promote the positive outcomes associated with coaching through education team newsletters and by sharing at various Committee levels.

5. **Integrate coaching with other people-management processes.**

   David believes this has real potential in terms of performance management in particular and suggests considering this approach when reviewing the current performance management system.

Will

What can be done to achieve this goal or another related goal?

Coaching adolescents

Back in the UK, James has continued his activities with schools, designing coaching courses and workshops for parents, and experimenting with how coaching skills can best support adolescents. He is also the Head of Training on our MOE Foundation courses for disadvantaged young adults, which is described in Chapter 14, 'Corporate social responsibility', where his role is to develop new trainers from the youngsters who attend the courses.

Throughout these years of taking coaching into schools, James has come to the conclusion that educators are quick to adapt to the coaching style of communication and already attuned to the coaching space of drawing learning from others rather than lecturing or telling. Graham's caveat on this is that teachers are brought up to be problem solvers – which can make for the type of 'level 3' listening described in Chapter 19, and quick fix solutions if coach training does not embed deeply. This is the school challenge.

Of course, teaching in schools is only one input of education, and children need consistency from parents, grandparents, relatives, youth leaders, and friends as well. Certainly parents have reported to James that the coaching approach is helping them to have longer and more insightful conversations with their children, of all ages, than was previously the case, particularly where they have had the not unusual experience of sliding into more reticent patterns of communication as the children reached adolescence. Graham witnessed a teacher transform his relationship with his own 15-year-old son by moving the locus of their interaction from parent/child to peer coach.

On practically every course I have delivered to managers in corporations there are several who share stories of how well their new-found coaching skills have helped their children, sometimes with life-changing effects. One had a son who had lapsed into depression for a year after failing to win a place at his chosen leading university. He seemed to have given up on life altogether until a 20-minute long coaching session from his parent, who had completed the first three days of our manager-as-coach course, resulted in a complete turnaround in attitude, after which the boy started to research and apply to less highly rated universities for a place.

As well as the skills of listening, questioning and clarifying, one of the key components of coaching is the GROW structure which provides an underlying framework for conversations. This is described fully in Chapter 23 and its fundamental purpose is to encourage the coachee to view situations from various perspectives in the future and the present before deciding how to proceed.

Having this structure for their conversations has proved particularly useful to the participants on the MOE courses, and it is evident that in daily life and education the benefit of such a structure is not as explicit as it needs to be. Constant, applied modelling of these skills throughout the school years can only serve to assist the teachers to create the ideal learning environments in which young adults of the future can flourish.

The full story of MOE is a wonderful example of the growing trend of corporate social responsibility, and the full story is told – among others – in Chapter 14.

One of the experiences that led to my commitment to MOE was a volunteer stint which I did for Crisis at Christmas, the organization which provides food and accommodation for the homeless at Christmas time and voluntary support all year round, and this is described in Chapter 13.

Coaching for Crisis at Christmas

'When a street stabbing happens it doesn't start with knives being drawn; there are words before the knives. With the coaching skills I have learned here, I can make a difference when the words start, and stop the knives from coming out.'

These words were the closing comments of a 26-year-old youth who had been sponsored to attend a coaching training course I delivered for Arts Council England described in Chapter 10. He lived in an area where gang violence was part of the landscape. His words made a change from hearing sales directors say their new skills would save time and make money, and got me thinking that coaching skills were most needed out in the wider world where there were no corporate funds to pay for them.

I started looking for ways to achieve this, and I am by no means the first to take this pathway: Tony Gordon, one of Sir John Whitmore's early colleagues, created the organization 'Youth at Risk' many years ago to use a coaching approach with youngsters from challenging backgrounds, and there are charities which provide coaching for prisoners.

To start my own journey, I approached Crisis, the extraordinary organization which has provided support for the homeless for the last 40 years. Their Christmas offering now extends to six days of 24-hour mental and physical care, including counselling, clothing, teachers, dentists, doctors, entertainers and Samaritans, all provided by volunteers. The operation I took part in extended across nine centres, employing 6,500 volunteers and accommodating 2,000 'guests', as the visitors are respectfully addressed, and I chose to base myself in the 'Rough Sleepers' building.

I arranged to run communication skills workshops in the period between Christmas and New Year, which seemed to me the optimum time when the guests would be focused on their next steps.

I delivered four workshops over the two-day period, consisting of simple coaching exercises for emotional intelligence and communication. I started by asking the participants to think of someone they had met during their stay with Crisis whom they liked being with; someone who had motivated and inspired them, made them feel good. We discussed as a group what qualities that person had and what the person had done that the participant liked so much. This is based on the exercise described in Chapter 10, which I undertake with business leaders from all over the world. The answers are always the same and they cut across language and culture: people mainly say that their 'special' person listened, supported, challenged and believed in them, and the homeless people were no different. The exercise demonstrated that getting along with people is about what one can give, not how much one can impress them.

There was one difference in the responses from the Crisis guests to the usual corporate ones: as well as the qualities mentioned above, the expression 'non-judgemental' came up at every workshop. It seems that the acceptance the guests encountered from the volunteers at Crisis outweighed the value of the food, warmth and health treatments, and it was a quality they did not encounter much on the streets. It seemed to be a key feature in inspiring them to change their lives. Crisis is not only non-judgemental, but non-religious and non-political too. Volunteers are asked to leave their personal views at home – we were not there to persuade, convert or pass judgement, which suited my coaching approach very well.

Then the workshop moved on to an interactive game to demonstrate 'the five levels of listening', described in Chapter 19, and I extended it to cover simple questioning techniques. Again, this is an exercise I use regularly with senior executives all over the world.

The guests seemed to find the workshops stimulating and they enjoyed the interaction with others. Most useful of all, I think, was the value of self-examination in a supportive environment. However, I found the key contribution to be the time in between my workshops, which I spent out on the floor. I would pick someone sitting alone and start an informal coaching conversation. We had been well briefed beforehand by Crisis to avoid the usual openers of 'Where do you live?' and 'What do you do?' So my opening question was 'How are you doing?' Coaching worked very well, because coaches talk in the present and the future, not the past, which would be painful for most of the guests. (Samaritans were present round the clock to help with past issues.)

The tough part was balancing the questions which would make people think, against the danger of highlighting the potential hopelessness of their situations. I met no small number of reformed crack addicts who were choosing to live rough in sub-zero temperatures rather than stay with still-addicted friends, because the danger of relapse was too great. There is a perception that people who live on the streets are there because they wish to, and could go to hostels and refuges if they chose. I was shocked to hear again and again that for a male over the age of 25, and not currently an addict, there are few beds available and, without an address, they could not apply for state benefits either. Crisis is working with Shelter to improve these conditions.

My most touching 'client' was a neat, elderly man who longed for a room of his own, where he could lay out his things and arrange his small life. He sat alone and sad in the same chair all day long. Coaching made him smile for a while but would not bring any real hope of being housed.

I think the most useful conversation I had was with a man with a very weathered face whose frequent laugh revealed broken teeth and a wicked sense of humour. He told me he had a room but his life was marred by an addiction to gambling. As opposed to most of those I coached, he was cheerful when not talking to me and became sad when we talked. Several times he said 'it's too late for me now'. Over the course of a few informal coaching sessions he gained a new insight that the gambling took the place of people in his life; he was lonely. He had carried around a helpline number for years and, towards the end of our session, he took it out, studied it and resolved to make the call. I hope he did.

Crisis say that most people today are only three pay slips away from homelessness. That was borne out by a number of the people I met, who only months before had had jobs, cars and somewhere to live, things that we all take for granted. But once homelessness has happened, the obstacles to rejoining society are sometimes insurmountable, particularly if there is an addiction involved. Where coaching can help is in breaking down those obstacles and the accompanying fear into manageable stages, so that the lucky ones can find a way forward and summon the determination to take it.

Crisis offers help to the homeless all year round, not just at Christmas, and always need volunteers. Of particular relevance to coaches is the mentor scheme, for which full details can be found on the Crisis website: www.crisis.org.uk.

14 Corporate social responsibility and shared value: bringing business and society back together

CO-WRITTEN WITH MICHELLE DRAPEAU

SUMMARY

- What is corporate social responsibility?
- Organizations who care
- Shared value
- The emergence of the 'social enterprise'

What is corporate social responsibility?

Corporate social responsibility (CSR) is about sustainability and corporate conscience, and the expectation placed on businesses to manage their operations in a way that makes a positive contribution to social and environmental concerns.

With CSR high on the global political agenda and public expectations of responsible business practices increasing, organizations are coming under pressure to demonstrate their CSR 'credentials' like never before.

Corporate responsibility recognizes that businesses have a responsibility to all stakeholders including: shareholders, employees and their families, customers, suppliers, distributors, local communities, and the wider, global community.

Central to the concept is the expectation that CSR should form an integral part of the overall company philosophy, structure and business processes. This demands an approach that is proactive rather than reactive. It requires businesses to take the lead, rather than respond purely to legislative requirements, and necessitates a level of authenticity and congruence that is possible only with complete commitment from shareholders and those at the top of the organizational tree.

CSR means different things to different people and different organizations, due at least in part to its voluntary nature. Being voluntary does of course allow for some truly creative thinking, but the downside can be a rather narrow view of what CSR truly means. For example, for some, CSR is purely about giving to charity or reducing the carbon footprint. While there are many organizations doing good work in these areas, and setting the standards as trailblazers, a company that sends a big cheque once a month to its favourite charity while failing to respond to the needs of its own employees may not be considered as truly fulfilling its CSR.

Within an organization seeking to fulfil its CSR, the welfare of employees must count. A safe and healthy working environment is essential and employees value supportive, family friendly policies, but CSR can also apply to the value businesses place on each and every employee as individuals with needs for personal fulfilment and self-development. An organization that fully embraces CSR into its business culture empowers its employees, taps into their creative potential and gives them the opportunity to stand up and make a difference.

For example, British retailer, Marks & Spencer has implemented its Plan A Innovation Fund which supports a range of CSR initiatives suggested by its employees, such as strategies for reducing food waste or improving energy efficiency. The company also allows employees paid leave to undertake volunteering activities of their choice, as do other organizations such as footwear and clothing retailer, Timberland, and international software company, Salesforce.com.

CSR can be considered to relate to any of the following, though the list is not exhaustive:

- supporting the local community;
- supporting the wider community;

- charitable donations of time, money or resources;
- support for employees and their families;
- minimizing the organization's impact on the environment;
- taking steps to proactively improve the environment;
- responding to diversity;
- Socially Responsible Investment (SRI);
- maintaining good relationships with customers;
- meeting customer needs; and
- activities which maintain or promote people's rights.

Organizations who care

There are some excellent examples of creative CSR initiatives: global financial services company, Citigroup, runs 'suit drives', collecting suits donated by employees for the charity Dress for Success, to support women on low incomes into work; ice cream manufacturer, Häagen-Dazs®, created a website to educate the public about the dwindling number of bumble bees and donates funds to honey bee research; and electronics giant Sony has expressed an ongoing commitment to 'usability and accessibility', adding features to a range of its products to make them more accessible to older people or people with disabilities.

Opponents of CSR believe that society's problems are not the responsibility of businesses and that commerce should primarily be concerned with making money for shareholders. Supporters argue that corporate responsibility does not remove the accountability to shareholders; central to CSR is the responsibility to survive financially and to contribute to economic development. Indeed, CSR done well can actually lead to a range of benefits, including cost savings and higher turnover, contributing to an increase in profits.

In terms of the benefits to business, CSR can potentially:

- act as a business differentiator;
- improve a company's reputation;
- motivate and engage staff;
- attract new staff and reduce staff turnover;

- generate PR opportunities;
- strengthen marketing campaigns;
- earn the trust and loyalty of customers;
- support entry into new markets – an ability to demonstrate social responsibility is becoming increasingly important worldwide;
- improve efficiency (such as from streamlining logistics);
- reduce costs (from energy savings); and
- enable access to Socially Responsible Investment (SRI) funds.

As Anita Roddick, Body Shop founder, famously said, 'Being good is good for business.' However, the benefits above are a positive by-product of CR, not the 'raison d'être'. As more and more businesses start to see the commercial advantages of CSR and take action to catch up with their competitors, the differentiators no longer exist. What happens then, or when public perception changes and CSR becomes a given, rather than a unique selling point? Those organizations 'signing up' to CSR as a potentially profitable PR exercise may in the end turn out to be disappointed.

The intention behind CSR was always about businesses recognizing their impact and reliance on society, taking steps to minimize any negative impacts and contributing to society's welfare. It was never intended as a PR-generating tool or a way of making businesses richer or more powerful.

However, there are those who believe that CSR puts society on the periphery of organizational operations and in doing so fails to acknowledge the two-way, interdependent relationship between society and business. And this is the starting point for *shared value*, an approach to business that enables society and business to profit from the progress of each other.

Shared value

According to authors Michael E Porter and Mark R Kramer in their *Harvard Business Review* article, 'Creating Shared Value: How to reinvent capitalism – and unleash a wave of innovation and growth' (2011), shared value is a 'new way to achieve economic success'. It is an approach to business that recognizes the interdependence of businesses and society and seeks business opportunities in social problems for the success of both.

In shared value, society rather than profit is at the heart of the business. However, it is not about charity or the redistribution of wealth. Rather, it is about a business having a thorough and intricate understanding of itself and the society within which it operates, identifying where the two meet and addressing concerns in a way that creates both value for society and economic value for the business. The key to shared value is the link between the business and the social concern it seeks to address, and without this factor there can be no shared value. This contrasts with CSR where there may be no link between an organization and the CSR activities it undertakes.

Porter and Kramer identify three ways that companies can create shared value:

1 The first is in relation to a company's products or services and the markets it serves. It requires the company to open its corporate mind, ask itself some searching questions and be willing to innovate (Porter and Kramer call this 'reconceiving products and markets'). Questions may include:

- Are we providing the right product?
- Is it relevant to this specific market?
- Does it benefit society?
- Is there something that this particular market needs that we could provide?
- Could we reduce costs to our customers by doing things differently?

With an open and creative mind, new business opportunities can be identified.

2 The second way is explained by Porter and Kramer as, 'redefining productivity in the value chain' and involves examining the influences that have an impact on a business's costs and productivity. For example, farmers struggling to produce quality products in sufficient quantity could potentially have an impact on a company's costs, the quality of its product and even its reputation. Similarly, poorly designed logistical systems or misuse of energy can have a big impact on a company's efficiency.

3 The third way relates to 'enabling local cluster development'. This is based on an understanding that the success of a business relies on the strength of its support network, both in relation to its suppliers as well as in terms of local specifics such as roads, schools, hospitals, water supply, telecoms and energy provision. Strengthening local clusters in a company's operational locations enables the organization to benefit from improved transport and logistics, more reliable energy supplies and healthier employees; indeed, a vast number of tangible benefits may be felt. For the local community, advantages can include greater employment opportunities, improved education and safer living conditions.

Food company Nestlé focuses its shared value activities on nutrition, water and rural development, all of which are intricately linked with Nestlé's core business activities. Among its numerous activities, Nestlé has implemented its 'Cocoa Plan' to support farmers who provide the company with the cocoa it uses for its range of chocolate products. The company runs agricultural education programmes, supplies farmers with good quality, high yield cocoa plants to improve crop production, and provides water wells to the local communities. The benefits to farmers and their families are increased revenue and better health while Nestlé benefits from a good supply of quality cocoa for their products.

Johnson and Johnson has introduced a range of employee wellness programmes designed both to support employees and their families and to reduce absenteeism due to ill health. Programmes include counselling and coaching services, the provision of nutritionally rich foods in their cafeterias and vending machines, a 'Move and Make it Better' campaign which encourages employees to take more exercise, resilience training to help employees better manage stress, and support for employees wishing to stop smoking. In one year alone, the health care company achieved savings of $15.9 million on its health care costs.

The emergence of the 'social enterprise'

Another type of business which has emerged in recent years is the 'social enterprise'. These organizations are run for a purpose that goes beyond simple shareholder value. They may be charities or commercial enterprises but are conducted along the lines of sustainable and successful principles. Examples include Leaders Quest and The Ministry of Entrepreneurship (MOE) Foundation.

Leaders' Quest is a social enterprise that was founded by entrepreneur Lindsay Levin in 2001. Her Quests are experiential learning journeys which take place in some of the most interesting and challenging parts of the world. A Quest is an intense journey of immersion, during which participants get to know the country and its culture and meet with a wide range of inspiring people from all walks of life. Quest programmes offer first-hand experience of issues on the ground – often in unusual and thought-provoking settings. These might range from a sprawling Mumbai slum to a South African prison or a boardroom in Shanghai. The core difference between Leaders' Quest and many charities is that everyone involved is encouraged to think like an entrepreneur and take responsibility for creating a better future. As a result, a Quest is also a search for insight and a larger sense of individual, and collective, purpose, and a chance to explore practical ways of making a difference.

Leaders' Quest works across sectors – business, civil society and government. Its participants are drawn from all backgrounds – CEOs of multinational companies, heads of non-profit organizations, entrepreneurs and grassroots community leaders. Leaders' Quest works with them to integrate social purpose with performance at the core of their companies, provides mentoring for high-calibre leaders, and empowers some of the poorest in society to tackle tough issues in their communities. The Leaders' Quest global community numbers some 6,000 leaders who are using their unique influence to create positive change in the world.

The Ministry of Entrepreneurship was founded more recently by Darren Robson, and its stated purpose is:

> '...to defeat the conditions that create a poverty mindset in society by stimulating conscious, purposeful entrepreneurial spirit in the current and future global generations. We aim to spin poverty on its head by helping young people realize their strengths, talents, gifts and potential. These young people then become community ambassadors and role models.'

MOE actively seeks to support young people, to break the rules of the game and positively disrupt their life experience by providing them with a supportive network, training, development, coaching, mentoring and leadership/entrepreneurial support.

For me, as a Trustee of MOE, the most exciting aspect is that we collaborate to provide coach training to young people sponsored by organizations such as Kidsco, Centrepoint, Action for Children and Foyer Federation. These youngsters have often been rescued from appalling backgrounds involving homelessness, crime, child abuse, gangland culture and drugs. They are typically aged between 18–25, at the point when they have largely overcome the difficulties created by their backgrounds and are ready to return to education, find a career or create businesses, both contributing to and benefiting from society. What we provide them with are communication skills that are absolutely crucial to someone who has grown up without good role models, and certification as a professional coach. Some go on to use coaching in their careers, particularly those who are helping others like themselves.

Even more exciting is the way MOE is growing the coach training faculty from within. After completing the course, every participant can volunteer to join our Trainers' Pathway at any level, from mentoring new students to delivering training, supported, developed and instructed on their journey by Head of Training, James Wright.

This experience and opportunity to hone their skills can lead to jobs and careers as trainers in the commercial world and, material benefits apart, it does wonders for their self-belief. At the start of our first course, several of the participants sidled up to me and whispered that I should not expect them to say much because they had no confidence, due to traumatic experiences like childhood beatings and mental as well as physical abuse. Yet three days later nearly every one of these youngsters stood in front of a camera and was filmed confidently expounding their plans for the future.

The courses are proliferating throughout the United Kingdom and there are plans to expand across the world. The programmes are attended both by the young people we aim to support and by their mentors. Some of our corporate clients attend as well, taking away a coaching qualification and contributing both financially and as mentors and role models. The mixed backgrounds of the participants provide rich learning for everyone, often leading to unexpected contacts and opportunities and, above all, new insights and a deeper sense of meaning and purpose.

Since its inception in 2012, the MOE Foundation has:

- gifted the equivalent of £150,000 in executive coach training to over 60 individuals;
- raised £40,000 that has been reinvested to support young people in the UK, India and Africa;
- supported two KidsCo MOE 'pioneer' programmes;
- micro-gifted £5,000 to a Tanzanian community, setting five female entrepreneurs up with a sustainable and profitable free running chicken farm that will feed their families and the infirm in the local community;
- successfully tested a ground-breaking approach to micro-gifting that builds a long-term and sustainable community fund to help small scale entrepreneurs in rural Tanzania ('Micro-gifting' means donating a sum of money to be used for setting up an ongoing series of small businesses within the village. These businesses then repay their loans to the village fund so that the money can be lent to other local micro-businesses. In this way the local community is responsible for

managing the money, motivated to repay the money, encouraged by the knowledge that they are helping to raise the individual and collective wealth and sustainability of lifestyle in their community, and they are empowered to make entrepreneurial decisions and take personal responsibility);

- certified over 60 people as professional coaches, providing a training development pathway to 10 people enabling them to learn transferable skills;
- gifted five laptops to support young entrepreneurs and leaders with their education and entrepreneurial learning pathway; and
- supported two successful young entrepreneurs through their entrepreneurial scholarship programme.

By the end of 2013 MOE Foundation will have 'gifted' over £250,000 in executive coach training to young people in the United Kingdom and the aim is to gift the equivalent of £1 million worth by 2015, which will positively impact over 400 young people.

Opponents of shared value believe that it is wrong to make a profit out of social concerns; proponents believe it re-establishes a relationship between businesses and society that has been absent for too long and that without the success of business, society cannot prosper, and vice versa. But whatever the position and whether we are talking about shared value or CSR, what is clear is that the relationship between businesses, communities and society at large is moving into a new era of greater awareness.

At the present time, neither shared value nor corporate social responsibility can possibly hold the solution to all of society's ills but we are away from the starting block and making progress. And that is a step forward in itself.

Bullying in the workplace

15

SUMMARY

- Bullying: nature or nurture? The neural perspective
- Reforming the bully
- Coaching the accidental bully
- How to cope with being bullied

Many of the young people we meet on MOE courses have had their confidence destroyed by extreme bullying in their own homes, both physical and mental. Happily the first change we notice when training them in coaching skills is a building up of that shattered personal self-esteem, a process which has usually already begun due to the dedicated work of their sponsor organizations and key workers. The type of bullying that takes place at work may not extend to physical violence but the effects of mental abuse can be severe.

Bullying: nature or nurture? The neural perspective

With as many as 50 per cent of workers having experienced workplace bullying, and legal cases brought by employees against organizations on the increase, I have sometimes been asked to 'fix' bullies. As a coach, I have taken the approach of enabling the bullies to fix themselves. I came to believe, as I listened to these coachees, that what they really wanted was to be liked and accepted. This is a universal place that everyone starts out from. The desire to be part of a tribe is in our genetic make-up, and is important in ensuring that people protect each other so that the human race survives.

But sometimes people get turned away from this natural desire to belong because of their life experiences. For example, if someone grows up with parents or carers who are aggressive, or perhaps physically violent, then that behaviour might become the child's blueprint for relationships. The lucky ones may meet role models outside of the home from whom they can absorb a more sympathetic way of communicating; others discover that replicating the intimidating environment of their own childhood, while providing a defence, also causes trouble at school and later at work, where they find it difficult to maintain positive relationships with others. The only method that succeeds for those people is to browbeat others into submission, something they became experts in from an early age, and they use these skills as a protection from the confusion, criticism and misery that is the response to their entrenched behaviour ... and the situation spirals.

I am not suggesting that these early experiences are an excuse for bullying people. Many people from violent backgrounds grow up to be gentle and seem to spend their lives trying to create the opposite of the atmosphere they came from. Others achieve a normal balance. What I am looking at here is how the bullying starts, and that will bring us to how we can help the bully to change.

My belief is that bullying is acquired rather than innate conduct, and the result of nurture rather than nature. This is borne out by research. Neuroscientist James Fallon studied the brains of psychopaths (Fallon, 2006) and discovered that there are three key ingredients common to the psychopathic killer:

- Genetics: psychopaths carry one or more (there are ten) high risk violence related genes.
- Loss of brain function in the pre-frontal cortex. This is the circuit that controls ethics, morality and impulse.
- A history of childhood abuse.

In an MRI brain scan, a normal brain is mostly lit up, signifying brain activity. However, a psychopathic brain appears to be dark in the pre-frontal cortex area, showing no activity at all in that area.

This suggests that such killers are therefore not responsible for their crimes or have no control over their actions. However, Fallon was unwilling to subscribe to that view. His interest was heightened by the discovery that there was a history of killers in his own family: the cousin of one of his ancestors was Lizzie Borden, the legendary killer who 'took an axe and gave her mother forty whacks', then dispatched her father in the same way.

There were other psychopaths in the family history as well, so Fallon thought a good place to start would be by examining the brains of his own current family members. He was in for a shock: out of the 40 or so brains he examined, only one had the psychopathic pattern of inactivity in the prefrontal cortex, and it was his own! He went on to discover that he has five major gene variants linked to aggression. So why is he not a serial killer? He concluded that the third ingredient was lacking: his had been a peaceful, happy childhood. He had never been exposed to any kind of abuse.

There were more surprises in store. When Fallon told his immediate family of his discovery, they said they were not surprised! His son confessed to being scared of him sometimes, with his hot-headed behaviour. His wife said there was a 'standoffish part' to him. Fallon reflected on all of this and realized that some of his reactions were somehow 'wrong' socially. But he found himself unable to care about it.

The big question for Fallon was that if he had the make-up and behaviour of a psychopath, why then was he not out killing people, nor feeling the urge to do so? He concluded that in the psychopathic brain, brutality is triggered by childhood abuse. If nothing activates the trigger, then the person grows up to be a normal member of society – except that his or her behaviour may deviate in small ways from the norm, explaining the comments of Fallon's own family.

A further study of CEOs from all over the world revealed that the majority of them have psychopathic brains as well, but although psychopathic bosses may seem lethal in the workplace, they are not actually killing people! However, they do sometimes take some hard business decisions, such as cutting down the workforce to increase profits, which many of us might find ourselves unable to implement.

So even if the nature argument is true, and preponderance to certain behaviour is dictated by neural make-up and genes, we can see that nurture makes all the difference. Can we assume then that learned behaviour can be reversed? In my experience this is possible and not always difficult. The bully must want to change, but I find that even a small exposure to coaching, particularly learning and practising the skills, is enough to create a desire to learn more about communicating in this way, simply because it feels better. A coaching skills course might not reform a psychopath, but for the average bullying manager it can be the key to a whole new leadership style.

For example, I once trained a group of managers who disliked their boss, also a participant on the course, to such an extent that they would avoid sitting next to him when possible. He was a known bully at work. We did two days of coaching skills training, then they all went away to practise with each other and out in the field. A month later, when we reconvened, the bullying manager said, 'I love this new way of communicating, but it feels awkward because it is not what people expect of me.'

A member of his team responded, 'It may feel awkward to you, but please go on doing it because to us it feels fantastic.'

Six months later I heard that the onetime bully was now judged by everyone in the organization to be kinder and gentler.

I believe that bullying is a habit that can be reversed. Recent findings in neuroscience show that the brain has 'neuroplasticity' – it can be rewired through experience (Doidge, 2007). New neural pathways can be formed and old ones de-conditioned through our choices and behaviour.

Reforming the bully

To achieve this type of change, our bully must be given the 'how to' skills, so that new neural pathways can be created to embed a new habit. By the 'how to' skills, I mean basic coaching techniques, like learning how to listen. What we are often doing when we think we are listening is either interrupting, hijacking the conversation to talk about ourselves or giving advice. True listening means paying attention when other people talk, and prompting for more when they run dry. Other effective approaches are to ask open, non-judgemental questions and to reduce defensiveness by asking permission. (See Chapters 19, 21 and 22 'Listening', 'Questioning' and 'Permission protocol'.)

There are of course times when a manager will have to direct or give feedback in order to develop and teach reports. (See Chapter 25, 'Coaching feedback', and Chapter 3, 'The directive–non-directive continuum'.) If the listening, questioning and permission skills have built a solid foundation to the relationship, the more directive elements will not have a jarring effect or reduce whatever trust has been established.

So how can a workplace bully be identified? Bullies who yell in the office, or take every opportunity to humiliate their staff, are easily recognized. Unfortunately the most painful type of bullying tends to go underground, being expressed in small ways, often in private, and continuing over a long period of time. Someone on the receiving end may become physically ill at the thought of going to work and having to face this workplace equivalent of Chinese water torture, not knowing when or where to expect the next piece of torment. This manipulative type of bully often has a Jekyll and Hyde nature, projecting bonhomie and selflessness to the people that he or she cannot get away with bullying. Victims can feel isolated because their experience is not shared or witnessed by colleagues.

During my time as a record company boss, I once had to deal regularly with a bully who managed one of our groups. Whenever we were in contact he would be rude or shout at me, even in public. Yet a male colleague once said, 'I don't know why you have a problem with him. He is always absolutely charming.' Fortunately I did not work for the bully, so was able to laugh it all off and, to be frank, I gave as good as I got. But I puzzled over his behaviour because it was potentially damaging for his own business. I discovered that he showed similar levels of aggression towards all the women in his office but never to men. He was in fact an old-fashioned misogynist and, in the 1970s, people at work could display their prejudices without restraint. This is not to imply that bullying is a male preserve; it is not gender specific and there are plenty of female bullies around, both the shouting kind and the manipulative ones.

A surreptitious way of bullying is by exclusion. I recall that a contemporary once shared with me that she had started to be excluded from meetings and events, like lunches, by not being issued with an invitation. She wilted under the pressure and eventually resigned, a situation that would now be regarded as constructive dismissal.

Other examples of covert bullying include overloading the victim with work, allotting menial tasks or denying requests for holiday dates, particularly compassionate leave. I recall one boss (fortunately I worked alongside her rather than as a report) refusing to grant permission for a member of her staff to attend a family funeral. Another example is constant criticism of someone's work and a refusal to recognize achievements, or a denial of deserved promotion. As an aside, the same manager eventually replaced this employee, but failed to make contact with him before he came to work to find his replacement sitting at his desk. This lack of empathy and respect for the feelings of others is a common trait in bullies, which aligns with the theories from neuroscience and psychopaths explored above.

It is the ongoing nature of the bullying which wears people down and makes the experience so very painful. Each incident may be trivial in itself and may not constitute grounds for a complaint, but when the anxiety reaches a point where the worker feels physically sick at the thought of facing work the next day, it is a good indication that a bully is in charge.

Coaching the accidental bully

Allard de Jong is a multilingual coach and trainer who works with senior leaders all over the world. He related to me his experience of coaching a Senior VP who was 'getting the results' and judged by top management as being an effective and valuable performer, but whose leadership style was regarded not only as too controlling, but actually distressing to those who reported to her. In unsolicited feedback, team members complained of burnout and pointed out their leader's manipulative, upsetting and threatening behaviours.

Allard started by carrying out a 360-degree assessment to help the coachee increase her self-awareness, evaluate her leadership effectiveness from multiple perspectives, and focus the development towards gaining maximum benefit. In order to optimize the quality of the 360 debrief, to start signalling a genuine coach–coachee 'alliance' and to maintain a minimum of psychological distance from what might be unexpectedly severe and potentially devastating feedback, it was decided to enlist the help of a qualified and professional third party expert to lead the one and a half hour debrief session. The process helped the coachee identify and understand her strengths, opportunities for improvement, blind spots that impeded effectiveness and her impact on others, without being shocked into an unproductive state of despair.

She also undertook the Bar-On EQ-i assessment (described in Chapter 35) to set the stage for focused development of emotional skills. This would help her to increase leadership effectiveness and demonstrate specific and observable behaviours at work that would result in winning without creating losers or causing collateral damage. Allard suggested using this tool as a response to the coachee's desire to work specifically on a series of soft skills such as empathy, impulse control and stress tolerance.

The coaching also focused on investigating the personal issues that were leading to her dysfunctional leadership behaviours, and then tactics for implementing new manners of conduct, so that she could learn from practising these behaviours.

After six months, at the end of the contracted coaching programme, both coachee and the project sponsors (her own line managers) reported marked improvements in her ability to build stronger, mutually satisfying relationships and connections with direct reports and peers, so that she could engage, enable and, above all, energize others.

The coachee was subsequently offered a position of increased responsibility within the organization and additional coaching sessions were put in place in order to accelerate her transition into the new role and enable her to form a coherent plan for the leadership challenges she may face in the future.

How to cope with being bullied

There remains the question of how to deal with a bullying boss when one is on the receiving end of the bullying, and not in a position to suggest that the perpetrator might think about creating some new neural pathways.

In such situations 'coaching up' is a useful skill to develop. If you pride yourself on being a coaching style manager to your own reports, next time you are feeling critical of the way your own boss behaves, address that boss by imagining he or she is one of your own reports. As a coaching manager, you will speak kindly and with respect, and provide positive feedback on the behaviour you would like to see more of rather than dwelling too much on what your report is doing wrong. When did you last give your boss any positive feedback? Tell bosses when they are managing you as you wish to be managed, and they are likely to repeat that behaviour. It is like giving dogs a biscuit when they jump through the right hoop:

Coaching up

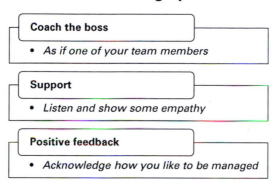

A useful remedy when you find yourself in an unpleasant situation where you have no control, like being the target of a bullying boss, is simply to recognize the strong emotions that the situation is arousing in you, but *without trying to change them*. Let them pass: 'Oh, I'm scared. Now I'm angry. She's still shouting. I feel it's not fair.' Acknowledging one's emotions in this way, and allowing them to be experienced without denying or trying to change them, helps us to function alongside them without being overwhelmed. This is based on the ancient Buddhist practice of mindfulness (Hall, 2013).

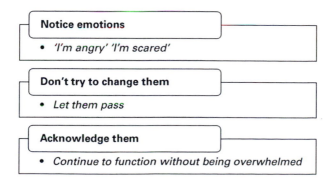

Finally, most organizations are running scared now in terms of workplace stress and bullying, because there is an increasing amount of legal help available from outside for unhappy employees. While I always advise legal action to be a last resort (because in my experience it is usually only the lawyers who gain, while the employee is faced with the stress and potential negative effects on his or her career prospects as a result of a protracted legal case) there is no need for people to suffer in silence. HR departments should be qualified to help, or can bring in an external coach or adviser.

There are more useful pointers in how to cope with bullying in our next chapter on 'Resilience'.

Resilience in leadership

16

CO-WRITTEN WITH MICHELLE DRAPEAU

SUMMARY

- What is resilience?
- Resilience in leaders
- What makes a resilient organization?
- Developing resilience

What is resilience?

Resilience is the ability to bounce back in the face of adversity. Wherever we are in our lives, at some stage we are likely to need an element of resilience in order to get through a difficult event, whether in our personal lives, such as when dealing with relationship, health or financial problems, or at work where we may face job insecurity, redundancy, bullying or periods of significant change.

Our ability to be resilient can be affected by a number of internal and external factors such as our view of ourselves, our belief systems and thought processes, and our external support network. A person with strong self-belief, a positive approach to life and a supportive network of family and friends will generally fare better when dealing with life's ups and downs than somebody without these sturdy foundations.

The good news is that wherever we are on the 'resilience scale', it is something we can get better at over time. While some people may seem to have a natural tendency to resilience, due to nurture or other life experiences, being resilient is not a fixed aspect of our personality. Nor is it an end goal.

Developing resilience is an ongoing personal journey, a journey that may at times involve emotional distress and uncertainty, but from which we can learn, adapt and grow stronger.

Resilience in leaders

Leaders are expected to deal with a range of problems or setbacks on a daily basis, all of which require a degree of resilience in order for the leader to come through the other side emotionally and physically 'intact'. In today's business environment, leaders may have to deal with cost cutting, downsizing, redundancies and restructuring, in addition to day-to-day issues such as juggling resources, managing risk, or addressing employee performance issues. An inability to remain strong in the face of such challenges can have an effect on both performance and health, so developing sound coping mechanisms is essential.

The level of resilience in a leader can be influenced by several factors:

- emotional intelligence;
- self-belief;
- personal thought processes;
- support networks;
- self-nurturing behaviour; and
- openness to learn.

It is estimated that the most successful CEOs and directors are a combination of 85 per cent EQ (emotional intelligence), and 15 per cent IQ. EQ is about self-awareness and our ability to build relationships with others (unlike IQ which, in the workplace, is about knowledge, skills and experience). Leaders with high EQ understand their own strengths and weaknesses, recognize their impact on the world around them and are better served to manage strong emotions and change unhelpful behaviours. In leadership terms, they communicate well, are responsive and adaptable, humble yet confident in approach, and have the skills to inspire loyalty and get the best from a team.

Closely linked with high EQ is a strong belief in oneself. Such leaders believe in their ability to make a difference, exhibiting high levels of authenticity and a commitment to see things through. Combining this with positive thought processes, which enable them to focus on reality and make clear decisions, and a willingness to learn from experience, such leaders prove to be purposeful, resourceful, proactive – and resilient.

All these elements are key contributors to both the development and maintenance of resilience, but perhaps one of the most important factors is the ability or willingness to look after ourselves. In times of difficulty, being physically and emotionally healthy is especially important. If we are not in optimum health, dealing with adversity becomes much harder. The most resilient leaders usually take time to charge their batteries, relax and enjoy life. They make healthy decisions in relation to food and exercise, and turn to their network of friends and family for support and companionship.

What makes a resilient organization?

Being a resilient leader naturally produces a style of leadership that promotes resilience in others and in the organization as a whole. Resilient leaders engage and empower their teams, providing a level of support and encouragement that promotes self-belief, purpose and positivity in others. A 2010 survey by Robertson Cooper and YouGov (Cooper, 2010) shows a link between the resilience of an organization and the level of support its employees receive from their managers: 65 per cent of the 2000+ respondents who believed their organization to be 'very resilient' also felt supported by their managers.

Likewise, an organization that is itself resilient enables the development of resilience in its employees through a non-blame culture where people have the space to make mistakes and learn from them. A resilient organization collaborates with its employees, sharing information and planning together so that all are working for the common good of the organization. The phrase 'stronger together' applies perfectly here.

A high level of organizational resilience is apparent in the ability of the organization to be proactive and plan for any potential future difficulties, as opposed to dealing with adversity on an ad hoc basis as and when it presents itself, or reacting in a knee jerk fashion. With a whole raft of internal and external factors potentially impacting on businesses, such as politics, new technology, finance, changing customer needs, societal changes, the employment market and competitor developments, an organization that does not assess its own resilience and plan for future challenges may find itself struggling more than necessary when adversity strikes.

A resilient organization regularly examines business trends for potential upcoming challenges and assesses its own capacity to change. It understands its capabilities and limitations but believes in its strengths and abilities to adapt in the face of adversity. As a result of this readiness, highly resilient organizations may even be able to transform serious setbacks into business opportunities by maximizing both the creative talent inherent within their workforce and their own ability to adapt.

Organizational resilience

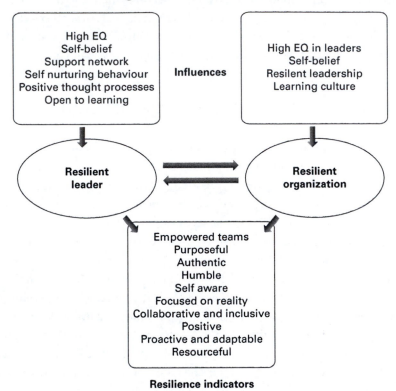

Resilience indicators

Developing resilience

It is important to remember that what works for one person may not work for another. There are many pathways to greater resilience; the following options are just a few:

- Believe in your ability to make a difference.
- Identify your goals in a positive way, ie what you want rather than what you do not, for example, 'I'm going to find a new job', rather than, 'I don't want to be in this job any more'.
- Accept the things you cannot change. Non-acceptance sets up an internal 'fight', causing stress, frustration and anger.

- Assess your situation objectively; is it reality, or your view of reality? Try to keep things in perspective.

- Be proactive. Taking positive action encourages a sense of control, which in turn promotes feelings of confidence and optimism. Remaining passive can bring about feelings of negativity and powerlessness.

- Develop a strong, supportive network of friends, family and colleagues.

- Understand those things that particularly impact on you in a negative way and plan your coping strategies in advance.

- Adapt. There is wisdom in the Japanese proverb which says, 'The bamboo that bends is stronger than the oak that resists.'

- Look after yourself, emotionally and physically.

- Learn from challenging situations and value them as an ongoing personal development tool.

When coaches have to deal with the strong emotions aroused during tough workplace situations, they sometimes face a variety of challenges. Is the coaching relationship straying into a psycho-dynamic territory which the coach is not qualified to deal with? Would the organization be happy about the way the coaching time is being spent? And above all there is a question which coaches sometimes ask themselves, because a one-to-one basis can feel isolating, which is: 'Am I doing it right?'

This is where coaching supervision has a role to play.

17 Coaching supervision: a workplace perspective

SUMMARY

- Differences between traditional and coaching supervision
- Supervision in therapy
- Coaching supervision in the workplace
- What to do in a coaching supervision session
- Types and frequency of supervision
- Credentials of the coaching supervisor

Differences between traditional and coaching supervision

The traditional meaning of the word 'supervision' concerns enforcing rules, checking, making judgements, demanding and rewarding compliance, and offering solutions.

Coaching supervision has very much the opposite meaning. It is about supporting, reflecting and occasionally mentoring the coach, and is more of a peer-to-peer relationship. The phrase itself can be interpreted as 'overview' and the question to ask in coaching supervision is: whose overview is being examined by whom? It is less a case of the coaching supervisor taking an overview of the coach's work than enabling coaches to take an overview of their own.

Although coaching supervisors may be aware of these definitions, there remains the risk that they might inadvertently carry some baggage attached to the traditional meaning of the word. I have noticed this from time to time while observing coaching supervisors and it must be recognized by the supervisor and put aside.

The Supervision Steering Group formed by the main coaching bodies defines coaching supervision as: 'A conversational process that helps coaches and mentors to manage their own learning and development in order to improve their coaching practice.'

Nancy Kline's elegant definition is: 'Supervision is an opportunity to bring someone back to their own mind, to show them how good they can be' (Kline, 1999).

Einstein has a famous quote that might be applied to coaching supervision: 'Problems cannot be solved at the same level of consciousness that created them.'

This emphasizes the value of moving into a special space to obtain different perspectives, which is arguably the core value of coaching supervision.

My personal view is that coaching supervision is a way of reflecting on one's own practice. Having another person present helps to focus the mind, view situations from different perspectives and gain some reassurance that we are making the best choices in how to support our clients. I do not believe that it is necessary for the supervisor to be more experienced than the supervisee, as that would be a throwback to the original meaning of 'supervision', where the supervisor is there to correct and instruct. On the other hand, there is an advantage in being able to consult someone more experienced, particularly for new coaches.

On our coaching skills training courses, one of the requirements is that participants supervise each other. The aim of this is to give them a personal understanding of the dynamics of peer-to-peer supervision and to bring home the value of it so that they will continue the practice in future.

I think that the supervisor should be a qualified and practising coach, in order to understand the nature of coaching and its challenges. However, I know of coaches who are supervised by therapists and who find the added perspective beneficial. Ultimately, the core nature of supervision is that it suits the coach being supervised and the supervisor who is delivering.

Supervision in therapy

Most of the work that has been published to define coaching supervision has so far been acquired from the field of psychotherapy. Some of the elements provide an effective framework for supporting and developing coaches, others less so, and many coaches believe that coaching requires a supervision model of its own because the requirements are different. Psychotherapists, whose role is prescriptive and diagnostic, must train for many years and be rigorously supervised to safeguard the mental health of the patients in their care. Coaching, however, is 100 per cent client-led, there are no judgements, prescriptions or diagnoses, and therefore no risk to the coachees. This is why coaches can practice safely and effectively after a minimal amount of training.

The guide that has gained the most credence for supervisors to follow is the Seven Eyed Model, created by Hawkins & Shohet in 1989. The Seven Eyed model provides some useful perspectives but can be too complex for some workplace coaches and leaning too far towards psychodynamic coaching and therapy.

Coaching supervision in the workplace

Here is the model I use for training coaching supervisors who work in or for organizations. The shaded circles identify the areas of focus, and the writing around the outside represents the skills that can be used during a coaching supervision session. The model is called a 'contract' because each party bears a responsibility to the others and has to be mindful of where boundaries lie:

The four-way contract

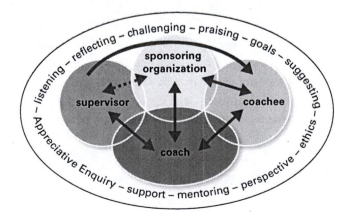

- The primary focus is the relationship between the coach and coachee.
- The supervisor needs also to be concerned with the benefit to the coachee, although they will never meet – notice how that arrow goes one way only.
- The supervisor needs to be aware of his or her own behaviour and attitudes during the session.
- As an organization is paying, both the coach and coachee have a relationship with and responsibility to the sponsor.
- If the supervisor is internal, or paid by the organization as an external supervisor, there will be a relationship with the sponsor there too.

Situations sometimes arise which relate to the benefit of the sponsor, or the ethics of the coach in relation to the sponsor. An extreme example is where a coach has been hired to work with a manager on the manager's performance. However, the manager tells the coach that he wants to leave the organization and use the coaching time to support him in finding another job. Can the coach ethically take the payment while working specifically against the organization's expectation? The coach cannot tell the organization because of the ethic of confidentiality in the coach–client relationship. There is no easy answer to this situation and this is where the coaching supervision session is likely to be helpful.

Two parts of Hawkins and Shohet's valuable model which I have found some resistance to from workplace coaches are elements 5 and 6. These seem to come from a process relating to transference in therapy, and it is a fact that many managers trained as workplace coaches shy away from anything too closely related to psychology and therapy. This is not to say that the ideas represented in these two sections have no value in coaching, nor that internal coaches never venture into these areas; it is about whether it is appropriate in workplace coaching supervision to emphasize them by naming them in the main model, when other processes peripheral to coaching are not named.

Although awareness of the potential for and existence of the parallel process is not confined to psychodynamic therapists, and can be informative to both coach, client and supervisor, one concern is that it may encourage coaches to venture into non-coaching, judgemental and prescriptive areas. Liz Macann, former Head of Coaching at the BBC, says:

'The exploration of some of the psychodynamic areas can take coaches into territory they are not qualified to work in, so it is important that the supervisor maintains agreed coaching boundaries which are also relevant to the job in hand.'

A simple and workplace-friendly way of describing the parallel process is offered by former Association for Coaching Supervision Lead, Benita Treanor:

> 'You begin to notice a relationship between what the coach talks about 'out there' and what actually happens in real time between the two of you. The supervisor can help the coach to become more aware and notice these patterns (parallels). This offers coaches an additional resource in helping clients become clearer about what happens within their organizations.
>
> A recent example of this was working with a coach who had felt undermined by the coaching sponsor within the business. This had led to a 'stand-off' between them. I noticed in the session as the coach relayed their story that their voice changed and became dictatorial and loud. I wondered if that is how they presented with the sponsor. This offered an opportunity to explore in the moment if that was the case. The coach was able to recognize their part in the dilemma and consider what different approaches may be required before the next meeting with the sponsor.'

Coaching supervisor Wendy Oliver has found the parallel process useful in situations where she experiences an emotion, such as confusion. In reflecting that back to the coach, she discovers that her confusion is sometimes a reflection of confusion felt by the coach at that moment, whose own confusion may be a reflection of what the coachee they are discussion was feeling.

However accurate these observations may be, it is hard to see where they align with coaching principles, being both judgemental and diagnostic. The coaching approach would be to ask permission to share an insight, thereby creating a clear boundary between the different agendas of coach and coachee. I think it would be advisable to observe this condition in the supervision session as well.

There exists a controversy over the raison d'être of coaching supervision and the fees charged. I have heard the following contentious questions raised in discussions:

- Has coaching supervision been promoted to lend some of the gravitas of therapy to the realm of coaching?
- Are its main supporters coaching supervisors and supervisor trainers who wish to profit from charging fees for their services?
- Are some coaches attracted to coaching supervision because it is easier to work with the coach than at 'the coal face' with real coachees?
- Do some coaches prefer to supervise because it presents more opportunities to offer solutions than when coaching?

Personally, I am neither for nor against coaching supervision and believe it can be useful to coaches. In any event, it is essential to have an arena where coaches can share their experiences with another practising coach because the profession can be isolating. However, the questions above are being raised and both coaches and supervisors need to be aware of the pitfalls. Some of the benefits which coaches recount are summed up by Benita Treanor as:

- Maintaining, supporting, sustaining and developing the coach and the coach's practice.
- Accountability to clients.
- Providing a confidential forum to discuss complex issues.
- Promoting and ensuring ethical best practice.
- Maintaining motivation and momentum.

What to do in a coaching supervision session

Now let us examine what might actually take place in a coaching supervision session. When we take the time out to think about any issue, we gain new insights and perspectives and this can come about through talking, sleeping on the problem, meditation, prayer, writing, research or any other kind of self-reflection. Having someone whose stated purpose is to focus attention on us for a defined amount of time maximizes the chance that we will experience some kind of breakthrough. It is part of the value of coaching, therapy, counselling, mentoring, teaching, friendship and parenting. The question then is which components are most effective in a coaching supervision situation?

Listening must score highly in any list. Being listened to, in a concentrated, caring and neutral way, is a luxury that grows rarer with every passing development in technology, travel and leisure – because these things take up our time. Our use of time affects the one who is listened to as much as it does to the listener – there is sometimes a reluctance, which may be borne out of laziness or a fear of exploring the unknown, to take the time to think our issues through, and the same lack of enthusiasm shows itself in a disinclination to work with a coach, mentor or supervisor. Hence there is a value in setting aside regular, formal times for supervision, where action is required to cancel the appointment, rather than informal supervision which can often be squeezed out of a busy schedule.

Once we are in the coaching supervision space, how can both coach and supervisor ensure that the time is used most effectively? Although supervision is not coaching, clearly the use of coaching skills by the supervisor will enhance the process. In particular, these can be:

Recognition

What's working well?

Sounds like you handled that well.

Use of the GROW model

What would be useful for you to get out of this session?

What is the situation?

What are your challenges?

What interventions/skills/tools have you used so far?

What else might you do?

What will you do differently?

Suggesting, mentoring and sharing experience

Could I suggest...?

Could I offer you my thoughts on this?

Could I share an experience which might be relevant to this?

Examining the coachee's goals

What is the measure/time frame?

Could that be stated more positively?

Is it what the coachee really wants, or is it what he thinks he 'should' want?

Kolb's learning cycle questions

How well do you perform at each stage?

Where do you sometimes get stuck?

How do you get stuck?

What are you experiencing when you get stuck?

What could you do to get unstuck?

AAR (After Action Review) – American Military Learning from Doing

What did we set out to do?

What happened?

What went well?

What tensions, puzzles and issues did we encounter?

What have we learned?

What will we do differently?

Nancy Kline's six-part thinking session

Nancy Kline's six-part thinking session is a framework based on uninterrupted listening and removal of limiting assumptions which can work equally well in a coaching supervision session or a coaching session (Kline, 1999).

Types and frequency of supervision

Finally, let us take a look at the different forms that coaching supervision can take:

Individual or group

Coaching supervision works well in a group setting where people can learn from each other. At the time of writing, the Association for Coaching runs free monthly Coach Supervisor/Mentor calls, where an AC Assessor hosts a call with up to eight coaches who discuss issues, share tips and benefit from exchanging their experiences. These calls are not intended to take the place of regular one-to-one coaching supervision.

Peer to peer or mentor

One of the key values of supervision is the creation of a space where coaches can reflect on their own work. Therefore, the practice of peer coaches supervising each other is a viable proposition and the supervisor does not necessarily have to be more knowledgeable or experienced than the supervisee.

Internal or external

Most of the coaches who regularly work with coaching supervisors are, at this point in time, probably independent consultants. However, organizations are becoming increasingly aware of the benefits of coaching supervision and, where there exists a sizeable force of internal coaches, coaching supervisors are trained to support them.

Paid or unpaid

Some coaches supervise each other without charge; others pay an experienced coach or qualified supervisor. In 2006, a CIPD survey revealed that 86 per cent of coaches saw the benefits of supervision but only 44 per cent actually undertook it. However, attitudes towards supervision within the profession have changed. According to a 2008 survey by the Association for Coaching, 71 per cent of respondents now receive coaching supervision, an increase of 23 per cent since their 2005 survey.

Frequency

Most coaching bodies recommend regular supervision, which might be interpreted as one hour a month or one hour to every 15 coaching sessions.

Credentials of the coaching supervisor

At the time of writing none of the coaching bodies requires the supervisor to be qualified specifically in supervision. However, it is generally recommended that the supervisor is a qualified and practising coach. Some coaches choose to be supervised by practitioners in different fields such as therapy, in order to receive another perspective.

ROI: Measuring the return on investment in coaching

18

SUMMARY

- Planning
- How to get quantifiable results from surveys
- Leveraging feedback
- Leveraging research
- Measuring the value of coaching at OFGEM

'You can't manage what you can't measure.' (Traditional business saying)

So far I have talked a great deal about the benefits of coaching and the results that can be obtained when an organization sets out to become a coaching culture. It is now widely recognized that coaching is a means of increasing employee motivation, retention and engagement, and that these factors are thought to contribute to raising profits or, in the case of not-for-profit organizations, better budget management. And coaching in organizations like MOE can turn people's lives around. But the question on the lips of the financial controllers in organizations remains: 'So everyone is feeling better – but are we making more money because of it?'

This chapter explores methods and tools for measuring the value of coaching programmes from the beginning to the end of the project, and how to express that value in quantitative figures where possible.

Planning

In a coaching approach, the goal is always identified before starting out. So the first step towards measuring a programme is to find out what its purpose is. The GROW model, described in Chapter 23, is an ideal framework for achieving this:

The GROW model

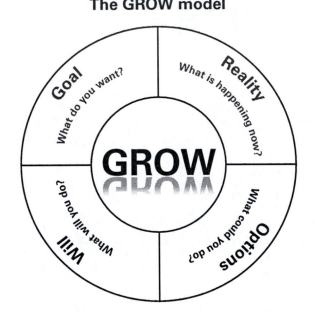

The following questions might be useful, modified slightly depending on whether they are delivered by the supplier or an internal executive:

GOAL
- What results do you want?
- What is the long-term goal?
- What is the short-term goal?
- Over what time periods?

REALITY
- What resources do you have/need?
- What are the challenges?
- What budgets are available?
- Who are the stakeholders?

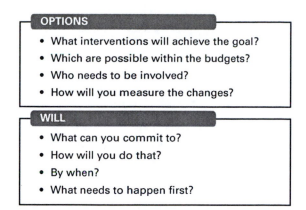

OPTIONS
- What interventions will achieve the goal?
- Which are possible within the budgets?
- Who needs to be involved?
- How will you measure the changes?

WILL
- What can you commit to?
- How will you do that?
- By when?
- What needs to happen first?

Once everyone is clear on what is to be achieved, it is possible to work back from that to put a measurement plan in place. It is a good idea, as in all good coaching exchanges, to begin by asking the stakeholders for their own solutions. They may well have measurement wholly or partially catered for in their existing practices, as explored below.

How to get quantifiable results from surveys

Most organizations run regular surveys with their workforce, whether about 'soft' items such as satisfaction and motivation, or 'hard' facts like absentee rates, target-meeting and turnover:

Survey results

QUANTITATIVE	QUALITATIVE
• Sales figures	• Motivation
• Absentee rates	• Leadership
• Staying on budget	• Engagement
• Retention rates	• Reduced stress

Some of these may be adapted to measure the benefits of coaching. To ensure that those benefits solely attributable to the coaching programme are identified, and not confused with benefits from other changes that may be happening, the following question should be used: 'What difference is due solely to the coaching programme?'

The answers can be proved to elicit more specific benefits and, where appropriate, it is possible to ask questions that place a figure on them:

- How much?
- How many?
- What percentage?

Various surveys can be used to measure the change in culture. My own preference for measuring culture change is Richard Barrett's Cultural Transformation Tools because it enables workers from all areas of the business to identify the strengths and weaknesses of leadership in an organization without pointing fingers at named individuals, or providing anonymous criticism that might be swayed by personal bias.

When conducted across sufficient numbers of employees, these surveys can show up trends. For example, if large numbers complain of confusion or bullying, a survey can be designed to work out what these factors are costing the business. The participants will estimate what percentage of say, turnover, is being lost as a result of the limiting factors. Taking the previous year's turnover, this percentage can be translated into a figure. A result like the one in the table below, although not statistically accurate, will be enough to attract the attention of those in charge of finance and budgets:

What percentage of turnover is lost through:	£
Bureaucracy?	-1,799,618
Confusion?	-3,178,636
Empire building?	-1,764,682
Information hoarding?	-624,327
Hierarchy?	-834,225
Bullying?	-2,280,607
Not delegating?	-1,200,211
TOTAL POTENTIAL BUSINESS VALUE LOST	-11,682,306
Annual turnover £333,000,000	

Leveraging feedback

A key contribution to measurement can be made during the coaching programme through collecting feedback, both on paper and verbally. Feedback forms can be filled in at the end of every day's training, providing an excellent basis for a report at the end of the programme. If the participants agree, they can be quoted by name, which carries a great deal of weight if they are senior in the organization in terms of justifying the spend and encouraging other staff to participate in future training.

The sooner feedback is given the better, and we allot ten minutes at the end of a coaching programme, or each day, to fill out the forms, while the experience is fresh in everyone's minds. If asked to complete feedback online or by e-mail after the course, probably most of the managers will not get round to doing it once they are back in their busy lives.

Some sample questions that might appear on a feedback form are:

Sample questions

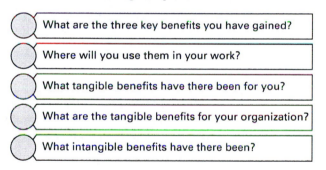

What are the three key benefits you have gained?

Where will you use them in your work?

What tangible benefits have there been for you?

What are the tangible benefits for your organization?

What intangible benefits have there been?

Verbal feedback is often more descriptive than what people put on a form. It can be noted by the coach or trainer and questions can be asked to draw out the specifics, including figures where possible. The answer can then be turned into a report to be presented to the organization, with the permission of the coachees or trainees concerned:

Verbal feedback

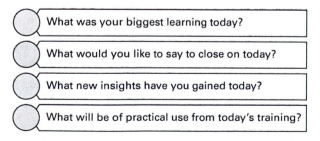

What was your biggest learning today?

What would you like to say to close on today?

What new insights have you gained today?

What will be of practical use from today's training?

Leveraging research

Another effective way of convincing organizations about the value of coaching is to present research. For example, the diagram below was compiled by US company Innovest.

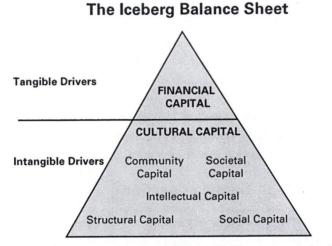

The Iceberg Balance Sheet

Intangible value drivers represent **60% – 85%** of a company's Market Value.

The research shows that, whereas an organization's worth might be expected to be gauged through inspecting its financial records, such as profits and share price, 60–85 per cent of its true value resides in the cultural capital – intangible drivers like relationships, communication, retaining knowledge and skill, behaviour within the company and to the external community, sustainability etc.

Various organizations including the Association for Coaching and CIPD publish relevant surveys from time to time, and these can be found through internet search engines.

Measuring the value of coaching at OFGEM

In March 2004, my colleague Wendy Oliver was approached by OFGEM (the government regulatory body for the gas and electricity market), who wished to increase staff retention. The request was triggered by an 'Investors in People' report which found that individuals at OFGEM, especially in the higher pay bands, were struggling to find time to train and consequently were not attending the management and leadership training courses already in place. As such, their personal development was not progressing as it might. In addition, an internal feedback report identified that there was a need for training and development to be 'more specific and linked more closely to individual Business Plan objectives'.

The Learning and Development team within OFGEM identified coaching as a potentially ideal solution, particularly because managers would be able to attend short sessions tailored to their own specific needs and style in line with the business's objectives.

Together with some other coaches, Wendy put in place a coaching programme. Prior to designing a scheme all parties recognized that evaluation of any programme was important to assess whether this was a viable learning intervention giving a return on investment. With this in mind the coaches and HR department defined the objectives of the scheme as an integral part of any post evaluation. Aims on a number of levels were identified:

- *Organizational aims*: the key organizational aim was to increase retention.
- *Departmental aims*: the main group identified were the leaders and managers and the key aims were to facilitate their career advancement within OFGEM and to improve their people management skills in line with the organization's leadership competencies and business objectives.
- *Individual aims*: to encourage self-awareness and personal development.

It was agreed that a pilot programme would be run, and then a lunchtime meeting was arranged where Wendy and three other coaches delivered a presentation on what coaching is, how it can be used, the aims of the scheme, the coaches' backgrounds, their styles of coaching, the coaching process and what would be expected from the coachees. Seven participants signed up and were asked to submit a business case that outlined the outcomes they wanted to achieve from the coaching. This was created in alliance with their directors so that business needs were taken into account and there was agreement surrounding the leadership competencies to be developed and goals to be achieved. The directors were now in a position to identify and encourage changes in behaviour and contribute to the evaluation at the end of the programme.

In March 2004 the coaching series began. Each person received a two-hour coaching session once a month for six months from a coach whom they had personally selected. During these early months more people joined the scheme until there were 22 people being coached, which represented 12 per cent of the management team. At the end of the coaching series, the results were assessed by going back to the original aims and noting what had taken place. Statistics were compiled through questionnaires and meetings with the coaches, coachees and the coachees' line managers. The types of questions asked of all groups were:

- To what extent were goals achieved?
- How had that contributed to business objectives?
- What were the changes in behaviour (particularly in relation to the management competencies) and what evidence did they have/had they seen?
- What difference had coaching made to their individual and department objectives?
- How did coaching compare with other management interventions?
- What worked, what didn't?
- What changes would they make to the process?
- Did they consider the scheme to be value for money?

The coaches' competencies were also assessed by the coachees, where their ability was rated from one to five covering a whole range of coaching competencies.

The evaluation showed that for those who were coached the following results were achieved:

Organizational aims

Retention of staff increased. This was quantified by the statistics: only 5 per cent (one person) of staff being coached left OFGEM during the coaching period, compared with 26 per cent of their peers who did not receive coaching.

Departmental aims

Career advancement within OFGEM increased dramatically. This was also evidenced from the statistics: 32 per cent of the people who received coaching either moved within OFGEM or were promoted, compared with 12 per cent of their peers who did not receive coaching. Feedback showed that coachees were able to identify which competencies they needed to work on, and that they were able to develop the new behaviours with the support of their coaches.

People management skills improved in line with the organization's leadership competencies and business objectives. This was substantiated by the coachees' self-assessment and achievement of goals, their director's observation and noted evidence of changes of behaviour in line with the leadership competencies. One hundred per cent of the participants were able to give evidence as to how their behaviour had developed in relation to the competencies, and areas included:

- delegation and trust;
- managing relationships assertively and influencing upwards;
- developing strategy and seeing the bigger picture;
- running and participating in team meetings;
- coaching;
- managing team performance;
- presentation skills;
- sharing knowledge; and
- time management.

A number of their directors said that coachees had requested meetings with them and expressed their views more openly, which would not have happened without the support of a coach. This had helped to resolve several internal frustrations.

Individual aims

There was an increase in self-awareness. Personal development: managers reported that participants' attitudes had shifted; they had benefited from the personalized nature of the support, gaining more self-awareness and focus in their roles and future careers and greater confidence in their abilities, and they had become generally more proactive. The individuals were choosing to shoulder greater responsibility for making decisions in their professional and personal lives, and taking action on things they had previously tended to avoid. There was also an increase in assertiveness, motivation, confidence, time management and risk-taking, and the ability to see situations from the perspectives of others.

As a result of the evaluation some valuable changes were made to the process – individuals could be flexible on where the sessions took place and over what duration. Coaches were also able to analyze and develop their coaching skills through reviewing on which competencies they are receiving the highest and lowest ratings.

The evaluation reported that the main aims of the programme had been met; that coachees found their expectations had been exceeded; and that short sharp sessions were an effective use of their time. Managers found that the majority of the objectives set out in the coachees' original business cases had been achieved, and hence development was in line with the business objectives of the organization.

It was concluded that coaching had been the most successful leadership intervention ever undertaken and good value for money. Without having some very measurable objectives before starting the scheme, which were agreed by all parties, these happy conclusions may never have been drawn. Wendy has continued to work with OFGEM for the last nine years. Due to the success of coaching over the years it still remains in place today and substantial numbers of people have now passed through a coaching series.

Conclusion

There is no quick fix for measuring the return on coaching, but it is possible to produce significant evidence of improvement, both qualitative and quantitative, through a combination of coaching, surveys, feedback and research. In practice I have often found it the case that although organizations often express a desire to measure results during the planning stages of their coaching programmes, the changes that occur as managers start to use their coaching skills are so much in evidence, and clearly adding value to the organization, that intentions to put an ROI structure in place are often set aside as being unnecessary.

Now, having covered the meaning of a coaching culture and the results and challenges that can be met along the way to acquiring one, Part 3 of this book outlines specific ways that people can communicate and behave with each other in order to make the necessary changes.

PART THREE
Skills for coaches and managers

Introduction

So far in this book I have concentrated on what a coaching approach means and what it can achieve, and I think I have made it clear that that a person's attitude, behaviour and intention behind the words have more to do with a coaching style than techniques that might be learned on a course. However, the best intentions in the world may not produce results if the 'how to' is missing. This part outlines methods that enable people to put those intentions into practice.

Training in coaching skills can be useful not only for managers who have a habitually directive style, which will have been acquired from role models like parents or bosses who were not coaching leaders; it may also be illuminating for the ones who are regarded as 'natural' coaches, enabling them to identify which of their abilities work well and why. They are likely to discover ways of refining their successful communication styles still further.

There are many guidelines available on the skills of listening, questioning and giving feedback. Something new to add to these skills is the 'permission protocol' described in Chapter 21. It explains how to use asking permission (as in 'Could we talk about xxx?' or 'Can I ask you about xxx?') as a technique to create rapport and reduce conflict, and I often hear that it is the most valuable technique that people have been taught on our courses.

I hope I have brought some new light to shine in the chapter on 'Feedback' (Chapter 25). There is no 'magic bullet', or secret set of words that will miraculously make people welcome negative feedback, although there are a lot of companies and managers out there looking for them. In a coaching culture, where people feel that they have the freedom to manage their own responsibilities and mistakes, what happens is that corrective comments are likely to be received as helpful suggestions rather than criticism. So the art of delivering motivating feedback lies in the attitude of the receiver more than the giver, and the state of the relationship between them. The rest of the techniques provide the means to achieving the desired type of relationship.

The final chapters in this part provide frameworks to underpin both coaching sessions and staff development meetings. They do not need to be strictly adhered to but provide support for coaches and managers who are newly embarking on their coaching journey.

Listening

19

SUMMARY

- The five levels of listening
- The power of listening
- Non-verbal signals

Way back in 1956, Dale Carnegie wrote: 'You can make more friends in two months by becoming interested in other people than you can in two years by trying to get other people interested in you.'

Most of the time, when people think they are listening, they are in reality interrupting, hijacking the conversation with their own stories, or giving advice. The luxury of hearing the words 'tell me more' is a rare gift.

The five levels of listening

I have identified five levels of listening. You can see that in the diagram on the next page, levels four and five are on a par. Level five without level four is not really listening at all:

Level one: interrupting

'I think we should arrange a staff meeting about that and ...'

'Yes, but first of all I want to talk about the research for our next campaign.'

The 'listener' is not only failing to listen, but not even allowing the speaker to finish. Have you ever felt that someone was simply waiting for your lips to stop moving, so that they could say their piece? That is another form of level one listening.

The five levels of listening

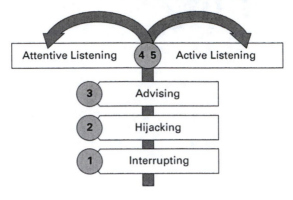

Attentive Listening   4 5   Active Listening

3   Advising

2   Hijacking

1   Interrupting

Level two: hijacking

'I'm having some difficulty being heard in meetings.'

'I find that too. Last month I came away from the marketing meeting without having said what I really needed to say.'

At least this time the listener has heard what the speaker said. But just like level 1, the agenda has been stolen. This is the most common form of non-listening and often occurs in everyday conversation.

Level three: advising

'I want to win a new account.'

'What you should do is...'

Giving advice can be valuable, but not until the issue has been explored and the ideas of the speaker have been heard. Firstly, there may be background information of which the advice giver is unaware, so the advice may be misplaced. Secondly, not many people like following advice; it can seem intrusive, particularly if unasked for. And thirdly, a solution that suits one person might not match the values, culture or learning style of another.

Level four: attentive listening

'I'm not sure how to restructure my department.'

'Would you like to tell me more about that?'

This is listening to what the speaker is saying and inviting more. The speaker is allowed time to think and knows that he or she is being listened to. What a luxury it is when someone replies simply by asking to hear more, and how rarely does it happen, both at home and at work?

Level five: active listening

'I really must get my report written but there's never any time.'

This time the listener will reply with a number of techniques, following the speaker's statements and prompting for more. Active listening means listening behind the words and between the words, listening to the silences, using one's intuition, helping the speaker to explore, facilitating self-learning, awareness and clarity, and making the occasional suggestion.

Levels 2 and 3 above have their time and their place in good management, particularly when mentoring, but they cannot be termed 'listening'. These two levels may also be appropriate in normal conversation, which is often a process of trading information and ideas. It is useful to be aware of where we are in the five levels during any exchange, so we can consciously decide which to use.

In a coaching session, we should almost always be in Levels 4 and 5; however, in a social situation Level 2 may be more comfortable a lot of the time, and Level 3 is sometimes useful, particularly when someone has come to us specifically asking for advice. Even then, though, the person will probably benefit from being asked exploratory questions about the dilemma to see if a self-directed solution can be found first.

Listening is probably the first coaching skill that any prospective coach or manager learns, and yet it is often the one that is least used, even by competent coaches, as it becomes buried under a profusion of more sophisticated tools and techniques. The reason for this is perhaps that most of us prefer to take action rather than observe; we want 'our turn' to come round. Using the coaching techniques of asking questions, repeating words back or even suggesting our own solutions, is sometimes easier than concentrating on what another person has to say.

The power of listening

The power of giving someone 'a good listening to' cannot be underestimated; in fact, sometimes people will coach themselves more effectively when allowed to talk unhindered. One of the values of having a coach is that the coach's attention focuses the coachee's mind. Trying to think through important issues alone can be difficult as our minds tend to stray, seemingly reluctant to face the facts, whereas an intent listener can return our focus to the issue in hand through incisive but non-leading questions. The required techniques of clarifying, reflecting and questioning are explored in Chapter 20, 'Clarifying, summarizing and reflecting' and Chapter 21, 'Questioning'.

Over several years of carrying out oral coaching assessments, I have noticed subtle habits that tend to get in the way of good listening. These include nodding too often, or using the same word in response to the coachee's statements, for example 'OK'. In coaching this is not a useful response as it implies either finality – 'OK, we've dealt with that, let's move on', or judgement, as in 'That was OK, you gave the right answer'.

Another common and overused response is 'excellent'. Like 'OK', 'excellent' implies judgemental approval, although it is often used when there is nothing particularly excellent at all about what has been said, and can place the coach slightly out of synch with the coachee, reducing the sense of being listened to. The authenticity of the session may be compromised.

Variations on these habitual responses are frequent interjections such as 'uh huh', 'right' and 'mm hmm' – particularly distracting when they interrupt a sentence.

Occasional use of all these responses is fine, and can demonstrate that the coach is listening; it is mindless repetition that must be avoided. When I have pointed it out during assessments, the coach usually replies either that they are unaware of the habit or that someone has mentioned it before.

In all of the above cases, what would be more appropriate when a response is needed is either to mirror back or paraphrase what the person has said, or – and quite often this is the best option – just stay quiet, keep one's eyes on the coachee, and wait for that train of thought to reach its conclusion.

Most coaches are happy to give advice in a coaching session where it seems useful. However, it is usually couched as a suggestion, for which permission is first requested, and not until the coachee has run dry of ideas. This is explored in Chapter 22, 'Permission protocol'.

Non-verbal signals

If the coach is concentrating entirely on what the coachee is saying, rather than what kind of question should be asked next, there is a greater opportunity to pick up on non-verbal signals. These might include hunching the shoulders (which usually indicates anxiety), smiling or sitting up straight (both of which often indicate a breakthrough), drumming of the fingers, and sighs, coughs or grunts. Such gestures often carry their own messages and when they appear, it can be fruitful to question the coachee about the phrase used just before the signal, or to ask a question like, 'What are your thoughts?' I once saw David Grove, the inventor of Clean Language (described in Chapter 28) ask the question, 'What does that foot know?' when a client's foot started wagging during a session.

It is not appropriate for the coach to interpret what the gesture means, but simply to honour it by stopping the coaching from moving on until the matter of exactly what is happening for the coachee, in that moment, has been explored.

One of the world's greatest experts on listening is Nancy Kline who, while working as a teacher, developed a practice similar to coaching which is based almost entirely on focused listening, plus a few prescribed 'insightful' questions (Kline, 1999).

There are more ways of listening than simply staying quiet, and one of these is to reflect people's words back to them, which is explored in Chapter 20.

20 Reflecting, summarizing and clarifying

SUMMARY

- Reflecting
- Summarizing
- Clarifying
- Benefits

This chapter explores some coaching tools that help coachees to think, and the first of these is repeating back what has been said in one form or another. The techniques described here are equally effective in formal coaching sessions or for managers running meetings in a coaching style.

These processes are often described simply as or reflecting, summarizing or clarifying:

Reflecting, summarizing or clarifying

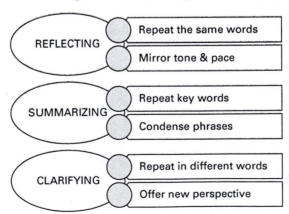

| REFLECTING | Repeat the same words |
| | Mirror tone & pace |

| SUMMARIZING | Repeat key words |
| | Condense phrases |

| CLARIFYING | Repeat in different words |
| | Offer new perspective |

Reflecting

Reflecting means simply repeating back exactly what has been said and is one of the most useful tools in coaching. It feels comforting and reassuring to the coachee and creates a homogeny with the coachee's values, cultural background and behaviour. It is less likely to interfere with the coachee's own ideas and train of thought than a question, for example:

Coachee: When I go into meetings I find it difficult to speak up.

Coach: You find it difficult to speak up.

Coachee: Yes, I tend to go along with the flow and agree with other people because I don't want any conflict.

Notice that the coachee has offered further insight and information without any new input from the coach.

The technique is also useful when coaching someone whose native language is different from the coach's own, something that happens increasingly in today's cross-cultural business world.

To make this technique really effective, not only words can be reflected but also tonality – the same pace and timbre of the voice as the coachee. Some practitioners recommend imitating the coachee's body language as well; however, in my experience, few people can do this without a sense of awkwardness. The theory arises from the fact that when two people are in rapport with each other, it is often the case that their body language will match – they may both have crossed legs or a hand under the chin, for example. However, I find that this is the outward manifestation of the relationship, not a means of creating it.

There is some value in noticing body language – if your positions do not match (particularly if you feel awkward, not sure where to put your hands, or you find your elbows keep slipping off the table, for example) you may ask yourself why there is a lack of rapport and look for verbal ways to improve it.

Summarizing

Summarizing is useful when someone provides a lot of information all at once. The key is to pick out words which seem to carry some sort of resonance for the coachee, or which have been repeated more than once, and make sure they are included in the summary presented back, for example:

> Coachee: When I go into meetings I find it difficult to speak up. I tend to go along with the flow and agree with other people because I don't want any conflict. Then I come out of the meeting very frustrated because I haven't got what I wanted.
>
> Coach: You go along with the flow and agree with other people because you don't want any conflict. Then you get frustrated.

Sometimes it is useful to summarize back key words or phrases later in a session or a series of sessions. Reflecting back in this way, after a period of time, can be useful in demonstrating to a coachee how far he or she has come, thereby raising confidence and motivation.

Clarifying

From time to time in a conversation, it can be useful if the coach paraphrases what the coachee has said, using the coach's own words. Hearing something stated in a different way can bring a new perspective, for example:

> Coachee: When I go into meetings I find it difficult to speak up. I tend to go along with the flow and agree with other people because I don't want any conflict. Then I come out of the meeting very frustrated because I haven't got what I wanted.
>
> Coach: Sounds like you have a problem asserting yourself?

This type of reflecting can be leading and is best used sparingly in a coaching session. It is most useful where a coachee seems to be having difficulty in identifying his or her true thoughts or feelings. The coachee may well reply 'No, it's not that', and then it is important for the coach to let go of the suggestion and follow the coachee's lead. There can be a value in contrasts. To use an analogy of colours, if the coach says, 'Is it blue?' the coachee may only then become aware that 'it' is in fact red.

Benefits

The benefits of using these techniques are:

- To show that the coach is listening: Repeating back assures people that they have your attention. Care should be taken that the use of these techniques does not descend to interrupting merely because the coach feels the need to do something. Always allow coachees plenty of silence to process their thoughts.

- To understand what the coachee has said: This is the function of the techniques in normal conversation as well as coaching.

- To help the coachee understand what he or she has said: The strange thing is that not only do we fail to listen to other people, but we have trouble listening to ourselves as well! Occasionally when I have repeated exact words back, the coachee has said, 'What a great idea, thank you!' or 'No, you've got that wrong!' This is one of the most powerful ways in which clarifying can help a coaching conversation.

- To validate what the coachee has said: This effect works mainly when reflecting back someone's exact words. Quite often in a coaching conversation, coachees will have a new insight, possibly something they were previously afraid to face. It can be daunting to put such thoughts into words for the first time and, when the coachee hears them repeated back, there is a sense of, 'I put the unmentionable into words, now someone else has said it too, so it must be OK. Now I can move on.'

- To move the conversation forward: There are times in a coaching session or meeting when we are working against the clock. One of the ways coaches can serve their coachees is to manage the time and keep the conversation on track. Reflecting or summarizing provides a way of interrupting which will not feel abrupt because the coach is not departing from the coachee's topic. Such an interruption will help to focus the minds both of coach and coachee.

These techniques can be used in all types of conversations, including coaching, problem solving, instructing and team building. It is particularly useful to repeat what someone has said during the course of a meeting, because others may be immersed in their own thoughts and miss something important. In addition, it will ensure that everyone who speaks feels validated and that they have been listened to. Repeating back also provides some relief from stock responses like 'OK' or 'Excellent!' which, as I mentioned earlier in the previous chapter, sometimes become an unconscious habit.

As with all coaching techniques, it is best to practise in safe situations until a new habit has been established, then follow one's own intuition about when to repeat back, or stay silent, or ask a question, which is explored in Chapter 21.

21 Questioning

SUMMARY

- Open and closed questions
- Judgemental questions
- Leading questions
- Multiple questions
- The significance of silence

Questions might be described as the 'precision tools' in the coach's tool-box. Effective coaching questions help people to think, to see situations from different perspectives and to enhance their awareness of self and others. Let us now examine the different types of questions used in coaching sessions, and the ones that coaches tend to avoid.

Questions

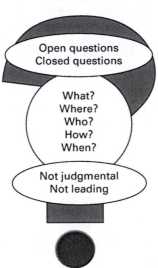

Open questions
Closed questions

What?
Where?
Who?
How?
When?

Not judgmental
Not leading

Open and closed questions

Closed questions elicit a short, 'yes' or 'no' answer. Open questions provide the space for people to find their own answers. Most of the questions used in coaching are open questions. Closed questions are used to tie down new insights and actions.

Closed questions are always used when asking permission (explored in Chapter 14), for example, 'Would you like to tell me more about that?'

Open questions:	Closed questions:
How important is that to you?	Can you commit to that?
What is happening at the moment?	Can I ask you about...?
When will you do that?	Do you want to explore that?
What would that look like?	Is there anything else about that?

Beware of judgemental questions

Most coaching questions begin with the words 'what', 'where', 'who', 'when' and 'how'. These open questions turn the focus inwards to help the coachee explore thoughts and feelings, and to gain new insights on how to move forwards.

Coaches tend to avoid questions starting with 'why' because such questions can put people on the defensive and sound judgemental; the obvious answer to 'why' is 'because'. We have to take care that a seemingly open question is not a judgemental question in disguise, for example, 'What did you do that for?' This begins with 'what', so ticks the coaching box, but in fact it is really a 'why' question, asking the person for justification.

Coaching questions

- What's stopping you from doing that?
- Who would you choose as a role model?
- Can I ask you about...?
- How important is that to you?
- Is there anything else about that?

Judgemental questions

- Why did you do that?
- What did you do that for?

It is acceptable to ask 'why' questions when asking for information that is not personal, for example, 'Why are the computers set up this way?' This question is not judgemental provided that it is not directed at the person responsible for setting up the computers. Then it would become personal.

An effective question is any question that is asked in the spirit of helping people to learn more about themselves without inviting judgement. As with all coaching rules, it is the intention behind the words that counts more than the actual words used. A person who is highly emotionally intelligent, who treats others with respect and cares about their development, can ask a 'why' question without putting people on the defensive. The opposite is also the case, that no matter how many coaching rules are followed, if the intention is to manipulate, damage or deceive, no coaching will take place, and there will be low trust and low rapport.

Beware of leading questions

Sometimes a manager's job is simply to tell someone what to do. That is fine. What is not fine is to manipulate people into making decisions by asking leading questions. For example, if a manager asks a report for a solution, but then does not accept an answer until it tallies with what the manager wants to hear, then trust will be lost.

Leading questions cannot be defined in isolation. Usually a question becomes leading because the coach has missed out on exploring a statement from the coachee.

Coachee: I find it hard to be heard at meetings.

Coach: How could you become more confident?

The coach has made an assumption that there is a lack of confidence, when the problem could be any number of issues. The most effective question here might be, 'Would you like to tell me more about that?' which is a totally open question encased in one of the closed 'permission' questions mentioned earlier, to relax the coachee and create rapport. However, if the coachee had already explored the situation and defined the core issue as a lack of confidence, then 'How could you become more confident?' might be an appropriate question to ask, because the avenue of thought has been opened by the coachee and the coach is simply following it.

Another useful response would be for the coach simply to repeat back the coachee's words:

Coachee: I find it hard to be heard at meetings.

Coach: You find it hard to be heard at meetings.

The more open the coach's response, the more helpful it will be to the coachee in identifying the core issue, which may turn out to be something the coachee could not have guessed at.

It could be said that the opposite of leading questions is 'clean' questions. Clean Language was devised by psychologist David Grove in the 1980s, and features a series of questions which he identified, over a period of years, as being the least likely to influence the thoughts and feelings of his clients. Grove's methods are described in Chapters 28 and 29.

Coachee: When I go into meetings I find it difficult to speak up.

Coach: And what kind of 'difficult' is that 'difficult'?

Coachee: I start to panic.

Coach: And is there anything else about 'difficult' and 'panic'?

Coachee: I tense up.

Coach: And whereabouts is that 'tense'?

Coachee: It's here (pointing to stomach).

This process is homogenous with the coachee's own words and provides a method for exploring the current reality of the coachee. (For the importance of exploring current reality see Chapter 23 on the GROW model.) Starting each sentence with 'And' implies that the coach's words are joined up to and following on from those of the coachee, rather than diverging. Clean Language is often concerned with locating feelings, thoughts and metaphors in terms of the coachee's mental sense of space. This seems to bring clarity and new insight.

Interestingly, in Clean Language the question, 'What will you do?' would be considered a leading question, as it implies that there is an action to be done. A completely clean question would be, 'Is there anything you want to do?' This conflicts with some coaching guidelines, which recommend avoiding closed questions on the grounds that they do not encourage people to think. I have not found this to be the case and wonder whether it was the manner of the question asked by the proponent of this theory, or perhaps the question itself, which produced the block to thinking, rather than the phraseology. As with all coaching guidelines, I believe that it is useful to know and understand all points of view, then make one's own decision about the appropriate course of action, accepting that it might differ from situation to situation.

Beware of multiple questions

When we are unsure of what to ask next, it is tempting to stumble through three or four questions in quick succession. It is worth taking time to frame your question and let it lie until it has been answered. Do not speak until you are sure that what you are going to say will be helpful to the coachee. If there is a period of silence while you do this, it will certainly be useful to the coachee, providing time to think.

The significance of silence

When people do not immediately reply to a question it is usually a sign that the question has given them something to think about. Silence is a valuable tool here to give people time to process their thoughts and come to a new awareness and understanding. If you are not sure whether someone is processing or simply stuck, just ask: 'Would you like more time to think about this or shall I ask you another question?'

There is a danger that coaches can become so wound up about what to ask next, that they stop listening and focus on their own performance instead of what their coachees are saying. We should never forget the power of simply listening, as propounded by Nancy Kline (1999) and explored in Chapter 19, 'Listening'.

Coaching questions have only one purpose: to enable coachees to find out information about or for themselves. This is different to asking questions in normal conversations, when the purpose is to find out information that the questioner wants to know. My colleague James Wright suggests asking oneself, as the coach, 'Do I want to ask this question because *I am interested* in the answer or because *it is useful to the coachee*?'

Interested or useful questions

There is a danger that being asked a series of questions can feel like a grilling, or that the coaching conversation can develop the rhythm of a tennis match, with the coachee feeling that the answer must be delivered at the same length as the question, which limits the coachee's opportunity to explore his or her thoughts. Some ways of breaking up this pattern have already been mentioned, such as clarifying and reflecting, or simply staying silent. Another useful technique to know for this situation and others is about asking permission.

22 Permission protocol

SUMMARY

- Permission as a tool
- Permission protocol
- When is permission not permission?
- Permission and the need for control

Permission as a tool

Permission is one of the most useful but unidentified tools in coaching and management. People who customarily have a high level of rapport with others tend to ask permission frequently, although they and their colleagues will probably be unaware of it.

Different countries have different cultures and habits which are not hard to identify and respect. However, people of similar race, culture and background may also have different customs, arising from their experiences in life. For example, two outwardly similar families may exhibit very different behaviour; in one home the culture may be cold and critical, while in another it is positive and easy going; in some families there is a lot of shouting, while in others voices are never raised. These values are less obvious than the ones we meet abroad when travelling, and it is easier to offend without realizing it. Asking permission respects the boundaries we cannot see, and can act as our passport requesting entry. Preceding a coaching question with the request 'Can I ask you...' softens the exchange, enabling people to feel safer and therefore think more clearly.

The diagram below shows the use of permission as a tool in five different ways, ranging from situations where trust is low to where trust is high:

Permission protocol

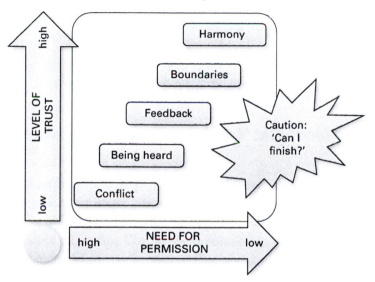

Permission protocol

1 Resolving conflict: Can I tell you?

Permission is the unsung hero of conflict resolution. Think of the person who irritates you the most. You may have promised yourself before a meeting that you will be ultra polite in order to avoid the usual conflict yet, in the event, the person becomes more upset with you than ever. What is missing here may well be the use of permission, both spoken and implied in your body language to each other. 'What I think we should do', however politely said, is not going to turn enemies into friends. If you can grit your teeth and rephrase it to: 'Can I tell you what I think we should do?' the barriers will start to crumble and rapport will grow.

2 Being heard: 'Can I add something to that?'

In a situation where one or more people are 'talking over' you, try the phrase, 'Can I add something to that?' People will stop talking and listen, because you are respecting what has just been said. 'Can I add?' carries the message that you have heard and understood what has been said and found it so valuable that you want to expand on the topic instead of introducing a new one. Other people will then have a sense that their own ideas have been found acceptable, and will feel validated.

The opposite of 'Can I add something to that?' is 'Yes, but ...' which implies dismissal not only of everything that has gone before, but of the person who said it, laying the foundation for resentment.

3 Giving feedback: 'Can I share something I have noticed?'

A coaching approach would be to ask people to give themselves feedback before offering any oneself. However, there are times when it is necessary to deliver some comment or advice on improving performance or behaviour. Asking permission to do so will soften the blow and relax the recipient, so that he or she will be more ready to listen and cooperate with you.

4 Respecting boundaries: 'Can I make a suggestion?'

In a coaching conversation, it is the coach's responsibility to manage the process, and it is up to the coachee to provide the content. If the coach strays inadvertently over this line, the coach is no longer helping the coachee.

However, if a coach has some useful information, experience or insight to offer, then passing it on makes sense. Preceding the offering with a question creates a boundary between eliciting information from the coachee and giving one's own. It eliminates intrusiveness and turns the contribution into a gift that can be used if helpful or discarded without any awkwardness if not.

The coach must not be attached to the outcome of his or her suggestion; if it does not appeal to the coachee, it must be put aside. A general rule of thumb is to offer suggestions no more than 10 per cent of the time, and only after the coachee's own ideas have been exhausted. This is explored further in Chapter 3, 'The directive–non-directive continuum'. Permission also works well in affirming boundaries in team situations, demonstrating respect and showing that people are willing to listen and take account of each other's views.

5 Harmony

Think of an exchange with your best friend or most trusted colleague; the actual words of permission are probably rarely used here because permission is inherent in the relationship. It will, however, be evident in voice tone and body language. The higher the level of trust, the less permission needs to be overtly stated and vice versa.

When is permission not permission?

We have all heard politicians say, 'Can I finish?' when interrupted by an interviewer or opponent. This is a statement which appears to comply with all the criteria of asking permission and yet which produces conflict. This is because of the intention behind the words; there is an implied criticism and the question is not a request but a demand.

Coaching is a mindset and attitude rather than a set of tools. The underlying intention must be aligned with coaching values, which include respecting people, advancing their development and building trust.

Permission and the need for control

Unlike most coaching questions, asking permission is of its essence a closed one. Its power lies in the fact that people are permitted to refuse. Although one has to be prepared to accept a 'no', that is unlikely to happen in practice because the person is being given control. Control is a fundamental need, going back to the time when humans lived in caves and were liable to be eaten alive or freeze to death if they did not have control of their environment.

When we feel control slipping away in the workplace today, it can also feel like a life or death situation and may trigger our defensive 'fight or flight' systems. Our sense of safety is increased when people ask permission. At work, the safer people feel, in terms of a blame-free and supportive environment, the more risks they will be prepared to take, the more confident they will feel and the higher their performance will be.

Fundamentally, permission is a tool which creates and respects the non-aggressive types of boundaries essential for harmony in relationships. The importance of positive boundaries has been recognized for centuries in different cultures all over the world.

> 'Good fences make good neighbours' – English proverb

> There must be a fence between good neighbours' – Norwegian proverb

> 'Between neighbours' gardens a fence is good' – German proverb

> 'Build a fence even between intimate friends' – Japanese proverb

> 'Love your neighbour, but do not throw down the dividing wall' – Hindi proverb

> 'Love your neighbour, but put up a fence' – Russian proverb

> 'It is good to erect hedges with the neighbours' – Medieval Latin proverb

Now we have explored the specific skills which ease the flow in both conversations and coaching sessions, it is time to address the fundamental structure which turns a conversation into an effective coaching transaction: the GROW model.

The GROW coaching model

23

SUMMARY

- The history of GROW
- Practical application
- Flexibility of GROW

The history of GROW

The GROW model

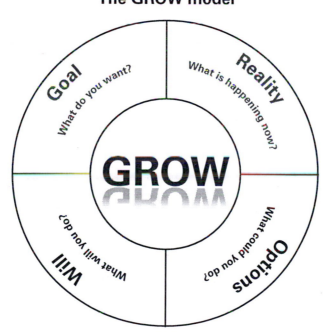

A coaching model provides a framework for a coaching session, a conversation, a meeting or a project.

The GROW model was developed some 30 years ago by Sir John Whitmore and his colleagues. It was publicized through his book *Coaching for Performance* (Whitmore, 2009) and, since the book has been translated into 19 languages, GROW has become the most prevalent coaching model in the world today. Other models have since been created but they are mostly similar to GROW.

Practical application

The sequence illustrates the solution focus of coaching and breaks down like this:

Goal

The Goal section of GROW is addressed at the beginning of each session and referred to again from time to time to keep the focus moving forward, especially if the coachee becomes stuck. It raises energy and clarifies thinking. Identifying what we want to achieve puts us on the path to accomplishing it by focusing on the solution rather than the problem.

Some Goal questions are:

- What do you want?
- Over what time frame?
- Where would you like to be on a scale of 1–10?
- Imagine you have achieved it:
  - What does it look like?
  - How do you feel?
  - What are people saying to you?
  - What are the benefits?
- What do you want to achieve in five years/one year/three months?
- How could you say your goal in a few words?
- Which part of that is the real focus?
- How will you know when you have achieved it?
- In an ideal world, what do you really want?

Reality

This is an exploration of the coachee's world at the moment. Time spent here helps people to recognize what is happening, how it affects them, and the impact on others. It provides an opportunity for viewing issues from different perspectives.

Some useful questions here are:

- What is happening at the moment?
- How important is this to you?
- If an ideal situation is 10, what number are you at now?
- What impact is this having on you/how do you feel?
- What have you done so far?
- Who else is affected?
- What are you doing that's working towards your goal?
- What are you doing that is getting in the way of your goal?

One of the precursors of coaching was the approach developed by Harvard sports coach Timothy Gallwey, author of the *Inner Game* series of books (Gallwey, 1997) described in Chapter 1. For example, he discovered that if he asked clients to 'watch the ball' they would tense up and under-perform. However, when asked to count how many times the ball spun as it went over the net, their shots improved significantly. The spin of the ball does not matter in terms of technique, but the process of focusing on the detail has the dual effect of forcing the coachee to watch the ball, and providing a distraction from limiting internal 'chatter', like 'I've failed before', or 'I never hit the ball'.

Exploring the current reality is one of the practices that differentiates coaching from normal conversation, where we tend to go straight from the past to the future, for example from, 'He said I was always late; I said I wasn't; he said I was unreliable,' to 'I'm going to resign!' In this statement, the speaker is taking the emotional baggage of the past into a crucial decision about the future. Reality questions (together with Goal questions, which can be thought of as 'future reality') enable coachees to step off the confusion track, gain some new perspectives, and make calm, informed decisions about how to move forward.

Asking Reality questions does not come naturally, and it is tempting to go straight to the Options or Actions stage of GROW. However, doing this without exploring the coachee's Goal and Reality may well result in the answer, 'I don't know what to do, that's why I'm here!'

All these questions help people to tap into their own awareness leading to a rise in energy which shows up in a lightness in the voice, brighter eyes, a smile and a more upright posture. That is the time to pin the new insights down to Options and Actions, and the chances are that by this time, coachees will spontaneously start originating actions where they were stuck before.

Note that we are exploring the present and, although we may ask what has been done so far, we are not dwelling on the past or listening to stories about it. We are focusing on what the situation means to the coachee more than on the facts. We are not asking questions to find out what has happened, but so that our coachees may find out more about the impact on themselves and their work, or life in general, and how to deal with it. When the coachee reaches a new insight or level of understanding, it is wise to explore the goals and realities of that, to embed the new awareness and to revisit the original Goal. Possibly a new Goal or direction will emerge. Then the GROW sequence starts again.

When the coachee reaches a new insight, these questions are useful:

- What do you know now that you did not know before?
- What is your insight about that?
- What have you learned about yourself from that?
- Where else could you use this?

Options

Coachees will move naturally towards the Options stage as their Reality becomes clearer. Often they display a new energy by sitting up and smiling, or through a lighter tone of voice. Then it is useful to ask some of these questions:

- What are your options?
- What could you do?
- What else?
- If there were anything else, what would it be?
- What has worked in the past?
- What steps could you take?
- What might someone else do in your shoes?
- Imagine you have achieved your goal; look back on the journey and tell me how you got here.

The following questions probe for more information and should be used only when the coachee has mentioned the subject in question, for example by saying, 'I need some help', or 'I don't have the information':

- Who could help you with this?
- Where could you find out the information?

Will

As opposed to 'Options', which brings to light all possibilities, 'Will' is about selecting actions which the coachee can commit to undertaking. When asked, 'What will you do about this?' there is a danger that the coachee will make a list of what they think they should do, rather than choosing a pathway which suits their talents and ways of behaviour. The classic example is where a man commits to joining a gym because he wants to lose weight. However, if he is never going to attend because he hates going to the gym, he would get more benefit from committing to walk his dog every morning, if that is something he would enjoy.

Some Will questions might be:

- What will you do about that?
- How will you do that?
- When?
- What will it take for you to commit to that action?
- What could you do to become more committed?
- Could you do more?
- How many?
- How much?
- How often?
- Where will you find that?
- Who will you talk to?
- What else you could you do?

If the coach senses a lack of commitment, a question like, 'How committed are you to doing that?' should be asked straight away. If there is any hesitation, it is best to go back into the GROW process to clear any blocks and find the most comfortable way forward.

Flexibility of GROW

It is crucial to understand that the components of GROW do not necessarily follow that order. An effective coaching conversation usually starts by exploring the Goal (which raises energy and provides a clear focus for the session) followed by some Reality questions to find out how the land lies. But then it moves between all four elements as required:

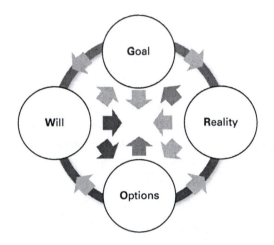

Since the GROW model was coined, other coaching models have emerged, including TGROW, where identifying the 'Topic' comes first, and the substitution of 'Wrap up' for 'Will'. Most of the models available work just as well as GROW – what matters is to have a framework, not to follow slavishly but to provide an awareness of which type of question will be the most productive, in terms of future aspiration, current reality or next steps. This is usually more important than the question itself. Goal questions raise energy, Reality questions provide clarity, and Options and Actions questions turn ideas into achievements.

Apart from GROW, which is so robust and all-encompassing, I am not a big fan of models and acronyms. I prefer to see people embed a skill by practising it than having to decipher a string of capital letters. However, I coined one further model for goal setting because without it managers in companies default to the SMART model. The benefits of each and their uses in different situations are described in Chapter 24.

The EXACT model: a coaching approach to goal setting

24

SUMMARY

- The EXACT goal-setting model
- Comparison between EXACT and SMART goals
- How to set a goal
- Goal setting with teams

The EXACT goal-setting model

One of the fundamental principles of coaching is to have a clear understanding of where the coachee wants to get to before starting on the coaching journey, hence the requirement for effective goal setting and the reason the GROW model starts with 'G' for Goal. Many of our goals are determined, perhaps unwittingly, by the agenda of others or by pressures upon us to be something we are not. The EXACT model on the next page describes an effective coaching goal, helping people to identify objectives which are congruent with their own values and performance style.

Setting a goal according to the above parameters provides energy and focus, and keeps people motivated in order to achieve what they may not have thought possible. It is said that the time period required to break an old

The EXACT model

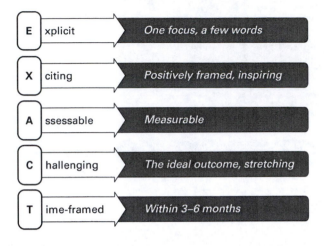

E	xplicit	One focus, a few words
X	citing	Positively framed, inspiring
A	ssessable	Measurable
C	hallenging	The ideal outcome, stretching
T	ime-framed	Within 3–6 months

habit is six weeks with a further six to ingrain a new one. Three to six months affords enough time to achieve a serious goal without losing motivation. The sessions during this period would ideally take place weekly or fortnightly, depending on the coachee's availability.

An effective goal is helped by the brain's own pattern matching system. This function allows us to notice only what is relevant to us at the current time, while filtering out the rest. For instance, in a busy airport, you will ignore constant announcements unless your own name is mentioned and this, miraculously, you will hear. Similarly, if someone has identified a powerful goal, the pattern matching system will highlight opportunities they might otherwise have missed.

Comparison between EXACT and SMART goals

The SMART goal-setting model is widely used by organizations. There are a number of variations, broadly listed below.

SMART goals show two significant differences from EXACT goals:

1. SMART goals are 'realistic' or 'achievable' whereas EXACT goals are 'challenging'. This is because the SMART model was created for managers who are setting goals for other people. There is a tendency to set them too high, which is demotivating for the people who have to achieve them.

The SMART goal-setting model

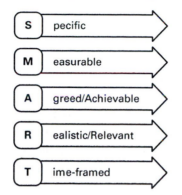

S | pecific

M | easurable

A | greed/Achievable

R | ealistic/Relevant

T | ime-framed

Therefore, SMART encourages managers to be realistic about the goals they are setting and to ensure that they are achievable.

However, in coaching, the goal is set by the coachee, and when we set goals for ourselves we tend to aim low through lack of clarity or confidence. Therefore it is important for the coach to facilitate the coachee in aiming high.

Another influencing factor is that company goals carry the possibility of public failure, whereas goals set in a coaching relationship should always remain confidential. In my experience, coachees find the coaching journey towards an EXACT goal more meaningful than whether they achieved the goal to the letter.

2. A SMART goal could be negative, such as, 'get out of the bottom league' instead of, 'move up a league'. In the former, the focus is on the bottom league, the place we want to get away from, but that is what will sit in the mind, prompting the brain's pattern matching system to pick up on external factors connected to the bottom league (Whitmore, 2009). It will also lower energy and motivation.

On the contrary, an EXACT goal must be positively framed, and something that excites the coachee or creates a feeling of significant relief. This raises energy and motivation, and engages the brain's pattern matching process to notice what might otherwise be missed.

So where EXACT differs from SMART is that:

- the goal has to be positively framed and inspiring; and
- the goal has to be challenging, stretching people to achieve their very best.

Whereas GROW is a set of stages, EXACT is a description of what an effective coaching goal might look like.

How to set a goal

Spend some time exploring what the coachee wants and what it will be like when the coachee has achieved it. It is not unusual for people to end a session with a goal quite different to the one they came to the coaching with, so this exploratory process is extremely important to ensure that the coachee will be working towards the most effective goal.

Another benefit of this process is an effect that is recognized in golf, where top players are encouraged by their coaches to visualize hitting the winning shot, to see the ball fly and to hear the cheers of the crowd. This works because, on one level, the brain is unable to tell fact from fiction (which is why sad movies make us cry). The new neural pathways formed by this imagined practice will be as real as those created by physical practice, creating a new habit of winning which will be easier to repeat a second time around.

Although the recommended period for an EXACT goal is 3–6 months, it is a good idea to establish what the long-term goals are as well – the end goal which might be 1–5 years ahead.

People tend to set goals according to what they think they should aim for, rather than what they truly want. The EXACT exploratory process will help them determine their true goals, and when this happens a shift in energy will show – a smile, an upright posture, brighter tone of voice, eyes lighting up etc.

Sometimes people come up with goals that are inspiring but have no clear measure. It is worth spending an extra 10 minutes or so brainstorming with the coachee to quantify the goal, because once a firm measure is in place the goal becomes more compelling. A goal without a measure is a dream, not a target. If it is not possible to get a real measure you can fall back on a percentage, such as '100 per cent efficient', or a comparison like, 'as fit as I was in '96', or 'as confident as Peter'.

We tend to set goals within self-imposed limitations. Coaching can help people to give themselves permission to admit to what they really want. One form of this is to set a goal which is part of the pathway to the target rather than being there.

Below are some examples:

A strategy is a means to an end, often carrying with it the burden of being an unwelcome chore. An EXACT goal is the end result – what the coachee wants to achieve within the next few months. On further exploration it may become clear that the original statement, marked above as 'strategy', turns out to be an end goal for the person. It is for the coach to explore this, not dictate. The test is whether the goal meets the EXACT criteria, particularly that of being inspiring to the coachee.

My colleague James Wright once coached a young, single mother of two autistic boys and who worked as a teacher in a special needs school for autistic children. In spite of being eminently qualified for her job, even holding a PhD in the field of autism, she encountered sarcasm, inappropriate comments and general lack of support from her Principal.

James started by helping her to set three goals, with the intention of working together over a 12-week period, meeting once a week. One was aligned specifically to her work situation and two others concerned personal issues. The work goal was about proving her worth to her boss, and she worded it provocatively: 'I'll show him!'

James voiced his concern that the outcome was to an extent controlled by a third party, namely the Principal; suppose he chose not to 'be shown?' Then the outcome of her goal would be in his hands, not hers. However, she insisted on this wording, saying she found it motivating.

During the second session, James helped the woman to work out a set of strategies, beginning with a written account of the current situation and how she felt about it, and a vision in writing of how her life would be when she achieved the goal. Other strategies were created around the issues of confidence and self-esteem, and it was here that her insights came thick and fast.

In the fourth week of coaching, however, it was proving difficult to create a really strong 'energy' about the goal in spite of its provocative title. Her commitment to this goal was dwindling, as she was finding that despite her efforts to support the pupils (including introducing some extra-curricular activities that had not been provided before), the Principal remained as ambivalent as ever towards her. She declared that she was considering giving up that goal and concentrating on the other two. James asked whether she might like to consider re-framing the goal in words that reflected outcomes entirely within her control, and she agreed to think about it.

Two days later, the woman phoned James to say she had something important to discuss. She went on to share that through exploring her confidence and self-esteem during the coaching, she had become aware of the extent to which she did in fact value herself, her academic and professional achievements and her remarkable energies as a single working mother to two demanding, autistic boys. Since the previous coaching session she had confronted herself with a number of challenging questions about what was truly important to her, writing down her responses and posting them up on the walls of her home as affirmations.

Through this process of self-exploration she had begun to see her life from a new viewpoint where she became the centre of her own world. This was new to her; a different perspective from her previous one, where other people's perceptions of her had always been at the centre. She said that her stated goal 'I'll show him!' no longer fitted and she had asked herself the question, 'How can I make this goal all about me?' She found that a revised goal had come naturally to her and she worded it in the present tense: 'I am an amazing Educational Consultant.'

She told James that just hearing herself say these words changed the way she felt. When James asked what she intended to do about it, she replied:

'Well, I hope it's all right but I've already taken a couple of actions that we didn't agree on in our coaching session. Yesterday, I went into school early and demanded a meeting with the Principal, told him what I thought of him and his methods and attitudes, and told him to shove his job! I handed him a resignation letter I'd brought with me and walked out there and then.'

James assured here it was indeed 'all right' and said, 'You know you're right – I definitely don't remember agreeing those actions with you! So tell me, what happened next?'

> 'Well I drove straight to the local Education Department and told them what I had done. They actually congratulated me and said they were impressed I had lasted even 18 months with that Principal, because his misogynism was well known. Two hours later I walked out with 77 days of consultancy booked in my diary at £750 per day, with more to follow.'

She reported that she felt elated and that by centering the goal specifically around herself, she was able to 'take back the reins' and 'chart her own course' with immediate and life-changing results. James asked what she had learned from this huge turnaround.

'In future,' she said, 'any time I set myself goals, I'll just remember to build them around me, remember who I am, what I want, and that nothing and no-one can stop me!'

So the simple but practical learning for coaches is that when setting goals with coachees, we must work on making sure those goals are phrased so that their success depends on the coachee – they must be *PERSONAL, and not about creating something for someone else.* That is where the motivation really lies when the going gets tough, as it invariably does with challenging goals.

An effective and practical way of achieving this is to ask searching questions about what is truly important to the coachee. Ask how they can put in place reminders of *what they personally can influence*, as James's coachee did with her post-its all over her walls.

Getting coachees to make 'I want …' or 'I am …' statements will help them reach a powerful, motivating goal.

Goal setting with teams

Although the SMART model is effective when setting goals for staff who are not involved in the process, the EXACT model can also be used successfully with teams to create a goal. I have known managers replace their usual practice of setting quarterly targets for their teams with EXACT goal setting meetings, where the team creates its own goals. Often these turn out to be more challenging than the ones the manager intended to set in the first place. Meanwhile, people feel more empowered because they have ownership of the goal.

Conclusion

Lewis Carroll wrote about a girl called Alice who was confronted with many pathways and asked a Cheshire cat for advice:

> 'Would you tell me please which way I ought to go from here?'
> 'That depends a good deal on where you want to get to,' said the cat.
> 'I don't much care where,' said Alice.
> 'Then it doesn't matter which way you go,' said the cat.
> 'So long as I get somewhere,' Alice added as an explanation.
> 'Oh you're sure to do that,' said the cat, 'If you only walk long enough.'
> — Alice in Wonderland, *Lewis Carroll*

Coaching feedback

SUMMARY

- Why feedback models don't work
- Eliciting self-feedback
- Relationship to the GROW model
- General feedback guidelines

Why feedback models don't work

One of the greatest hurdles that managers say they face in today's workplace is the giving and receiving of feedback. Gone are the days when bosses acted as supervisors who were there to chastise and correct, but many now flounder when it comes to putting a more interactive style of management into place while ensuring that everything gets done.

I often meet managers who are looking for the 'magic bullet' that will turn corrective feedback into an inspiring and motivating experience for whoever is on the receiving end. But whichever of the techniques learned on courses that they put into action, feedback encounters seem to fall flat or generate antagonism.

During the 1980s, positive psychology gained pace in filtering into the workplace. Managers were encouraged to praise their staff on a regular basis instead of speaking up only when something was wrong, and this proved a welcome break from the critical hierarchy that once prevailed. It was promoted by thought leaders like Ken Blanchard (whose 1981 book *The One Minute Manager* and its slogan 'Catch people doing something right' I still rate highly today) and Bob Nelson's *You get what you reward* (Nelson, 2005), which made the point that praise could be an even more effective reward than money. However, this approach faltered when indiscriminate praise started to be bandied about at work, using unspecific words like 'Great!' and 'Super!' One manager I coached told me he thought his boss must have been on a feedback course because at the end of each day the man walked round the office thanking and praising people, as if fulfilling a 'feedback quota' for the day. This approach reduces the quality of relationships rather than enhancing them.

Another approach to feedback is the 'sandwich', now discredited, where managers were advised to package their negative feedback in between two positive observations. Users of this method found that staff quickly cottoned on and, at the first sign of a compliment, would brace themselves for the nasty filling in the middle.

Although the sandwich fails when practised in isolation, I think the principle on which it was formed is sound. In the inspiring and liberating atmosphere of a true coaching culture there is no such thing as negative feedback; every pointer or piece of advice is regarded as a useful tip and people feel free to discard what is of no use to them. Imagine someone building a castle. If that person's role is simply to be a bricklayer for the castle owner, without any creative input, a demand to rebuild a section may demotivate the bricklayer. However, if the castle is *owned* by the bricklayer, advice might be welcomed or at least the bricklayer will not feel under any obligation to follow it.

In a true coaching culture, workers feel as if they are running their own businesses and that the boss is there to turn to for support when it is needed. They have a sense of owning their part of the castle, not being merely bricklayers. I experienced this myself at Virgin and it was particularly exhilarating in those authoritarian times. More recently Branson wrote:

> 'I think if people are properly and regularly recognised for their initiative, then the business has to flourish. Why? Because it's their business, an extension of their personality. They have a stake in its success.' (Branson, 2009)

This style of management requires a high level of trust in the relationship, and some subtle communication skills, which are what this book is all about. There is an apocryphal story about a worker who was retiring after a lifetime's employment in a factory. 'For 20 years,' he said, 'you have had the use of my hands. If you had asked, you could have had my brain as well.'

Eliciting self-feedback

The easiest way to approach feedback is to ask people to give it to themselves. The danger that the words used may feel awkward to the recipient, or not be aligned with his or her learning style, is eliminated. This applies both to positive feedback and what has come to be known as 'learning' or 'improving' (rather than 'negative') feedback.

This technique would apply to a conversation about an action, a project, behaviour, a staff appraisal, or any situation where people might be asked to reflect on their personal performance. The questions and statements given below are guidelines to a series of areas to be explored and can be modified to suit a particular context, vernacular or style of communication:

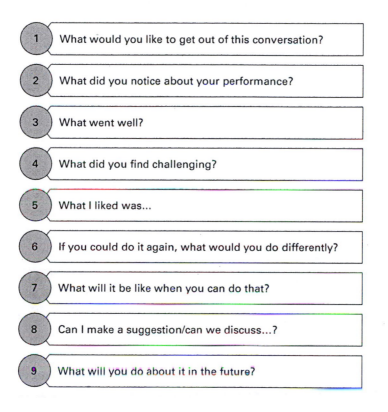

1. What would you like to get out of this conversation?
2. What did you notice about your performance?
3. What went well?
4. What did you find challenging?
5. What I liked was...
6. If you could do it again, what would you do differently?
7. What will it be like when you can do that?
8. Can I make a suggestion/can we discuss...?
9. What will you do about it in the future?

Relationship to the GROW model

The significance of each question or statement listed above lies in its purpose, rather than in the actual words used. Most of the questions are not chronological and can be mixed into a different order, although it is always useful to start with a future focused question and end with a plan of action. Let us now explore each question one by one:

1 What would you like to get out of this conversation?

It is usually effective to start any undertaking by looking ahead to what all parties want to achieve before setting out. This focuses people's minds and highlights any differences or misunderstandings in terms of intention. Looking to the future has a side benefit of raising energy and clarity of purpose (see Chapter 23, 'The GROW coaching model').

2 What did you notice about your performance?

Asking 'What did you think of your performance?' invites judgement, which tends to put people on the defensive. 'What did you notice?' is a neutral question requesting information rather than assessment. This can be rephrased to suit the context of the situation and explored with several questions, such as:

- What was your experience of that?
- What is happening at the moment?
- What have you done so far?
- Would you like to tell me where you are at?

3 What went well?

Even if a neutral question is asked at (2), people tend to answer by describing what went wrong. However, it is important to recognize strengths as much as weaknesses, therefore this question is intended to highlight what is going well.

Alternative questions could be:

- What are your strengths?
- What are you enjoying about this?
- What have you achieved so far?
- What does knowing you can do this tell you about yourself?
- Where else could you apply this?

4 What did you find challenging?

Occasionally, particularly during a manager-report performance review, someone might admit only to achievements and avoid mentioning any problem areas. These are best approached as neutrally and openly as possible.

So rather than zeroing in directly on the problem, eg 'Why are you missing targets?' a broad question like the one above allows the person to explore the situation and approach it in the way that he or she finds most comfortable. While talking it through, the person is likely to gain new insights and start to address any failings. An alternative question might be: 'What difficulties are you experiencing?'

Another scenario is where people reply by talking about why the failures were all someone else's fault. In this case I would make the questions more personal and include:

- What was your own contribution to the success/failure of the project?
- What might you personally have done that would have produced a different result?

If the person continues to avoid admitting to any problem areas, there is a place for direct feedback later in the conversation.

5 What I liked was...

Because people tend to dwell on what went wrong and overlook their accomplishments, it is useful to give some positive feedback where it is authentic and deserved. How often have you walked away from an event where your performance was impeccable except for one small flaw? Perhaps you forgot to cover a point or mixed something up. These events can stay with us for days, blotting out the sense of what went well.

These comments could happen anywhere in the conversation and as often as deserved:

- Sounds like you have made real headway there.
- How are people responding differently now you are doing that?
- I've noticed how far you've come on this over the last year.

6 If you could do it again, what would you do differently?

This can be explored at length and asked several times. Each answer might benefit from being explored through the GROW questions explored in Chapter 15:

- And where are you with that now?
- Where would you like to be?

- What is getting in the way?
- How might you change this?
- How will you do that?
- What else would you do differently?

The intention of this question is to look to the future, so it is in effect a Goal question in terms of GROW. The beneficial effect of this future focus can be intensified by the question in the section below.

7 What will it be like when you can do that?

This is an extremely important part of the process. It directs the person's thoughts to the future, bypassing obstacles that may be obscuring their vision. This area can usefully be explored at length using questions like:

- What will the benefits be?
- How will it impact others?
- Imagine you have achieved it – what do you see/hear/feel?

Help the person to place him or herself into the future and gain a practical sense of how the achievement feels. This process raises energy, motivation and confidence. It is far more likely to improve personal performance than an analysis of what went wrong and who was to blame.

8 Can I make a suggestion?

Depending upon the context of the conversation, this is an opportunity for the coaching manager to offer advice or to deliver any 'learning' feedback that needs to be given. With any luck, the person will already have come up with his or her own learning feedback, negating the need for the manager to deliver it at all.

Notice that this question is placed near the end of the list. People perform best when they are in control of their own ideas and working at their own pace, so once they have said all they want to say, they will be more receptive to input from others. Alternatives to this question might be:

- Would it help to hear something from my own experience?
- Could we discuss the feedback we have received from your customers?
- Could I share with you what is coming up for me here?
- I have an idea that might help. Would you like to hear it?

Notice that all the above questions are prefaced by asking permission. This helps people to relax and think more clearly in sensitive situations because they feel more in control. This is covered in Chapter 21, 'Permission protocol'.

9 *What will you do about it in the future?*

Finally we embark upon the 'Options' and 'Will' (actions) part of GROW, to tie down reflections and ideas into a solid pathway forward. If this is attempted too soon, without a thorough exploration of the present situation and the future, people will tend to remain 'stuck' and not know how to resolve their dilemmas or change their behaviour. Other questions might be:

- What could you do about that?
- What would you advise someone else in your position to do?
- How/when/where/with whom will you do that?
- How committed are you to that course of action?

The GROW model, upon which this coaching feedback is based, is covered in Chapter 23.

The key to the whole process of coaching feedback is that people give themselves the feedback first, and for most of the time. This is more effective because they will own it, deliver it in a way that will least jar or upset them, and will feel more enthusiastic about making changes. However there are still times when feedback has to be given and received, and the guidelines which follow may prove useful.

General feedback guidelines

Many managers are challenged both by giving and receiving feedback. As a result they wait too long to provide learning feedback or do not provide it at all. Another common pitfall is failing to set out clear expectations and guidelines in the first place.

Most people are their own worst critics and it is impossible to chastise them more than they do themselves. So where people are aware of their error and perhaps need more time and practice to do better, it is more productive to focus feedback on what they are doing well, leaving them to work out the problems in their own way or ask for help if they need it. This will raise their energy and confidence instead of making them feel like giving up.

When we receive unwelcome feedback it is worth remembering that all feedback is usually offered as a well-meaning gift. However inappropriate, it is likely to arise from generosity and a desire to help rather than malice. Whether positive or negative, we may think it is one of the following:

- undeserved;
- of no use to us; or
- of great value to us.

In all cases, the best response is a simple 'thank you'. Giving feedback on feedback to justify one's own position can make both parties feel uncomfortable. It is of course acceptable to ask for more detail if you feel it will be useful to you.

Feedback is most effective when it is:

Specific

These statements are too vague to mean much to the recipient:

- That was great.
- That didn't really work for me.

These statements give the recipient useful pointers:

- You were effective during the meeting when you made the analogy between our team and a pride of lions.
- Your report gives some good facts and figures and I think it would benefit from being more succinct.

Notice that the word 'and' has been used in the above sentence in a position where people might often use 'but'. As we explored in Chapter 21 'Permission protocol', the word 'but' tends to dismiss what has gone before, which in turn makes the recipient feel as if he or she has been dismissed too. Using 'and' here validates what has been said about the report and implies that the suggestion is intended to add to the previous statement, rather than negate it.

Personal

Present the feedback as coming from you personally, not as a judgement from the world in general. You are entitled to your own opinion but presenting yourself as an authority may be resented. In these statements the speaker is taking ownership of the opinions:

- I think you did that well.
- What would have worked better for me is...

The following statements dismiss the whole person and imply that the speaker's judgement holds more value than the opinion of the person on the receiving end:

- You're not much good at handling customers.
- You should spend less time thinking about it and more time taking action.

Some managers fail to realize that seniority adds weight to their words. So whether their opinion is right or not, it will carry extra significance purely because it has come from a senior member of staff rather than from a peer.

Accentuating the positive

Because, as mentioned at the beginning of this chapter, we tend to take more notice of negative feedback than positive, it is important to give positive feedback wherever possible, as long as it is authentic, specific and deserved. Building people's self-belief is part of the coaching approach and provides energy and confidence to change.

- What I liked was...
- Can I suggest something you might do differently?
- You are always so good at...

Surveys show that many people value satisfaction at work even more than money. One of the best ways to raise employee satisfaction is to tell them specifically the difference they have made and where they are good at their jobs, every day and as often as is appropriate.

Self-directed

Coaching feedback, as described at the beginning of this chapter, is the most effective way to begin any feedback situation.

Invited

People will be more receptive to your feedback if they have asked for it. When you are asked you must tell the truth, while always remembering to accentuate the positive. They are more likely to ask for feedback if you have given them a chance to feedback on themselves first.

Appropriate

Negative or learning feedback is always best given in private to the person concerned but there are times and places for giving positive feedback. These are the parameters:

- As often as you can.
- Only when it is deserved.
- Immediately.
- In public if the recipient is not shy and if it will not belittle the contribution of other members of the team.
- Direct to the recipient.
- To the recipient's boss.

The structure of coaching

SUMMARY

- The coaching contract
- Structure of a coaching session
- Structure for a series of coaching sessions

Coaching sessions usually take place as part of a series of sessions over a period of time but can also be stand-alone. This chapter provides a framework for single or multiple sessions. The framework is by no means mandatory and must be varied according to the client's needs, but having an underlying structure to follow is often helpful, particularly to novice coaches.

This chapter is primarily concerned with formal coaching sessions rather than manager-as-coach meetings, where coaching skills may be used but formal coaching does not take place. However, the principles of the structure may be useful for ongoing development and appraisal meetings with employees.

The coaching contract

Prior to embarking on a formal coaching programme, both parties will benefit from an agreement on the parameters, creating a contract either verbally or in writing. The contract should cover items like the number of sessions agreed, length and whereabouts of sessions, expectations of each party, cancellation terms and any other agreements between them. There are plenty of examples available on Google (enter 'executive coaching contract'), or from the Association for Coaching.

Ideally, there will be a series of sessions over a period of time to ensure that:

- the groundwork is effectively laid for change;
- plans can be worked out and followed through;
- the coachee is supported through unexpected challenges; and
- old habits are permanently replaced by new ones.

An ideal length of time for a coaching series is likely to be 3–6 months, because that is the most effective time period for working towards a goal, as described in Chapter 24. Whereas a one-off session may produce high motivation and results in the short term, new habits, attitudes and way of behaving need to be firmly embedded, and this will take time.

It is not uncommon for sessions to take place on a monthly basis, particularly for busy executives or in organizations where budgets are restricted. However this will be a different experience from sessions at shorter intervals, because the landscape is likely to have changed so much that reviewing actions from a previous session may no longer be relevant.

Some executives like to see a coach at monthly or longer intervals in order to review and reflect on what is happening. In this case it is still advisable to have some long-term goals but they may be set over a longer period of time than 3–6 months.

There are advantages to setting goals to work on over a fixed period, in that coachees will have a sense of what can be achieved, how much time and effort will be required and, where working with an external coach, what the cost will be.

Another reason for adopting the fixed period approach is so that the coachee does not become 'coach dependent'. The nature of coaching itself should eliminate this possibility, because the responsibility for change lies with the coachee. If at the end of the fixed period there remains more work to be done, another fixed period of coaching can be commenced. What is important is that the coaching programme has an identifiable beginning, middle and end. The regularity of the sessions is dictated by the amount of time a coachee has available and what issues are being addressed.

Structure of a coaching session

I recommend a plan consisting of three types of session:

First session

This is spent identifying goals in all the areas of work and/or life where the coachee would like to see some change. Two or three of these will be complex goals in separate areas, to be worked on at every session. The rest are likely to be simpler goals, such as 'sort out the filing system', which the coachee can write down on a list. Because of the energy that coaching generates, the coachee is likely to tackle tasks that have been hanging around for years, even if they are not visited at every session. This list should be reviewed two or three times throughout the coaching series and specific actions can be set if required.

Transitional sessions

The next 3–6 months are spent working towards the goals through insights and actions. On a surface level, this process resembles working towards the target on any project. However, the coaching processes turn this into a voyage of self-discovery, where new insights are uncovered and new habits put into place.

Final session

This is a consolidation of the new learning, measuring how far the coachee has come and celebrating achievements. Whether or not the goals set at the beginning of the coaching series have been achieved, it is often the case that self-awareness uncovered on the journey has become more significant than the end result in practical terms.

Structure for a series of coaching sessions

Below is a brief description of the framework for each session in a series like the one described above. This can be adapted according to the context of the situation.

First session

1 Establish the contract between the two parties (ideally this will have been done beforehand).

2   Identify areas where the coachee would like to see change. Encourage the coachee to examine all areas of work and/or life areas.

3   Prioritize these areas into complex goals, namely those which will require months of work (usually up to four goals), and simple goals, which can be retained on a list and checked on from time to time (usually up to ten).

Some examples of complex goals might be:

- 10 per cent increase on sales;
- be a coaching manager;
- be in my ideal job;
- six new accounts.

A simple goal might be 'order my new laptop' – something that does not require intricate strategies or great effort.

4   Set the complex goals. The EXACT model described in Chapter 24 is helpful here:

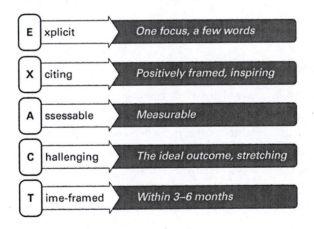

E	xplicit	*One focus, a few words*
X	citing	*Positively framed, inspiring*
A	ssessable	*Measurable*
C	hallenging	*The ideal outcome, stretching*
T	ime-framed	*Within 3–6 months*

As we explored in Chapter 24, this varies from the conventional SMART (Specific, Measurable, Agreed/Achievable, Relevant/Realistic, and Time-framed) in two ways: coaching goals should be challenging, instead of achievable or realistic, and always positively framed, exciting and inspiring.

It is more effective not to think about how to achieve the goals in the first session. The time is best spent exploring and defining clear outcomes for the future, because this will ensure that the coaching time is well spent and raise the coachee's motivation.

It is not uncommon for people to leave a coaching session with quite different goals to those they came in with. I recommend that this first session is spent exploring what coachees really want – as opposed to what they think they should want – and what it will be like when they have achieved it.

The EXACT model above is a description of the G part of GROW. It is used when the session is the first of a series, in order to identify the goal or goals that are to be worked on over the coaching period. If a session is taking place in isolation, the coach would not normally spend so long exploring the goal.

Finally, the session can be brought to a comfortable close by asking the coachee to reflect on what has been achieved, perhaps asking for feedback, or inviting anything else that needs to be said.

Transitional sessions

After the first session, there will be a series of further sessions over the agreed period. These are spent working towards the goals, identifying and eliminating obstacles, gathering resources, amassing new insights and changing habits. The GROW model (described in Chapter 23) is an excellent framework for these sessions, both to support whole sessions and explore each element of it.

An effective way of running a series of coaching sessions is to start each one by briefly reviewing each goal, setting an outcome for the particular session, and then exploring the goals one by one, reviewing previous actions, gaining new insight and setting new ones. Setting and reviewing actions is covered in the next chapter.

Final session

This is a time for consolidation, review, celebration and feedback. Any actions set previously should be reviewed, but no new ones set unless they happen naturally. Ask the coachee to measure how far he or she has come in terms of his goals and what new insights have been gained along the way.

Throughout all the sessions, it is the coach's responsibility to manage the time – the coach may be free to run over but the coachee may not, and may well leave mid-sentence if due at another meeting. Always ensure there is enough time to bring the session to a comfortable close.

As is the case with all coaching, the structure used should follow the needs of the coachee and be used as a support, not a prescription.

27 Setting and reviewing actions

SUMMARY

- Exploring the 'Will' part of GROW
- Setting actions
- Reviewing actions

Exploring the 'Will' part of GROW

Below is the solution-focused GROW framework explored in Chapter 23, which underlies most coaching and coaching models.

The 'W' in GROW represents action, and is so-named because it describes not just what is to be done, but the will to commit to an action. There is a danger that on being asked what to do, coachees will come up with a list of what they think 'should' be done, without taking into account whether they will find the time and motivation to carry the named actions out. Ways of exploring this commitment are described below.

Setting actions

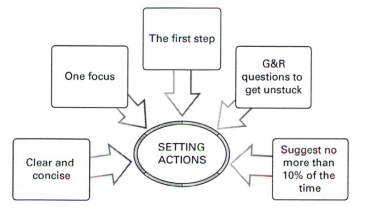

Actions are the simple steps by which we move towards the goal.

- **Clear and Concise:** It should be obvious to coach and coachee what the coachee has to do and how they will do it.

- **One focus:** Each action should cover just one step at a time.

- **The first step:** It is important that an action is the first step. If someone sets an action such as 'write my proposal' they may not get around to it. But if it is broken down into a number of actions and the first one is 'go to three different offices to assemble the necessary documents', the action is easier to achieve, one action leads to another, and the proposal will get written.

- **G & R questions to get unstuck:** If enough Goal, Reality and Options questions have been asked, actions will arise naturally and the coach's job is to ensure these actions are specific and well thought through, and that the coachee is completely aligned to and committed to carrying them out.

- **Suggest no more than 10 per cent of the time:** The content of the action is entirely up to the coachee. The coach may occasionally suggest an action but only after the coachee has had time to come up with his or her own. Coaches should have no attachment to their own suggestions. If the action does not appeal to the coachee, let it go.

Example:

Coachee: I'll write the paper.

Coach: Is there anything you need to do before you write the paper?

Coachee: Yes. I need to collate all my research.

Coach: So what would be the very first step?

Coachee: Set aside a morning to collate the research.

Coach: And when will you do that?

Coachee: Tuesday morning.

Coach: So what action are you writing down?

Coachee: Collate the research on Tuesday morning.

Sometimes coachees or employees will come up with an action they feel is expected of them, without any real buy-in, particularly if the coach is their boss. You can tell when this is happening because there will be no energy in their voice or their body language. If you think they are not buying into an action, ask some open questions. We may not realize ourselves that we do not have buy-in, until questioned. This usually happens when we have not spent enough time exploring the 'Reality' or 'Options' stages of the **GROW** model. It is fine to back-track at any time and a good rule of thumb is 'When in doubt, check on *the Reality*:

An example of an unhelpful conversation:

Coachee: I'm so untidy. There are papers all over my desk, piles of filing to do, magazines all over the floor at home. I can never find anything.

Coach: What would you like to do about that?

Coachee: I could do my filing.

Coach: When will you do that?

Coachee: Tuesday morning.

Nothing has changed; no new insight has been gained; no coaching has taken place. It is quite likely that Tuesday will come and go with no filing done and leaving the coachee feeling worse than before. A coaching conversation is successful when the coachee gains new insight which brings about change.

Example:

Coachee:	I'm so untidy. There are papers all over my desk, piles of filing to do, magazines all over the floor at home. I can never find anything.
Coach:	Is it okay if we talk about that for a few minutes?
Coachee:	That would be good.
Coach:	So you're untidy. And how do you feel about being untidy?
Coachee:	I hate myself.
Coach:	What's it about for you, being untidy?
Coachee:	I put things off. If I'm fiddling around looking for things, I don't have to face the big challenges.
Coach:	And how do you feel about facing the big challenges?
Coachee:	I guess I'm afraid.
Coach:	And is there anything else about being afraid?
Coachee:	Yes. I'm afraid that if I get myself sorted out I will have to perform and I might fail. It's an excuse. Being messy, no-one expects very much of me. I never saw that before.
Coach:	So it's that if you get yourself sorted out, you will have to perform and you might fail. How would you like it to be?
Coachee:	I'd like to be Miss Tidy. Be ahead of myself.
Coach:	And is there anything else about being Miss Tidy?
Coachee:	It would feel great. It's worth the risk.
Coach:	So what would you like to do about that?

Reviewing actions

After actions have been set during a coaching conversation or meeting, there will usually be a follow-up meeting one or more weeks later where the results are reviewed. In coaching, the purpose of reviewing coachees' actions is to increase their self-knowledge, help them to see clearly where there may be any blocks and support them in moving forward:

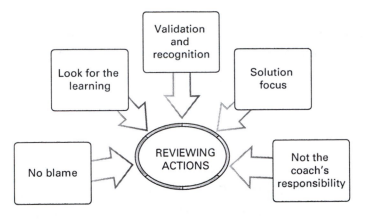

- **No blame:** reviewing actions is not about blaming coachees or making them feel guilty, but about learning and awareness.

- **Look for the learning:** ask Goal and Reality questions to help the coachee understand the impact of what he or she has done and not done.

- **Look for the real problem:** people often say they have not had time to do an action, or other things got in the way. Sometimes they fill up their time with 'other things' in order to avoid doing the action. Help them to understand what is in the background. If an action seems to be a strain, it may be because the path they have put themselves on is not appropriate for them. Ask open questions to create space for new insights. Never decide that you know best or be tempted to ask leading questions.

- **Look for insights,** eg What did you learn about yourself? What impact will it have if you don't do this? What will be the impact if you do? How do you feel about yourself having done this?

- **Clarify the learning:** reflect back any insights the coachee discovers and offer your own, always asking permission. Build on what has been learned, eg Now you know you can do this, where else could it be useful?

- **Validation and recognition:** give specific positive feedback where it is due and make sure the coachee appreciates what he or she has achieved.

- **Solution focus:** rather than worrying about failure, look for the way forward. After the situation has been explored using Goal and Reality questions, move into Options and Will, asking questions like: What would move this forward? Are you ready to commit to doing that? What would you be able to commit to?

- **Not the coach's responsibility:** although it is easy to understand that as a coach we do not offer solutions, even experienced coaches make the mistake of feeling they are responsible for ensuring that the coachee finds a solution. This attitude can affect the quality of the coaching and make the coachee feel under pressure. The coach's responsibility is only to create a space where the coachee can think more clearly. Then it is possible that a solution will emerge; but if it no solution is reached that does not mean that the coach has failed.

All of the foundation skills that coaches use have been covered in this part. However, as they develop, learn and become more advanced, coaches tend to bring other tools into play wherever they seem appropriate. Another reason for this is that many coaches have come to coaching from other disciplines and find that the skills they already have may be useful from time to time in coaching sessions.

When I began coaching I found the array of possible tools that could be studied and added to the toolbox bewildering. So in the next part I have provided a summary of the most common ones that have been found to be useful in coaching, together with any pitfalls that might arise when using them in this way.

PART FOUR
Tools of the trade: continuing professional development

Introduction

Coaching is fundamentally a simple process, a way of being and communicating which is defined by a small number of guidelines and rules. It is possible, and indeed quite common, for a coach to deliver a session that can change the course of someone's work or life using no more than the foundation coaching skills of listening, questioning and clarifying, supported by a structured coaching model like GROW.

After mastering these basics, coaches usually start to discover other tools and methods that may be complementary to coaching and can be applied in conjunction with it. These may come from a coach's previous learning, for example if he or she has trained and practised as a psychologist, or they may come about through further reading, research and continuing professional development. There are an abundance of useful techniques to choose from, but to learn them requires time and money, both of which may be in short supply for the average coach.

Organizations face similar challenges when deciding which development programmes to introduce for their managers. Would 360-degree feedback be useful, and does it need to be supported by costly external coaches? Can a force of internal coaches be trained up to take the role? Will managers benefit from identifying their MBTI profiles? Is Situational Leadership helpful? Again, the key limitations are time and money, particularly in today's business where budgets are shrinking.

This part of my book is specifically aimed at helping both professionals and organizations to identify which pathways to choose in terms of development. Each chapter gives an overview of a particular model or technique, and some are matched with case histories contributed by experts in the field.

The various topics have mostly been created during the last 40 years and we can assume that they all carry some value, having stood the test of time. However, the efficacy of each tool depends on the context in which it is used and how it is administered. There are pitfalls to be aware of and I have highlighted these wherever relevant.

Another intended use for this Part is as a reference guide for novice coaches and training executives, who may hear various tools and techniques being mentioned in meetings with clients and colleagues, and will benefit from having some knowledge of what is being talked about.

I believe that each of the methods, including coaching itself, must be regarded as a tool, not a master. The master should be the practitioner, who should trust his or her own intuition, experience and wisdom. All of the topics covered are relatively untried and untested and none has ever been subjected to any kind of academic scrutiny or scientific evaluation. This is not to say they are not effective, but it does lead me to advocate that, after becoming thoroughly well versed in a field, one should throw away the rule book and recreate the technique in the light of the situation and the learning styles of both the practitioner and the client.

It is also important for the practitioner to approach the use of the tools in a coaching style, avoiding judgement, treating people with respect and honouring their right to privacy.

David Grove's Clean Language

28

SUMMARY

- History and principles of Clean Language
- Metaphor
- Traumatic memory
- Clean Language questions
- Reflecting words back
- Clean conversations
- Clean Language in coaching
- Clean Language at the BBC
- Grovian techniques in industry
- Research into Clean Language

History and principles of Clean Language

Clean Language is a process that uses metaphor and neutral questioning to ease emotional blocks and resulting limiting behaviour patterns. It was created by psychologist David Grove (1950–2008) in the 1980s. The techniques were originally developed to help patients suffering from traumatic memories and coaches have found them useful in facilitating clients to resolve blocks and phobias. I worked with Grove from 2005 until his death in adapting his techniques into training courses specifically designed for coaches. These courses continue to be developed and delivered by our colleague Angela Dunbar.

Metaphor

Unlike the guided visualizations widely used in psychotherapy and healing processes, in Clean Language practitioners are led by metaphors created entirely by their clients, through the use of questions which will elicit the metaphors and develop them with the least possible influence from the practitioner. The techniques are useful in human interaction in general, in the workplace and outside, as well as in more formal situations where it may be used in therapy, coaching and other related fields.

Metaphors are an inherent part of our daily life, both in our waking and sleeping states. We use them consciously to convey a feeling, description or situation. Unconsciously, during sleep, our dreams string together metaphors and symbols, some of which are easily attributable and others so obscure that they remain a mystery. Metaphors we often use include:

- A millstone round my neck.
- Flat as a pancake.
- I'm freezing.
- I'm boiling.
- Throw some light on.

Less obvious metaphors are:

- What's your view?
- I'm under pressure.
- I can't get through to you.
- I'm in a relationship.

Metaphor has played a significant part in therapy and self-development for many years, contributing to Jungian therapy, NLP, Transpersonal Psychology, psycho-synthesis and ancient healing rituals.

Grove identified a series of questions that would least influence his clients while on their metaphorical journey. He asked only these questions at least 80 per cent of the time and coupled this questioning with frequent repeating back of the client's exact words. He termed this process 'Clean Language' as opposed to language that would interfere with, or 'dirty' the client's experience. There is a strong parallel here with the coaching principle of being on the client's agenda rather than that of the coach.

Not only is it unnecessary for the coach to understand what the client's metaphors relate to, but the client does not need to understand them either.

This is a key breakthrough in Grove's work, because deeply embedded trauma may be something that one's consciousness will protectively block out from memory; hence, if asked to interpret what their metaphors represent, people may be unable to do so and the process will stop there. Grove's Clean Language framework allows the client to move through the effects of the trauma and out the other side, without ever having to consciously remember the trauma itself.

Traumatic memory

Blocks, fears and phobias are often the result of traumatic experience that happened when one was too young, or damaged too severely to recall them. In real terms, the trauma may or may not have been serious. It could arise from child abuse, or a difficult birth, or simply being frightened by a dog. The effect of the trauma may be much more intense than the original event.

What happens is that a protective framework is set up by the psyche, for example to shield against the sound of parents fighting with each other when the child is too young to understand what is happening, or a more serious trauma like child abuse. As the years go by, the framework may be triggered by situations where it is not useful, and that reaction will create another small or large trauma that renders the framework more complex.

By the time the child becomes an adult there is an impenetrable structure in place which causes what Jung described as 'neuroses' or which in layman's terms we might call 'hang ups'. By then, the mechanism might be triggered by any number of situations unrelated to the original trauma, such as conflict in a business meeting, and the adult will revert to limiting behaviour dictated by a psychological construction which is obsolete but still functioning.

These illogical reactions sometimes cause overwhelming emotional responses, such as anger against colleagues or family members, fear of authority or public speaking, phobias like fear of heights or spiders, and even dependency addictions to alcohol, drugs or particular types of relationships. Such a framework has an additional disadvantage in that it is likely to be blocking off and limiting some part of the adult's emotions, skills or potential.

The Clean Language process effortlessly dismantles such frameworks and allows people to access all of their inherent energy, talents and resources. For example, it is highly effective in alleviating the fear of public speaking, social shyness, fear of authority or uncontrollable anger, as well as helping concentration and alleviating stress. Clean Language is a healing process that allows the unconscious mind or intuition to home in on wherever it is most needed. The metaphors that come into people's minds develop as if they are watching a film and may result in improved function and capacity in areas different to the ones that they originally entered the process to improve.

Clean principles treat the client's psyche as a system and, if one part of that system changes, it will affect all the other parts. During our lives, particularly in the early years, we may be turned away from the paths with which we might feel a sense of congruence by external circumstances, such as parental control, bereavement, schooling or illness. These experiences can modify the systems of our internal landscape, or 'psychescape', causing us to lose sight of our natural paths, and this in turn can create feelings of loss and frustration. These internal reactions and counter-reactions create barriers that cause some of our original self-knowledge to be lost from view, so that our full potential and strengths can no longer be accessed.

Clean methods have proved useful to coaches when it comes to breaking down blocks, phobias and repeating behaviour in their clients. The techniques are increasingly used in business and fit smoothly into a coaching session, being particularly effective where a client seems mentally stuck.

Through the exploration of client-led metaphor, issues are tackled at a deeper level than the conscious mind can reach, and changes in behaviour take effect immediately. Being 100 per cent client led, the process is non-invasive and can be performed safely by relatively inexperienced practitioners.

Clean Language questions

Clean Language questions are delivered with a slower and more rhythmic cadence than normal conversation. A typical Clean Language question is as follows, with [xxx] representing the client's own words:

'And what kind of a [xxx] is that [xxx]?'

The slow, rhythmic pace directs the question to land at a deeper level than the client's conscious mind, tapping into the unconscious mind and intuition.

Clean Language questions often start with 'And' or 'So'. Tacking one of these prefixes on to the front, particularly 'and', makes the question kinder and less invasive. The client is less likely to become defensive.

Clean Language questions are often closed, eg:

'And is there anything else about that?'

Phrasing this question as an open one, for example, 'What else is there?' would not be clean, as it implies that there must be something else.

Reflecting words back

In Clean Language, only the client's own words are reflected back. There is no paraphrasing or inserting the coach's words, for example:

Client: It is a forest. A thick, dark forest.

Coach: And what kind of a **forest** is a **forest** which is **thick** and **dark**?

Client: It's very shady, with sun above dappling through the trees. There's a sound of birdsong and it's very peaceful. There's water running, a river. Quite a wide river.

Coach: And is there anything else about a **river** that runs through a **forest** which is **thick, dark** and **peaceful** with **birdsong**?

Or:

Coach: And when it's a **thick, dark** and **peaceful forest** with **water running** and **birdsong**, whereabouts is that **forest**?

If the client uses too many words to repeat back, the coach selects those words that seem to be the most significant, or have the greatest resonance with the client.

The main questions currently used are set out below:

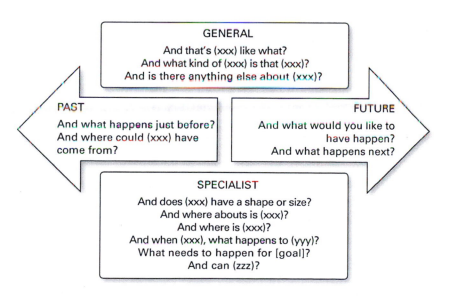

GENERAL
And that's (xxx) like what?
And what kind of (xxx) is that (xxx)?
And is there anything else about (xxx)?

PAST
And what happens just before?
And where could (xxx) have come from?

FUTURE
And what would you like to have happen?
And what happens next?

SPECIALIST
And does (xxx) have a shape or size?
And where abouts is (xxx)?
And where is (xxx)?
And when (xxx), what happens to (yyy)?
What needs to happen for [goal]?
And can (zzz)?

In addition, the client's words would frequently be added to the coach's question, for example:

Client: It's like a railway track.

Coach: And it's like a railway track. And when it's like a railway track, is there anything else about a railway track?

The questions loosely adhere to the framework above, in terms of when each is asked. The principles of being Clean require that certain questions are asked only when the client has introduced the concept. For example, 'And does it have a shape or a size' would be asked only when the client has implied that there is an 'it'. For example, the statement 'I feel fear', labels 'fear' as an object, so a question about the size or location of the object 'fear' could be asked:

- And whereabouts is fear?
- And does fear have a shape or a size?

However, if the client says 'I am afraid', a more appropriate clean response would be:

'And when "afraid", what kind of "afraid" could that "afraid" be?'

It is best not to use the word 'you' if avoidable, because it tends to elicit a conscious 'real-world' response from the client. The sentence above would be delivered with an emphasis and pause around the first 'afraid'.

This is clearer than trying to repeat the client's exact words:

'And when "I am afraid", what kind of afraid is that afraid?'

This might cause a moment of confusion about to whom 'I' refers, the client or coach.

Notice the phrasing of 'And does it have a shape or size?' which varies from the traditional way this question would be posed, 'size or shape?'. This is typical of the way in which Grove's questions were developed over a period of years, and the most effective version selected. Grove said that in this case, he had tested the two versions and found the unconventional phrasing to be the most efficient because the question landed more freshly and was less likely to tap into habits and assumptions, due to its unusual phrasing.

Other questions may be asked if they relate directly to a statement from the client. For example:

Client: The birds are chasing me.

Coach: And when the birds are chasing you, how many birds are chasing?

Because the client has implied a number, it is clean to ask what that number might be.

Grove went on to develop his work from a linguistic approach to a spatial one, called Clean Space, where he had the client literally move around the room. He found that clients could unearth new self-knowledge in different positions, and that they seemed to have an instinctive knowledge of which space in the room would enable them to do this.

This work developed into Emergent Knowledge, which is explored in the next chapter. Where the aim of Clean Language was to use words that would least contaminate the client's experience, in Emergent Knowledge he eventually dispensed with words that contained any content altogether, and the client's experience became almost entirely spatial.

It was at this point, in 2004 and after having used Clean Language techniques in my coaching for five years, that I met Grove and became one of a small number of practitioners who helped him to identify and record the new techniques.

The underlying principles behind all of Grove's work are well aligned with coaching.

Being 'Clean' means:

- staying out of the client's way and focusing on the client's agenda;
- following the client in tone and pace and reflecting back the client's own words and gestures; and
- focusing on the solution more than the problem.

One major difference between clean and conventional coaching is that in clean, suggestions are never made and the coach's own insights are never presented back. In this way, as Grove used to put it, clients can trust their intuition to be their guide. The unconscious mind is in control and will take the client only where it is safe to explore in order to alleviate any psychological tangles or traumas and move forward.

Clean conversations

The principles of Clean Language can be useful in everyday life, particularly at work. For example, take this conversation:

Report: I'd like to introduce a coaching programme.

Boss: What kind of a coaching programme?

Report: So that our leaders will manage in a coaching style.

Boss: What kind of leaders?

Report: The team leaders.

Boss: Is there anything else about the leaders?

Report: They want to coach but think they don't have time.

The boss could instead have advised what type of programme to introduce, a suggestion which may have been unsuitable for the managers in question and their particular challenges. Notice how much time has been saved by taking the Clean approach.

To ensure the conversation sounds normal, the rules of Clean Language have been relaxed. For example, a strictly clean response to the second statement would have been 'And what kind of managers are those managers?'

Clean Language in coaching

When people talk in 'real world' (non-metaphor) language they are speaking from the conscious mind, which is clouded by all kinds of baggage, such as fear, past failure and agendas which, over the years, have been implanted by role models like parents or teachers. When people talk in metaphors they are communicating directly with their unconscious minds. So if the coach coaches the metaphors, then he or she is enabling the coachee to explore on an unconscious level rather than being blocked by conscious limitations.

This formed the basis of twentieth-century psychologist Jung's work. He prefaces his autobiography, which is largely an account of the symbols which appeared in his dreams contained within a sparse account of his life (Jung, 1964) by stating:

'Recollection of the outward events of my life has largely faded or disappeared. But my encounters with the 'other' reality, my bouts with the unconscious, are indelibly engraved upon my memory. In that realm there has always been wealth in abundance, and everything else has lost importance by comparison. I can understand myself in the light of inner happenings. It is these that make up the singularity of my life, and with these my autobiography deals.'

However, there is one key difference between Jung's work and Grove's: Grove placed no importance whatsoever on interpreting the symbols which appeared. He maintained that merely identifying the symbols and watching them unfold was sufficient to alleviate the traumas they represented. Jung, however, believed that interpretation was not only crucial, but a duty of the therapist towards his patients:

> 'It is equally a grave mistake to think that it is enough to gain some understanding of the images and that knowledge can here make a halt. Insight into them must be converted into an ethical obligation. Not to do so is to fall prey to the power principle, and this produces dangerous effects which are destructive not only to others but even to the knower. The images of the unconscious place a great responsibility upon a man. Failure to understand them, or a shirking of ethical responsibility, deprives him of his wholeness and imposes a painful fragmentariness on his life.'

The potential difficulty with this obligation to interpret the symbols is that issues are often presented in symbols either because they represent traumas that are too painful or damaging for the person to face, or arise from a situation that occurred at a young age, before the person had words. Jung assisted his patients in recalling and describing their dreams, and then he interpreted the symbols for them, diagnosing their origin. The first process is in line with coaching principles, the second is not. Coaches do not diagnose their coachees' problems and these principles hold particularly true in David Grove's Clean work. This demonstrates the shift in attitude that occurred in the second half of the twentieth century across all areas of life, including psychology, work and personal development, which encouraged people to start taking responsibility for themselves, and to look towards the future with a positive, solution-focused approach.

Many people sense that they have a 'real me', which is not always the one they show to the world. They may feel that this 'real me' is not good enough, or perhaps too bright or too strong, and they are afraid to shine. Or a sense of duty has been bred into them along with 'rules' about how they should behave or what they should think. I once heard a client exclaim, 'It was my mother who married him, not me!' as she realized, during a Clean session, that her whole life had been lived according to her over-controlling mother's agenda, not her own.

People often have a sense that there is a 'path' or a 'life's purpose', a calling they could be following if they could only identify it. Clean processes

help people uncover these vague senses and eliminate what is not necessary or no longer of use to them.

Through working with Clean Language I have become more aware of picking up on these symbols or labels. They are like gifts from the person's unconscious mind, as if it is saying, 'You may be talking about schedules but this is what really needs to be examined'. Whenever one crops up I stop and ask it some questions.

Someone might use a word like 'recognition': 'What I want is the *recognition* for what I'm doing at work. The *recognition* of the hours I am putting in.' As soon as a word like this is repeated twice I will ask a question like, 'And what does *recognition* mean to you?' This is not phrased in a purely clean way, because that might sound odd in the middle of a coaching conversation, and anything that sounds odd might make the coachee uncomfortable. However, it follows Clean principles, which can be applied in any situation.

At other times, a coachee might use an obvious metaphor, like 'It's as if I'm on an *express train*'. This is another gift and the coaching should stop here and explore what is being offered: 'What kind of *express train*?' The responses may continue in metaphors, which should be explored until a sense of completion or new insight is reached. Then the coaching can resume in its normal way.

Sometimes the label is not an obvious metaphor. On one occasion, I heard a client refer to herself in the third person. She said (name changed):

'**Sally** will pass her exams and **Sally** will get **her** promotion.'

So I asked:

'What kind of a **Sally** is that **Sally** that will pass her exams and get **her** promotion?'

As she described this Sally she became visibly more confident and energized.

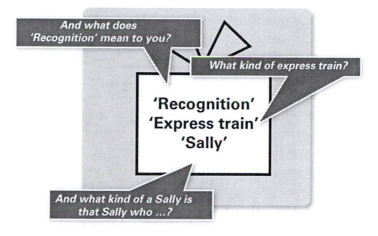

Someone may be coached about a situation that cannot be changed, particularly in today's climate of cuts. Conversations that explore symbols and metaphors help alleviate pressure when no action can be taken, enabling the person to feel more comfortable and to manage the situation more effectively.

It is not advisable to insert a formal Clean Language process into a session without the coachee's permission, as it might feel awkward or invasive. The coach could say 'I know a process using metaphors which might help here. Would you like to try it?' There is no need to explain all the background and technicalities, but a boundary should be established between this technique and what the coach regularly does with this coachee.

Clean Language at the BBC

The techniques are not widely known in business but have been highly effective on the occasions I know of when they have been applied. I have run two courses at the BBC, one to extend the skills of their internal coaches, and the other as a project in my doctoral research, which is described at the end of the next chapter, 'Emergent Knowledge'.

The BBC has trained and accredited a group of internal executive coaches to a high level, as described in Chapter 9. Guided by former BBC Head of

Coaching, Liz Macann, these lucky coaches have received a wide variety of training for their continuing professional development and in 2009 I was asked to design a Clean Language course for them, which was delivered in conjunction with my colleagues Angela Dunbar and Wendy Oliver.

We called the course 'Transformational change through metaphor' and delivered it to 24 internal executive coaches in two days spread over a month long period where the coaches practised the skills with each other.

The participants came from a wide range of backgrounds including departmental heads and programme makers. On the first day there was some healthy scepticism in the room, which is not unusual in media organizations, but when we all regrouped a month later, after the coaches had the opportunity to put the skills into practice with their course partners and their clients, this had completely disappeared, to be replaced by a new found passion and respect for the techniques. Coaching head Liz herself found that Clean Language gave her 'a way to explore emotions and feelings safely, staying within the boundary that separates coaching from therapy. It was also a revelation to see where the client's mind went to when it was freed from its usual verbal restrictions when exploring an issue'.

The general reaction was that Clean Language provided not only a key tool in the coach's toolbox, but enhanced leadership skills as well as coaching ones. Their experience in being coached with the methods proved valuable in terms of personal development as well.

Grovian techniques in industry

One of the leading practitioners who worked extensively with Grove is Caitlin Walker, who uses his techniques with groups and organizations in a process she calls 'Metaphors at work – transformation through Systemic Modelling'.

An example of her work is a project she designed and delivered with nine senior managers whose job is to connect around the world with leading experts in a variety of fields, including anthropologists, economists and scientists, to remodel the way the world does business, so that the world does not get destroyed in the process.

Her work with them has a dual purpose:

1 To use the elicitation and development of metaphors as a tool for better understanding of themselves and one another, so that they function as a high performing team.

2 To introduce the process of Clean questions and metaphors as tools they can use in their wider external networks.

Caitlin concentrates on building metaphors within a theme, for example 'time'. She might ask the managers to form a circle of nine nodes, and pose the question: 'Time is like what?'

She then asks six iterations of questions, for example:

- What kind of future is your future?
- Is there anything else about your future?
- Where is your future?
- Does it have a size or a shape?
- Whereabouts is a week, month or year?
- Your future is like what?

Then they move on to metaphors for the past and the present, as in, 'Your past is like what?'

The participants self-model, creating their own metaphors, then they map out and share in space their metaphor model, for example one might say: 'My past is a big cloud, with nothing but grey mist and it is full of question marks. I question everything I think that I believe.' Another might say: 'My past is like a clear road, I know exactly where I come from, what I'm here for and exactly where I'm going. There's no room for doubt.'

A third might say: 'My past has changed over time. I used to be so sure of what I wanted and then there was a point where I ran out of road and realized it was all baubles and trinkets and that what I had didn't really matter. Then there's a change and I found my own new path and I use my values to guide my way.'

The managers realize, from the diversity in their metaphors, why there is such diversity in the way they react to one another and respond to business situations.

Another set of metaphors could be 'Making decisions is like what?' and the process develops like before with each manager developing his or her own metaphor model for decisions.

By the third set of metaphors, the managers start to detect patterns in themselves and in one another. Patterns are where the various metaphors for one individual for each themed iteration are congruent with one another and it becomes possible to start making predictions based on the patterns.

The fourth and fifth metaphors create new dimensions of understanding and often result in innovative ideas about how to work together.

By the sixth iteration the beginnings of a self-organizing system start to emerge. The group will have been through a process of deconstruction, and new knowledge becomes possible. Once a quarter Caitlin visits the group to help them create a new metaphor, until they have six.

Caitlin worked with Grove frequently after attending a workshop in 1997. She combines all forms of his work, including Clean Language, Clean Space and Emergent Knowledge, into her Systemic Modelling.

Research into Clean Language

No piece on Clean Language would be complete without mention of Penny Tompkins and James Lawley, a dynamic pair of therapists who discovered Grove's work in the 1990s and prodigiously transcribed hundreds of hours of his sessions. Their work was key in identifying the Clean Language questions and how Grove applied them, and they have amassed all of the accumulated knowledge of Clean Language and its practitioners and published it on their comprehensive website www.cleanlanguage.co.uk.

Grove's work continued to change and progress up to his death in 2008, moving from linguistic methods into spatial ones, and eventually known by the term 'Emergent Knowledge', which is described in Chapter 29.

David Grove's Emergent Knowledge

29

SUMMARY

- Clean Space
- Principles of Emergent Knowledge
- Science of Emergence
- Small world networks
- Emergent Knowledge processes
- Clean Language and Emergent Knowledge for BBC internal coaches
- Emergent Knowledge in one-to-one coaching

David Grove pioneered the ground-breaking technique of Clean Language (covered in the previous chapter) while working with traumatic memory cases during the 1980s. He discovered that patients (typically Vietnam veterans or victims of child abuse) tended to speak in metaphor to describe their experience and that the most effective way of resolving their trauma was to encourage exploration of these metaphors with the least possible interference from the therapist, hence the term 'Clean' because his words did not contaminate the client's experience.

Grove went on to develop his work from a linguistic approach to a spatial one, called Clean Space, where the client would literally move around the room to unearth new self-knowledge. This work developed into Emergent Knowledge for which he used the symbol ΣK. It was at this point, in 2004, that I met Grove and helped him to identify and record the new techniques, with a particular emphasis on ensuring that coaches and other practitioners who are not trained therapists could safely use them.

Clean Space

By the early part of this century, Grove's work, introduced in the previous chapter, had progressed away from linguistic techniques and into spatial ones, which he originally termed 'Clean Space'. Whereas Clean Language explored the psyche through Clean questions and reflecting words back, Clean Space explored it by asking clients to move to another location of their choice. This could mean another spot in the room, or even outside of it. Clients were known to leave the building because the position they needed to be in was outside and across the street.

Have you ever been stuck for a solution and felt the need to go out for a walk 'to clear your head'? Do you understand the phrase 'a change is as good as a rest'? Have you found that moving into another environment seems to refresh your mind and give you new ideas? Have you noticed that when you walk into an empty room that is laid out with chairs for a meeting, you always have a sense of where you want to sit?

These were the propensities into which Grove tapped for Clean Space. The technique treats geography as the landscape of one's psyche; therefore if one moves to another part of the room, it is like moving to another area in one's mind, from where it is possible to unearth knowledge, skills and resources that were hidden in the previous position.

Here is a framework for a Clean Space session:

Coach: And what would you like to have happen?

Coachee: I would like to manage my time better.

Coach: Can you find a space that knows something about that?

Coachee moves to another place in the room.

Coach: And what do you know from that space there?

Coachee: I'm juggling too many things.

Coach: And when you're juggling too many things, what kind of juggling is that juggling?

Coachee: The things are spinning in the air too fast. They're in danger of hitting me.

The coach develops the metaphor using several Clean Language questions (described in the previous chapter) and then asks:

Coach: And is there a space which knows about that?

Coachee moves to another space.

This continues for approximately six spaces, developing the metaphors at each. After an average of six moves, the client has usually reached some kind of resolution or new insight.

When asked to move to another space, people seem to know exactly where to go in order to uncover new insight – knowledge which existed but which they were previously unable to access. The knowledge may be about oneself, or may turn up options and ideas not previously thought of.

Grove did not spend much time working in Clean Space. It partly formed the ground for his final work in Emergent Knowledge.

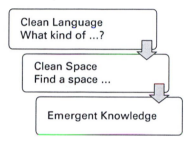

Principles of Emergent Knowledge

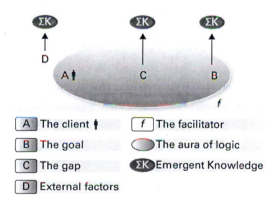

A The client	**f** The facilitator
B The goal	The aura of logic
C The gap	ΣK Emergent Knowledge
D External factors	

This diagram maps out the theory behind Emergent Knowledge. If we take the client as being at A, the client's goal at B, and the gap in between as C, C is the place where we are likely to find all kinds of resistance built up from habits, memories, previous unsuccessful experiences, fear and the other hurdles which stop us in our tracks. We will also find resources in C, which the client may have lost sight of, but which can now be rediscovered and used to reach the goal. The facilitator is marked as f, outside of the process altogether. Emergent Knowledge is represented by the symbol ΣK, and the arrows show the areas from where knowledge can emerge. Note that none of the ΣK areas include the conscious mind – from there all we will get is what the client already knows.

Map of a client's world

Whoever the client is at A, and whatever the goal at B, it will be fairly obvious to most people how to go about achieving the goal. However, if it were that easy, A would be at B and there would be no gap. As A and B are not in the same place, there must be something in between. This may be something that A has not recognized, or even dared to hope for, and it is the unknown obstacle which Emergent Knowledge seeks to identify and resolve.

Throughout his life, Grove drew on knowledge from many sources to further his own theories, and Emergent Knowledge incorporates principles from the science of Emergence, the theory of the six degrees of separation, chaos theory and Grove's own Clean Language and Clean Space.

> 'Emergence creates boundary conditions by laying the problem out in space and engages the individual's intuition as the primary guide to finding a solution. The facilitator stands outside of this process and does not add, comment, discuss or analyse any of the Client's content. The facilitator is engaged at the operating systems level, asking a series of questions several times over, independent of the content offered by the replies of the Client. Emergent Knowledge holds that the expression that is inherent in the nature of the problem also contains everything that is necessary for its solution. Conventional knowledge moves you from A to B and is goal oriented: Emergent Knowledge changes both the nature of the person at A and the nature at the problem or goal at B, such that, to a new world order, getting from A to B is irrelevant.' (Grove, 2005 in Wilson, 2014)

Science of Emergence

Emergence is a science particularly appropriate to the age of technology and explains:

- how Google works through a process of iterative algorithms (repetitive questions which change slightly each time);

- how ant colonies are formed in a logical way, for example positioning the rubbish dump as far away from the food supply as possible (it was once thought that there must be a 'leader' ant communicating the master plan, but it is now understood that the ants act as a collective, constantly exchanging signals with each other, and that decisions emerge from this process); and

- how our own cities have evolved through the ages using a similar logic.

'Emergent Knowledge is an information centred process developed as a theory of self-discovery, to facilitate an individual's journey into the inner landscapes of mind, body and soul. This information contains knowledge which, when drawn on, provides a solution to whatever problems have been identified. This knowledge or wisdom resides in the inner world of the individual and can be used to resolve life's challenges or problems.' (Grove, 2004 in Wilson, 2014)

Small world networks

The 'six degrees of separation' is a theory developed in 1967 by sociology professor Stanley Milgram, which suggests that on average one person anywhere in the world is no more than six degrees of contact away from another specific person. Perhaps surprisingly, the links are often the least likely ones, not the most obvious.

Grove drew on this for a questioning process that he termed 'six degrees of freedom'. This works on the premise that creating a 'small network' of moves will enable the client to reach the goal more quickly and with less effort than taking the obvious route; sometimes it is through the most obscure links that the most effective connections are made.

The weak ties are like shortcuts to the solution. For example, if there are 50 points on a circle, one might imagine that it would be necessary to go through each point to complete the circuit, but if there are a number of 'weak' links in the circle, ie where one link has a vague connection to another, then all of a sudden it is possible to jump to a place where less links are required to reach the target, as illustrated in the diagram on the next page.

A 'weak link' might appear in an offhand remark, gesture or sound, which, if explored, can take a client to what Grove likened to the 'sweet spot' in tennis. By this, he meant a new perspective or solution that might

Small world networks

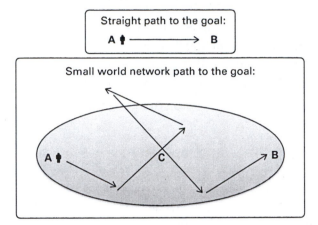

not have appeared if the most obvious line of enquiry were followed; he also acknowledged the feelings of wellbeing, satisfaction and happiness which often accompany such a discovery.

The exploration process involves a series of iterative questions (meaning repetitive, similar questions) asked in groups of approximately six. Grove found that this was the average number of questions required for a new insight or solution to be reached.

'If the client's issue can be thought of metaphorically as an egg type problem, then conventional knowledge processes look for an egg type solution. The application of the Emergent Knowledge system creates a non-ordered, non-linear small world network of seemingly unrelated, irrelevant, red herring type data points that coalesce at a sweet spot, in which the mantle of a non-scaling, profound knowledge experience changes the very core of the client. In this moment emerges a new world order solution, one which confers the wisdom of a chicken's cosmology rather than that of the egg. Hence, Emergence creates opportunities to solve egg type problems with chicken type solutions.' (David Grove, 2004)

Emergent Knowledge processes

During 2005, Grove formed his theories into a series of new processes that incorporate the Emergent Knowledge principles. When metaphors arose as clients changed position, he reduced the number of questions asked about them. He theorized that the more questions asked of a metaphor, the deeper the person would probe the issue represented by the symbols, and that this was not necessary. He decided that the metaphor need only be acknowledged with two to three questions, before returning to the iterative series of approximately six spatial questions in order to move forward.

This was inspired by the principles of sampling theory:

'In sampling theory, the minimum amount of pieces of information required to pick up from one place and to be able to faithfully reproduce the original information in another place is 2.3. In the same way, if we ask approximately two to three questions we can create a sufficient amount of information in a metaphoric landscape so that it can be an accurate representation of the meaning of what the client was trying to convey in words. This could extend to asking one question or four questions.

If you keep asking questions around the same metaphor, you will get deeper into it. The more information you get, the harder it will be to move on. This is why on average we only ask two to three questions maximum on each metaphor. If you ask more you will create a larger emotional dwelling spot, a memory will have been invoked and the person will have been gripped by that feeling.' (David Grove, 2005)

At the start of his work in Emergent Knowledge, Grove would spend time downloading metaphors from each position. However, towards the end of the time we worked together, he moved away from exploring metaphors and eliminated words completely, except for some basic commands like 'Find a space which knows about that'. His belief was that words, even without content, carry some baggage, and that the cleanest interaction a coachee could experience with his or her unconscious mind must be purely spatial. He came to the conclusion that people enjoy exploring their metaphors because the practice provides an emotional high, and that this emotion was a distraction from the real process of discovery.

Not enough research has been done to evaluate which of the methods is most effective, and it is probably the case that different amounts of exploration of metaphors suit different clients, so it is perfectly acceptable to experiment and decide how much of the metaphors to explore using one's own intuition. Personally, I hold all of the techniques that Grove devised over 30 years in equal regard, and use them according to the needs of the clients.

During 2005, Grove created 11 new techniques which incorporated Emergent Knowledge:

Name	Function
Clean Start	To ensure that the client and the goal are in the most productive physical position from which to emerge knowledge.
Clean Pronouns	For the client to understand that there is more than one self that may respond in any situation ('I', 'Me', 'You', 'Myself'). Each of these selves is asked discovery questions. Some selves may be parts of the client's psychological system which have become disassociated at some point in their lives. The questions help to acknowledge and reintegrate the parts.
Clean Time	To re-align or re-scale the client's internal time signature to match that of his or her current reality. Time can 'stop' when we experience a trauma, locking up energy and resources, and creating inappropriate patterns of response which may be triggered years later by a stressful situation.
Clean Hieroglyphics	To find the psychological origin of words which have been written down by the client. Each of the letters has an inner history to it relating to past experiences. A case history is included in this chapter.
Clean History of Goals	To emerge knowledge which may have been lost when the client was deflected from his or her life's congruent purpose through stressful or traumatic events or influences, which may have occurred particularly during the client's early years.
Clean Scanning	This comprises a short burst of several of the techniques, to identify the one to which the client is most responsive.
Clean Action Space	To tie any new knowledge and energy which may have emerged during the session into tangible changes which will move the client forward.

Name	Function
Clean Scapes	Drawing pictures and symbols downloads the client's information and provides clarity.
Clean Networks	As we move through life we accumulate layers of knowledge. Some layers become separated through time, or circumstances, or disturbing experiences. When the client physically moves to a different space, previously lost knowledge can be regained.
Clean Spinning	To emerge knowledge which may be uncovered when the client faces different directions.
Clean Aid	To bring the client back to a safe place if an intense emotional reaction is experienced.

All of the above processes are based on Grove's observations of how the 'psychological map' of his clients tends to be linked to their physical senses, for example their position in a room, the direction they face, the height at which they are standing or sitting and even the way in which they express themselves in written words.

Clean Language and Emergent Knowledge for BBC internal coaches

In 2010, I embarked on a Doctorate in Professional Studies at Middlesex University's Work Based Learning Unit. This exciting programme recognizes workplace achievements in place of academic qualifications and supports learning through work based projects. I chose to explore David Grove's techniques for my thesis and felt that the BBC offered the ideal conditions for my project, because the coaches there had been trained to a high standard and I knew they would be objective and unafraid to challenge the learning and experiment with it. I also knew that they coached clients who had the same robust attitudes. The very nature of a doctoral thesis requires constant questioning and evidencing, which was the water these exceptionally talented coaches already swam in. The diversity of their coaches and their clients, who came from all areas of the BBC including production, management and administration, was another bonus.

Happily, Head of Coaching Liz Macann agreed to support the project and assembled a group of highly competent, intelligent internal coaches who were also passionate learners. I designed the training to take place over two days, during which the coaches would learn Clean Language techniques on one day and Emergent Knowledge techniques on the next. This would be followed by seven months of practice and experimental fieldwork, culminating in a day of consolidation. Cramming the initial learning into two days was a very intensive way of learning, as a course in each subject could easily last for a week. However, I had enough confidence in the abilities of these coaches to take the risk.

During their first two days of training, the coaches learned all of the techniques David had invented through seeing me demonstrate and then practising with each other. Then they chose partners to work with for the next seven months and agreed to deliver the techniques systematically, according to a plan of assignments I provided, to their course partners and their clients, and to provide me with written accounts of each session. At two-monthly intervals we met on conference calls to discuss achievements, challenges and any questions the coaches might have.

I started with 16 coaches to allow for dropouts and hoped to complete the project with a minimum of eight. In the event, there were only two dropouts and almost all of the rest returned descriptions of their sessions on a regular basis.

Grovian techniques are in their infancy and largely untested, but practitioners (myself included) share universal stories of exciting 'magic bullet' type achievements of their work with their clients, in alleviating emotional blocks through simple, non-invasive methods. However, it is natural that exponents should all talk about their most interesting and productive cases, and I wanted to find out whether there were times when the techniques fell down, or produced unexpected results.

I did not feel the knowledge of the practice had reached the state where I could set out to prove anything. The purpose of the doctorate is to gather information about what actually happens during sessions and how they are experienced by the coach and the client in a workplace setting. The advantage to the BBC of being involved in the doctoral project was that its coaches received several months of free professional development because I did not charge a fee for delivering the training.

The case history that follows is an account of the sessions between two of those BBC coaches, Claire Taylor, acting as coach, and Vali Lalioti as the client. The session combines Clean Language and its metaphors with an Emergent Knowledge technique called Clean boundaries. The framework for the questions is:

CLEAN START

- Enables the client to find the right space from which to start the session

CLEAN BOUNDARIES

- *And what kind of space is the space around [xxx]?*
- *And is there anything else about that space?*
- *And does that space have a shape or a size?*
- *And how far does that space go?*
- *And what kind of boundary or edge does [xxx] have?*
- *And is there anything else about that boundary?*
- *And what does that boundary know?*
- *And what does the space between those two boundaries know?*

CLEAN FINISH

- Enables the client to finish the session comfortably and consolidate what has been learned.

Vali described her situation as follows:

'I was faced with a relocation decision that felt like a zero-sum situation, rationally positive but emotionally negative. Logically thinking it was clear to me that the relocation presented a great opportunity, but there was an emotional aspect that made it feel very negative too.'

Claire asked questions using the Clean Boundaries framework above and this is how Vali described her journey during the session:

'I initially found it difficult to look outside the ugly rock that this "zero-sums" felt like. The coach continued with the questions and I was able to move away from the rock and look at the space outside it that felt vast and beautiful like the universe and the milky-way. At some point the word "edge" sounded louder in my head. I think that was a shift moment that just the sound of the word somehow unlocked something, and I was holding a baseball bat, swinging it to hit the rock (that had already turned into a somewhat more flexible, semi-milky transparent object that I was pushing to expand from within) to effortlessly see it move in space and become one with the milky-way. It felt that it always belonged there and I didn't need to hit it, I only had to grasp the bat and swing in a dance kind of movement for it to get in its place, and this will make ripples in my world to move what felt like an ugly, solid, difficult to change semi-milky inflexible blob/rock into an amazingly beautiful milky-way. Writing the previous paragraph, I am smiling and my whole mood is lifted. I don't play baseball, although this symbol was present in this journey and is linked to my kinaesthetic-self.'

The changes brought about by Clean sessions take place at the deepest level, below consciousness, and can continue to effect changes for days, months or years after the session. Five days after the session Vali reported:

'What happened in the following days was like a flood that started and was impossible to stop and I had to experience it fully and hold on and see what would come on the other end, when the flood waters subside. I spend two days mourning deeply for what had happened, crying and sobbing at times that I least expected, being unable to move forward, frozen by the irrational fear of what would happen if I relocate and I feel utterly miserable. But at the same time, something was healing, something deeply traumatic has come back but it was healing itself. I am not yet at peace with it, but at least through this process I was able to understand that my research and professor past was screaming to be part of me again. My technology expert self, so eagerly abandoned to escape an "ugly blob" of the past, has lifted its head thinking that there is an opportunity to find ways to become whole again and all this thanks to the impossible challenge of relocating and the journey through feelings and emotions and the help of Clean boundaries and metaphors.'

The 'becoming whole' comment that Vali made crops up frequently in Grove's work. Traumas are often embedded at a young age and then forgotten by the conscious mind. Meanwhile, defensive mechanisms are set up deep within the psyche, growing more convoluted and irrelevant over the years, and grinding into action when triggered by events reminiscent of the original trauma. These mechanisms use energy and resources that could be put to a positive use and when resolved often result in the client uncovering a talent or ability previously unknown to them.

Claire, the coach, commented:

'One of the areas I want to improve as coach is to allow and help the client explore more their space, issue and thinking and avoid a tendency to get to action space too quickly. I found the boundary approach gave me this

'"permission" to explore almost for the sake of exploration. The client presented
an amazing richness of metaphors and visual spaces. I was almost lost for
choices and the boundaries gave me the tool to explore this richness rather than
feeling lost in the wealth presented to me by the client. It also felt more natural
to mix questions from Clean Language with the Clean boundaries, and the client
commented that this helped her and felt like a richer coaching experience too.'

This type of exploring 'for the sake of exploration' is required more frequently from coaches now that clients often find themselves in uncomfortable situations that they have no control over: all that can be altered is how
the clients feel about and react to the pressure they are under. Clean Language and Emergent Knowledge techniques help people develop greater
resilience in such times of stress and uncertainty.

Emergent Knowledge in one-to-one coaching

Angela Dunbar, my colleague in Clean work, trained Jane (not her real
name) who works as a business coach within a consultancy on one of the
Emergent Knowledge courses Angela delivers. As part of this training, Jane
wrote and drew a goal on which Angela coached her using the Clean Hiero-
glyphics technique mentioned in the list on page 208. In this exercise, the
client is encouraged to keep adding words, phrases or pictures as they come
up, to the same piece of paper. This has the effect of building up the layers
of information necessary for knowledge to emerge.

Jane came across as a confident, assertive and highly competent woman
but she had an issue with being occasionally unable to hold direct eye contact with people. She had explored this with various practitioners but had
not yet found a solution.

Angela began by asking which letters on the page in her drawing most
captured her attention, and she replied that it was the letter 'I'. So Angela
explored the various 'I's on the paper, asking the Emergent Knowledge question: 'And what does that "*I*" know?'

The purpose of this question was to tap into the client's deeper wisdom
in her unconscious mind.

Jane replied, 'It knows but it won't tell me.'

Angela continued to ask if there was anything else that the '*I*' knew. After
six attempts, Jane realized that what she needed to do was trust herself to

admit, out loud, that sometimes she feels small and insignificant. This was quite at odds with the strong, confident persona she normally presented.

Jane continued that the eyes drawn on the paper seemed to hold significance. 'Eye' and 'I' sound the same and during these sessions, which engage the unconscious, there often seemed to be connections between both meanings.

After they had explored the eyes, Angela asked what words could come after the words that were on the paper. Jane responded by becoming emotional and angry. 'How dare you make me feel like that!' she said, but almost immediately added, 'But it's only me making me feel this.'

Angela asked Jane to put everything she was saying onto the piece of paper. When Jane had done that, Angela asked, 'And where could all those words have come from?'

Jane quickly replied, 'Me'... but then, a few seconds later, she shared a realization that most of the words were actually from someone in her past who had made her feel small and insignificant. Having recognized this, she found herself able to deal with it, and did so by obliterating some of the words on the paper.

Angela concluded by asking 'And what do you know now?'

Jane replied: 'I feel taller. I am stood next to the wall and there is a place where I have previously marked my height, and, weirdly, I seem to be looking down on that … how strange!'

Jane later told Angela that her problem with direct eye contact is a thing of the past.

The underlying principles behind all of Grove's work are well aligned with coaching:

- Remain neutral, focusing on the coachee's agenda and without making assumptions.
- Follow the coachee in tone and pace and reflect back the coachee's own words and gestures.
- Focus on the solution more than the problem.

Being Clean

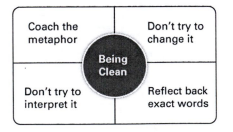

David Grove's work continues to be progressed by therapists, practitioners and coaches all over the world. I deliver the courses we devised together to corporations and our colleague, Angela Dunbar delivers open distant courses (website).

30 Transpersonal Coaching

SUMMARY

- Origins of transpersonal psychology
- Sub-personalities
- Transcript of a coaching session by Sir John Whitmore
- Commentary by Sir John Whitmore

Origins of transpersonal psychology

Transpersonal Coaching owes its origins to transpersonal psychology and draws from the earlier explorations of psychologists like Psychosynthesis founder Roberto Assagioli (Assagioli, Girelli and Bartoli, 2008) and Abram Maslow (Maslow, 1998). The main exponent of Transpersonal Coaching is performance coaching pioneer Sir John Whitmore, who was filmed delivering an insightful transpersonal session with me as the coachee, which is reproduced below. The word 'transpersonal' means 'beyond the personal', and Transpersonal Coaching helps coachees to discover meaning and purpose in their lives, and to become more consistent and integrated in their behaviour and desires for the future.

Sub-personalities

Whitmore sometimes uses the analogy of an orchestra to describe his approach. He calls the players in the orchestra our 'sub-personalities', which are the things we are identified with, such as our roles, relationships or possessions. For instance, in answer to the question 'Who are you?' most people might reply with answers such as 'I'm a doctor', 'I'm a father' or 'I'm a good listener'. Transpersonal Coaching challenges that these labels describe us but do not define who we are.

As we evolve we dis-identify from these things, and then we become the 'orchestra conductor', who ensures that the instruments are played in harmony. This represents the centred state we can reach when all of our sub-personalities are working together. Yet there is something else behind that conductor and orchestra – the composer who writes the score. This could be called the 'self' or 'higher self', and represents universality and individuality. It is where our ultimate potential lies, our innovation and creativity, the things we would like to tap into.

One transpersonal approach is to identify these sub-personalities. The coach facilitates the coachee in examining the various aspects and roles of the most active players, how and when each sub-personality appears, and how the coachee's behaviour is affected, whether in empowering or limiting ways.

It seeks to synthesize the sub-personalities so that they work together in harmony instead of stifling each other, and to uncover not only the orchestra leader but occasionally the self who writes the score.

The transpersonal approach can help relieve conflict, when it is realized that it is not 'I' who is in conflict with 'you' but one of my sub-personalities which is in conflict with one of yours. Once it is realized that only a part of ourselves is not in agreement, it is possible to make a conscious decision to draw on a different sub-personality, which might be able to agree with a different one of yours.

Transcript of a coaching session by Sir John Whitmore

Below is an abridged version of Whitmore's Transpersonal Coaching session with me, filmed for the Oxford School of Coaching and Mentoring in 2007. What cannot be conveyed in the transcript is the lightness and humour of the session. At the time of writing the film is available for viewing on www .theocm-store.com/72-transpersonal-coaching.html. To the right of the transcript are some comments I have noted about what John Whitmore is doing as a coach, and after the session John gives his own account of what he was doing as the coach.

Coach	Coachee	Notes
John:	So, Carol, I'd like to know what you'd like to work on in this session.	
Carol:	The key thing for me at the moment is about my business model and life model and aligning the way I'm spending my time.	
John:	So how are the business model and the life model related to each other?	Coach focuses immediately on coachee's keywords without leading in any direction.
Carol:	Completely related. All of my work involves things I'm passionate about, but I tend to be doing so much that I can't keep moving forward.	
John:	So what you'd like to have a look at is how you can unblock that and move forward to wherever that might take you. Is that what you're looking for?	Coach clarifies to check the purpose of the session.
Carol:	Yes. It has got to the point where there are things going on in half a dozen areas, none of which I want to give up, all of which I'm passionate about.	This clarifying elicits further thoughts from coachee.
John:	You mentioned 'passion' just then. Can you give me an idea of the sort of things, even before you started your current career, that you got passionate about?	Coachee has mentioned 'passion' several times. Coach picks up on this and explores it with an open question.
Carol:	My whole life has been about taking risks and challenges. I ended up running record companies which was a great challenge. I realized early on that what I loved about doing it was the opportunity for developing people – both artistes and staff.	
John:	The pattern here is about stretching and supporting people. Are there any other words you would say that you like to do with people?	Coach presents back a pattern he has noticed.
Carol:	I like to see them enjoying themselves.	
John:	So, going back to you personally, what are your personal values, the sorts of things that you really value in life, to get a sense of what's going on behind that passion?	Coach returns the focus to the coachee's interior life.
Carol:	The key thing is freedom – people being in a situation where they have the freedom to express themselves and develop.	Coachee evades the personal focus by talking about other people.
John:	You are talking about people there in an objective sense – what about you?	Coach persists.
Carol:	For me it is essential to have the freedom to	

	develop myself.	
John:	Are you suggesting that in your present situation, and why we're doing this coaching, that there is some restriction on that freedom? And would you like to elaborate or build on that?	
Carol:	I have managed to get myself into the position where it can all be developing and stretching. The only constriction now is time.	
John:	In terms of your skills, Carol, what would you be able to put your hand on your heart and say 'I'm good at this'?	Coach avoids the temptation to ask about 'time', which often hides deeper blocks, and approaches from a more oblique angle. Lack of time is not referred to again during the session, confirming that it was not the real issue.
Carol:	I'm good at writing, listening, working in a facilitator or public speaking role, engaging people, maintaining my health and being disciplined about work–life balance.	
John:	So if we put those three together, your passion, your values and your skills, what stops you being able to exercise the full range in what you're doing at the moment? I'm talking about internally now, not external circumstances.	With these new insights, coach asks again what is getting in the way.
Carol:	Can I start with external and move in? I run a business in training, leadership and coaching and my big passion is writing. But when interesting work comes in, I'm drawn by the challenge of doing something new, and I don't put enough into the other areas. Does that answer your question?	Coachee evades the question.
John:	It does, but I'm looking a little deeper here. What inside you stops you doing things in exactly the way you want to? There are always external circumstances and they will always be there. But it really all begins internally, so what is it inside you that has not changed things to exactly the way you'd like them to be?	Coach persists in looking for the inner answers.
Carol:	That's a very good question. I think there is a battle between the Introvert and the challenge of going out and developing people. And in our work we get a lot positive feedback, so there's a bit of 'feeding the ego' there too.	Coachee confirms this is a question that makes her think, and finally focuses more inwardly.
John:	You've mentioned three parts of yourself: the Introvert; then there's the person who's 'out there'; then there's that other part that needs and likes to get good feedback. If we just look at those three parts of yourself, to what extent do you notice some degree of conflict between them?	Coach has now heard a response he thinks worth exploring further and presents back the coachee's words.
Carol:	That's interesting, because there's quite a lot of conflict. If I have a few days writing, it is quite	Coachee confirms the value of this line of questioning.

	hard to go into training. Yet after three days of training I look forward to the writing.	
John:	So that way is the easy one, the other way is not so easy?	Clarifying with a closed question.
Carol:	Yes.	
John:	What does your writing give you?	Breaking down the areas to focus on more detail.
Carol:	Good question. If I start the day by writing, I feel buoyant, free, happy and flowing. I don't function so well without it.	
John:	So that part of you is very important to you? That part of you that has that need, so to speak, and you're clear that it serves you to have that. What's the downside of the fact that you like that part so much?	Clarifying and further exploration.
Carol:	The down side of the introverted self – and this is probably a key thing that you have uncovered here, John – is that if I did give up the delivery I am afraid that the Introvert would take over and I would never be able to go out again!	
John:	This extroverted bit – in what other ways does that enrich you?	Coach has identified rich ground for exploration and continues to question each aspect.
Carol:	Intellectually, it is the very fabric of the stuff I write. Out of that comes the new development.	
John:	So these two parts of yourself, the introverted part and the extroverted part, they serve each other?	Clarifying by presenting back what the coachee has said.
Carol:	Yes. They do, don't they?	
John:	If you were not out there ...	
Carol:	... I wouldn't have anything to write about.	
John:	It sounded as if these bits were in conflict with each other, but perhaps we're seeing now that they need each other in some way.	
Carol:	Yes, you're quite right – one couldn't exist without the other.	Clearly, coachee had not realised this as she is crediting the coach with the insight.
John:	Can they be friends?	Coach challenges coachee.
Carol:	I think they are friends ...	
John:	You don't sound very convincing when you say that.	
Carol:	I'm just wondering. I've never thought about whether they were friends or not.	This reveals new information to the coachee.

John:	Just imagine they were totally collaborative these two parts, and worked together, what do you think that would feel like?	
Carol:	I don't know what the reason is, but there is a reason why that can't be. I can sense there is a barrier between them but I don't know what it is.	
John:	Let's go away from that for a moment. The bit that you described – the ego, the liking good feedback – tell me more about that. What does that give you?	As coachee was unable to answer, coach does not persist but takes coachee's conscious attention to another area she has raised. Again, the oblique approach.
Carol:	It raises my energy and the validation gives me confidence to stick my neck out.	
John:	And what's the downside of that bit of you?	Further exploration.
Carol:	It takes up more energy than it gives. It raises short term energy, but I pay for it with long term energy. Writing is the opposite and raises long term energy.	
John:	So are there any other areas where that ego part affects you? Relationships?	Broadening the field of exploration.
Carol:	I'm sure it does!	
John:	Tell me in what way.	Further exploration.
Carol:	I think of myself as a good listener, but sometimes I don't listen because I'm waiting for someone to stop speaking so I can tell them my big idea.	
John:	So there are these three obvious parts of yourself that you've talked about. Have you got another what we sometimes call 'sub personality' in there which is different to those? I don't want any other parts of you to be ignored. What else comes to mind? When you go away on holiday or when you do things completely differently, is there another part of you that comes in there?	Coach tries some clarifying. Coach makes a suggestion. Note how rarely he does this.
Carol:	Yes, there's a person who slobs out. That's the space where you recharge because you are not making any demands on yourself. I do yoga, walk and swim. Without those the rest couldn't happen.	It provides a welcome new perspective and aids the coachee in seeing exactly where she stands.
John:	So you're comfortable with that part of yourself?	Coach clarifies, recognising and validating what coachee has said.
Carol:	Yes.	
John:	Any other parts that are lying around there somewhere that we haven't uncovered yet?	
Carol:	There's the Shopper! And the Friend.	

John:	So it sounds like you feel a lot of pressure from all the different things you are doing out there. That pressure comes from inside because of not being able to fulfil all the things that you would like to fulfil in yourself.	Coach makes a second suggestion – notice that this happens a long way into the session and only after coachee has unearthed her own insights.
Carol:	It is pressure but very exhilarated and energetic pressure-pressure in the sense that there isn't enough time to follow all the avenues.	
John:	Certainly what you've indicated is a degree of collaboration between these different parts of you, and you recognise that one is meeting the needs of another. What I'm also hearing is that there is a competition for time between these parts of yourself. Can you imagine these parts negotiating with each other and coming to a kind of an agreement about a way forward that you don't have to stick to, but could say, 'Let's make this sort of agreement between ourselves and try that out for a month or six weeks', or something like that, so that each could get their needs met without pulling on each other? Could you envisage these parts negotiating with each other?	Coach challenges coachee.
Carol:	I think it would be a really good idea. Whether I can get them to the table I'm not sure.	Coachee resists the challenge.
John:	If we were having another session in future, the sort of thing I would suggest we work on would be that negotiation process, and we have methods for doing that and getting you to negotiate between those. I suspect that because they are, in principle, supporting each other, and you are recognizing that, that they are not really in conflict. There would be a lot of benefit for smoothing that out.	
Carol:	I can sense as you are saying it there would be a huge benefit. I think now you have identified it…	Coachee has credited coach with her new insights several times; this time coach alerts her to this.
John:	Who identified it?	
Carol:	You identified what you heard me saying and hearing it back from you has made me identify that that process has already started happening.	Coach persists.
John:	Can you just say 'I, Carol, identified'?	
Carol:	I identified it – with your help John!	
John:	Let's look at stepping back from that. Those are all parts of you but they're not you. Who are you underneath this?	Now that a lot of clarity has been attained, coach encourages coachee to delve further, instead of moving into options and actions at this point.
Carol:	I hate this question.	

John:	It's a great question for you then!
Carol:	I've never been able to answer it.
John:	You might want to run through those and say – 'there is this part, but that's not me'. Can you actually say that – 'There's an introverted part of me but that's not who I am'? Try to say that out loud.
Carol:	Ok. There's an introverted part of me but that's not who I am.
John:	So that's true for each of these parts is it?
Carol:	It may be that the introverted part of me <u>is</u> who I am.
John:	OK, so just take a look at it now. Just take thirty seconds on your own to say that slowly to yourself for each of those parts and see which is the strong one.
Carol:	OK [*pause*]. What came out about the extroverted one was 'Leader'. Leader hasn't been mentioned, but it's part of the extroverted one. What came to me – it was a really good exercise – was that the introverted person was introverted because it was comfortable, and actually the real person wanted and needed to lead. Becoming an Extrovert enabled the Leader to operate where the Leader couldn't operate from the introverted position.
John:	So the good news is that you sound rather clear about that – what emerged here is leadership and it looks...
Carol:	It's astonishing. I've never seen that before. It's almost something I have to give myself permission to do.
John:	So you've got to give yourself permission to be who you are, and leadership is definitely a part of that. Of course the Leader in you is another sub-personality. So who are you? Again can you step back from that and say 'this is a part of me, there's a Leader here but that's not who I am'?
Carol:	[Silence]. Then the Explorer comes up.
John:	So at a level beneath the Leader...
Carol:	Actually a metaphor came into my mind of the Explorer – it's about exploring who I am and exploring life, but I saw a picture of someone setting off in a ship.

Coachee's assertion 'I hate this question!' confirms it is a challenging, and therefore productive, area of exploration.

Coach assists coachee in unpicking some confusion which has arisen for her.

Coachee reaches a major new insight through this process and has uncovered a key sub-personality which has not been mentioned before. She has also shed some light on the question she was not able to answer when asked directly earlier.

An 'astonishing' insight for the coachee about giving herself permission to be who she really is.

Coach clarifies this very important insight, embedding and validating it for coachee.

Further exploration, bringing in previous elements.

John:	Sometimes those images that come up like that are very valuable. Because the kind of questions I'm asking are taking you a little bit outside your rational mind. And that's where there is great wealth in this non-rational part, because what comes up are images that have great meaning for you. I should caution you not to get frustrated because you can't answer fully that question 'who are you?', because very often we discover who we are by discovering who we are not, so you never actually find out who you are. That in itself is an exploration and what it sounds like to me is that you are on that journey of exploration of yourself and you are using these other activities that you have as a way of that exploration. Does that make any sense?	Coach recognizes the value of a metaphor as messages from the unconscious mind (which he refers to as 'non-rational')
Carol:	Yes, that's what was coming up for me, definitely.	
John:	So now that has happened and you have talked out your issues, how might that understanding help you to balance the different activities that you get involved in, that cause you so much time pressure and so on? Can you imagine how you can use that deeper part of yourself to maybe 'conduct the orchestra' so to speak?	
Carol:	I'm sorry to say that what's coming up is how to contain the other things so I can put more things in. The Explorer wants to explore! I have a feeling that now we have identified all this, the component parts may start reorganizing themselves and I will follow what the outcome is. Does that make sense?	
John:	Absolutely. What we are moving towards here is that you are the conductor of the orchestra. The conductor doesn't play an instrument, but manages the orchestra. As you go further down this you may begin to find that you can manage these components more and balance them, including the possibility of what you have suggested, which is another one coming to disrupt the process. If you can step back from that a little bit, and become more the observer, and manage the whole process from that place, the deeper you go into that question 'who am I?' the stronger that conductor capability emerges. Does that make sense?	
Carol:	I have a feeling that's what will emerge. Just by identifying all these things it's enabled me to step back and now, having stepped back and seen all these parts, I can't step back into the middle of them and not see them.	

John:	Just before we conclude here I would like to jump you forward in time: if you could fully express the things that have emerged here, and you could lead that process, what would be your positive fantasy of say five years or ten years from now?	Coach starts to consolidate the process and asks a Goal-oriented question.
Carol:	The fantasy would look like doing more creative writing, being somewhere on a beach so I get my swim every day, and be invited to speak at conferences and run workshops all over the world. I think the leadership would express through the workshops and conferences; it is leading people into developing themselves rather than day-to-day management.	
John:	So the leadership retains its importance. You played it down for a bit in the scenario, and then it seemed to rise up again. In this life, five or however many years ahead, if it was perfect, when someone asked you what your life is like, what would you say?	Coach presents to coachee the significant discoveries during the session.
Carol:	You know that expression 'quality time'? I would say 'quality freedom'.	
John:	Maybe that's a good place to stop on 'quality freedom'.	
Carol:	Thank you John, that was fantastic. Extraordinary!	
John:	Thank you for being open.	

Commentary by Sir John Whitmore

After the session, John explained the structure and thinking behind his approach:

'So what I was doing in that session was, first of all, exploring with Carol the deeper parts of herself that had always been there. I referred back to earlier things, to find out what qualities she had, what passions she had, and the values she had, because we were trying to establish the underlying drivers that manifest themselves in her different activities. If we imagined we all had some kind of role or purpose, it shows up in those things so, in order to help Carol move forward, it was important that we identified what these core things were in her that had been there for some time.

What began to happen was that she herself came up with the conflicting different parts of herself – the introvert, the one who wanted to be out there and so on – and so I moved at that moment on to what we would call the sub-personality model.

I did notice that she was reluctant to go inside when she described her sub-personalities, all these conflicting parts of herself. So I was using the opportunity to follow certain words that she used to go inside, because I felt quite strongly she needed to go to a level beneath all the external circumstances that she was readily talking about. Then I wanted her to establish the degree to which these parts of her were in conflict with each other and the degree to which they supported each other, so that's why we explored their relationship and the different components.

Now, one of the places you can go off track is to just focus on the things that first come up. So it was important that I went back there at some point and said "are there any other parts of you here that are not being expressed?" We wanted to broaden the picture to include that, and then looked at the degree to which there could be some improvement in the relationship between these components.

All the time I was taking the lead from the different words she was saying. I'm looking at her face and her body expressions, so to speak, but listening to the timing of her responses – when there's a slight hesitation, what does that hesitation mean? I was trying to pick up all those messages, and she was passing quite a lot of messages in that way. And then I was going in on particular terminology that she used, because I want to go where she has expressed an interest; there were certain words she kept repeating and I would follow down those words. I then began this process of trying to see to what extent these could be further integrated with each other and I think she had some insights that they could be integrated, they support each other and so on.

At that point we started a process of becoming the observer, standing back from these different components of herself and her recognizing that they are not her – not to get caught up with any of these pieces and have that part of the person completely dominate, because that's what can happen, and then the others feel frustrated. And I wanted to avoid that and then move into a more stepped back position. And that's why I went into more of a subconscious process of getting her to say to herself "I have this part of me but it's not me". I wanted her to do that silently to herself so she could hear what she was saying and digest that, and that's working at a deeper level.

What happened then was that some insights came up from that – the other part of herself, the Explorer, came up. I felt we had moved towards helping her discover more of who she was – this "Leader" that emerged, and the Explorer beyond the Leader was now becoming a stronger part of her – but it's still not who she is.

I wanted to point out that this is just another sub-personality; it is a deeper sub-personality and closer to who you are but it's not who you are – because that is a long way down the road, if you ever get there. I felt she was in quite a good place with this. I think she had some realizations and recognitions. I felt there was some clarity emerging and that was showing on her face and some of her expressions.

I wanted to take her forward from these qualities we had started with, and that had blended themselves into leadership, to then say where are you going with this? I wanted her to see that there's a future, something to point towards, something to move toward. I wanted to end up on this high note with this aspiration towards a couple of qualities she had expressed right at the end.'

On a final note, from my own perspective as coachee several years after this session took place, the session was prophetic: I went on to 'contain' things so that the Explorer could 'fit more things in' and am now undertaking a doctorate, updating this book and writing another. Meanwhile the other 'things' have grown in themselves, yet the sense of pressure has abated. I do indeed feel that the conductor is managing the orchestra!

31 An introduction to neuro-linguistic programming

SUMMARY

- The origins of neuro-linguistic programming
- NLP processes
- NLP at work

The origins of NLP

Neuro-linguistic programming, or NLP as it is commonly known, is widely used in coaching. NLP comprises an abundance of theories and processes drawn from many sources and its fundamental principle is that it is possible to re-programme the brain to change behaviour mainly by visual, auditory and kinaesthetic processes.

NLP was devised in the 1970s by psychologists Richard Bandler and John Grinder whose theories grew mainly from the work of psychologists Milton Erickson, Fritz Perls, Virginia Satyr and other prominent thinkers of the era. After an acrimonious split from Bandler, Grinder went on to develop New Code NLP firstly with Judith DeLozier, then with Carmen Bostic St Clair. DeLozier also continued to develop New Code with Robert Dilts, a practitioner originally trained by Grinder and Bandler. The main difference with New Code is that instead of trying to re-programme the subject from the outside in, it attempts to reach the unconscious mind to effect a reprogramming from the inside out, because it was found that the conscious reprogramming did not last – eventually the unconscious mind would fight back and the new state achieved through the reprogramming would fail.

The most widely used NLP processes are meta model, mirroring and matching, VAK, perceptual positions, logical levels, anchors and time line, which are summarized below. In addition there are some new code techniques which are said to cause changes in brainwave patterns akin to meditation, purporting to deliver a higher performance state.

NLP processes

Meta model

The meta model examines the subject's words and phraseology to identify deletions, distortions, generalizations and limiting beliefs, and then to reframe them into less limiting words, for example:

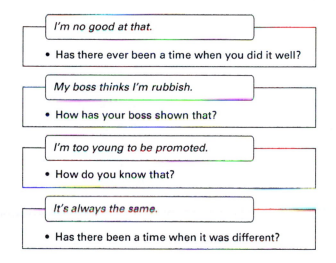

This is highly useful as long as the practitioner bears in mind that a limiting belief must be honoured as real because it is real to the subject. The coach's job is to ask questions that will enable their coachees to gain new awareness, not to dismiss their statements as a limiting belief, which would be judgemental and out of place in a coaching style.

Mirroring and matching

Mirroring and matching are core practices in NLP and are applied to words, tone, body language and size, in terms of talking about a situation in the same sized 'chunks' as the subject. There is particular emphasis on mirroring body language, including the claim that rapport can be created in this way, even from across a room. My own experiments over the last ten years appear to conclude that while people who are in rapport do indeed mirror body language, this results from a relationship created mainly by eye contact, tone of voice, choice of words and – most important of all – the intention behind the words. If the intention of the manager or coach is genuinely focused on the development and wellbeing of the subject, and the communication skills of the manager/coach are sufficient to enable this, then rapport will be created and mirrored in body language. If the former aspects are absent, then no amount of artificially mirrored body language will create rapport. Indeed, physical mirroring may have the opposite effect by feeling inauthentic to the one being mirrored, while the effort involved detracts from the coach's ability to be 'present' with and listen to another person.

A further question here is whether it is healthy in any relationship to put oneself in the 'supplicant' position by copying anything at all; it is akin to agreeing with a statement we do not believe in order to curry favour. We tend to like and respect people who are congruent, honest and have a strong sense of self, and this applies as much to those who work for us or want to sell to us as it does to those we wish to impress. Therefore the idea of making our body language copy someone else's instead of reflecting our own innate self would seem to be the least effective way of building a strong relationship. I believe that this is because words are formed by the conscious mind, while body language arises from the unconscious and, if faked, may send out conflicting messages, one from the conscious and another from the unconscious.

Where mirroring can be effective is in repeating people's words back to them, or matching the 'chunks size' of what they are saying. Both are a form of giving attention and demonstrating listening, without carrying a risk of incongruence because they are both conscious processes.

Visual, auditory and kinaesthetic modalities

Commonly referred to in NLP as 'VAK', this model divides people into three main types in terms of their responses. It proposes that people have a tendency to one or more of these types, for example a visually oriented person would speak in visual terms, such as 'What I am looking for is...', while a primarily auditory person might have difficulty in answering the question, 'How do you see it?' and would need to be asked 'What is this telling you?'. There are two more types: gustatory and olfactory:

⊙	VISUAL:	How does it look?
👂	AUDITORY:	What are you telling yourself?
✋	KINAESTHETIC:	How do you feel?
👅	GUSTATORY:	That leaves a bad taste.
👃	OLFACTORY:	Something smells fishy to me.

Together with mirroring and matching, VAK provides the tools for what NLP terms 'calibration' – assessing the coachee's state and using processes to alter it. As this invites judgement, care must be exercised by the coach not to extend the judgement to the subject's content or ask leading questions, which would be contrary to the ethos of coaching.

Like many NLP procedures, this approach has benefits but can be limiting if taken to extremes. The theory, which is scientifically unproven, is that people have an innate preference to communicate in one particular style, and the extreme assumption would be that if visual people are asked auditory questions, they will not be able to answer. Neuroscientists do not support the theory behind the model, or indeed any learning styles models, and this is examined more fully in Chapter 49. However, there will always be an effect whenever a technique is introduced, and I find the value of making use of VAK in coaching is that it encourages the coachee to look at issues from different perspectives.

In my experience most people function well at all five levels and, if they do happen to have an innate preference, asking questions from another type can make them think just a bit harder, which brings about new insights. Occasionally I come across someone who struggles to answer a question (usually 'how do you feel?'), and the awareness of this theory can cause me to try another line of questioning.

Where the danger lurks for a coach is in focusing on categorizing coachees instead of listening to the meaning in what they are saying and asking insightful questions. Where this technique always proves useful is that asking questions from at least the first three categories helps people see things from different perspectives.

Submodalities

Submodalities are used to change someone's experience of a situation, and refer to the five senses, or modalities, described in VAK. For example, the coachee would explore his or her VAK responses to a positive experience and then to a negative experience. Then the metaphor of the negative experience would be viewed using the modalities of the positive experience in order to overlay a more positive state on the issue.

Perceptual positions

Perceptual positions draws on Perls' Gestalt therapy (Perls, 1989) and is often used where there is conflict. Let us take as an example a conflict between a male executive and his female boss.

The facilitator asks the executive to look at the situation first as himself (position A), then as his boss (position B), then as an impartial observer. In each position the facilitator asks questions which will bring the experience to life for the executive and explore that perspective in depth.

In the first position, where the executive is playing himself, the facilitator asks him to relive a particular interaction with his boss that left him feeling unfairly treated. The following questions might be useful:

- What did you say?
- What did she say?
- What did you see?
- What did you feel?
- What impact does it have on you/her/others?
- What do you want to have happen?

It is best not to spend too much time on this part, or the resentment the executive is feeling will become more embedded and it will be harder for him to see the situation from the boss's point of view – this first step is simply an overview and reminder of what happened. From a coaching perspective, the solution focus of the last question will help move the subject forward and raise his energy to look at the problem with new eyes. It might also result in a realization that the executive is not actually prepared to resolve the situation, in which case that very insight may change his attitude, or at worst result in a decision to find another job.

The questions are asked from the perspectives of the VAK modalities described above.

Once the scene is set from the executive's point of view, the facilitator asks him to 'become' his boss. Ideally he will do this by moving to another place of his choosing in the room; some people prefer to stay in one place and go through the exercise mentally. Another way of getting a clean transition is to use an NLP technique called 'breaking state', which means doing something entirely different for a few moments. This could be as simple as standing up and stretching, or another technique is to ask people to repeat a phone number backwards, which puts the brain to different use and refreshes perspective.

Then the executive is asked to try to put himself into the boss's body, even to the point of imagining he has the same physiology, looking through her eyes and experiencing what she saw and felt. The facilitator asks what she, the boss, is seeing the executive do, his gestures, facial expressions and what message is coming across. Some further useful questions might be:

- What did you feel?
- What did you mean when you said...?
- What did you hear?
- How do you see the situation?
- What do you want to achieve here?
- What are the contingent factors for you?
- What impact is it having on your work?
- What impact might this have on the executive's work?
- Who/what else is affected?
- What advice would you give the executive on how to handle this situation?
- What do you want to achieve in the situation?

This part is trickier because for it to work, the subject has to make a real effort to 'be' his boss and not just project his own views, although this is not a mind reading exercise and there is bound to be some transference. I remember one particularly truculent executive who on moving to the boss's position would give no more enlightening answers than 'I'm acting like a prat; I'm talking rubbish; I can't see any further than my own nose!' However, it is more common at this point for subjects to start saying things like: 'I (the boss) am under time pressure and probably didn't explain this as clearly as I could have done, but I didn't mean to confuse him.'

When this has been thoroughly explored, break state again and ask some questions to develop insight:

- What did you learn from that experience of 'walking a mile in your boss's shoes'?
- What will you do differently as a result of it?
- What outcome would you like, knowing what you know now?

Now the executive will move into the third position, as if he is a fly on the wall observing both himself and his boss going through the same exchange. As before, the body language of both parties is explored, plus their facial expressions and their tone of voice. Some pertinent additional coaching questions might be:

- What advice would you give these two people to resolve their situation?
- What do you think would be the most positive outcome?
- What benefits could come out of the relationship?
- What needs to happen for those benefits to be realized?

Finally, after a thorough exploration, break state again. This is a good time to ask some insightful coaching questions such as:

- What do you know now?
- What else have you learned?
- On a scale of 1–10, how effective is your relationship with your boss at the moment?
- What number do you want that to rise to?
- How important is it to you?
- Imagine you have reached that level of improvement in the relationship. What is different?
  - What do you see/hear/feel?
  - What is the impact on you/her/others?
  - What is the impact on the business/your career?
- What could you do to bring this about?
- What will you do?
- How/when/where/who with?

There can be some benefit in repeating the whole exercise before the final list of questions above; the subject should find it easier to enter the other two perspectives and more insights will be uncovered. Another NLP technique called 'anchoring' can be used here, where the subject is asked to come up with, say, a gesture that represents one of the other states. When under pressure in his next encounter with his boss, he could imperceptibly make the gesture and bring himself immediately into a state where he can more clearly see her point of view.

The perceptual positions technique has been developed in other ways, including a timeline version where subjects place themselves in the past, present and future, bringing each to life with similar exploratory questions, and capturing insights along the way:

- What are you seeing now regarding B?
- What are you feeling about B?
- What are you hearing from and saying to B?
- What do you want from B?
- What would be your ideal relationship with B?
- Imagine you have your ideal relationship with B: how does that look/ sound/feel? What has changed?

The technique can also be used to explore different aspects of the self, by having the coachee choose as second position either an object in the room which represents the area of exploration, or metaphor, or a character from a film or book, or an animal, bird or plant.

The process helps people gain different perspectives on a situation and is suitable for use during a coaching session or a mentoring conversation. The metaphoric element tends to access the unconscious mind and can deliver new insight and awareness.

Perceptual positions at work: Anne's story

Lynne Cooper is a coach, coaching supervisor and team coach who finds that when coaching senior people in organizations, it is rare to come across anyone who is not facing at least one challenging relationship at work. Leaders come to coaching with a variety of objectives and a frequent theme is that they are stuck and frustrated in terms of achieving them. Somewhere in the complexity of the problem there is likely to be an issue that centres on their relationships with other people.

Anne came to coaching with just such an issue. She was a newly-appointed director in a public sector organization, performing well in her new role but experiencing some difficulty with a colleague on the executive team called Sally (both names have been changed to protect confidentiality).

Anne respected Sally's capabilities but found their relationship challenging. In team meetings Sally was warm and cooperative but in one-to-one contact Anne found Sally strong-willed, forthright and stubborn. Anne's personal style of compromise and collaboration was being overwhelmed by Sally and she found herself acquiescing to things she did not agree with and taking on tasks delegated by Sally, all of which she resented.

Lynne used the perceptual positions technique to facilitate Anne to explore her interactions with Sally. Anne stepped into each position in turn, first as herself, then as her colleague. In each she imagined an interaction between the two of them, trying to see and hear what might typically happen, and noticing her resultant feelings.

Anne then stepped into a third position, as an observer of the other two. When asked what she noticed from this perspective, she immediately identified that the relationship was stuck, that the Anne she observed in her mind's eye was passive and that the Sally she saw seemed quite frustrated. She decided it would be useful for the Anne of her imagination to be more confident and relaxed.

Anne then moved into the first position again and imagined a conversation with Sally in which she herself felt confident and relaxed. She quickly noticed that this brought about a transformation in their imaginary exchange. When she then revisited Sally's position, the real Anne found herself able to see and hear a change in imaginary Anne. Accordingly, the imaginary Sally seemed to feel reassured by Anne's confidence, regarding her as capable and enjoying the possibility of a good debate, instead of being faced with submissive behaviour.

When Anne stepped into the final position she was impressed by the change that she realized she had made so far. In a few minutes she had succeeded in creating a whole new attitude towards her colleague. Within a month Anne called Lynne to tell her that the relationship was transformed. Sally was now Anne's greatest ally on the executive team, and they had jointly taken on a new project – with gusto!

One interesting result that Lynne has found by facilitating her clients in this exercise is that they seem to be able to run it again autonomously for any tricky relationship in which they may find themselves. And once the technique is embedded, it is not even necessary to move physically – the process can be performed solely in one's imagination. Similarly, people are able to combine the techniques with other ideas to make them more useful, and Anne provided an example of this.

In a later coaching session Anne and Lynne were sitting near a table in a meeting room. Anne was struggling with big decisions she needed to make that affected her home and work life. Lynne suggested that she move her position in order to get a different perspective on the issue.

Anne went to the other side of the meeting table and sat down. She looked back to where she had been sitting and said: 'Wow. This is my father.' Anne had not only found a new perspective but her unconscious mind had given it an identity. Acting as if she were her father, Anne explained what she could see, hear and feel about the 'Anne' that she was observing, and gave some positive messages.

From there, she in turn sat in two further seats, in which she again took on the imagined perspectives of other people she knew, watching and hearing 'Anne' describe her current dilemma. As coach, Lynne asked some questions and then asked Anne to step back into her own shoes, in the first position.

After returning to 'herself', Anne sat quietly, integrating all the insights from the perceptual positions that she had explored which incorporated the imagined views of people who were important to her. As she spoke, her physiology changed – her face and shoulders relaxed, some colour came to her cheeks and she sat back in her chair and looked up.

'I know what I need to do,' Anne declared, and smiled.

Perceptual positions at work: John's story

John (name changed), a director in a professional services organization, was leading an important business development project. Agreed at board level, the implementation was given to a cross-functional group of five people at the next level down in the organization. However, John found their progress frustratingly slow. Two people seemed to be giving low priority to the project, another was actively blocking progress, a fourth cooperated but somehow failed to be effective, while the fifth, at least, proved reliable and was meeting all his commitments.

This was a complex situation with multiple stakeholders. Lynne coached him using an exercise developed by Mariette Castellino, which incorporates elements of David Grove's Clean Space (which is described in Chapter 29) combined with some principles of perceptual positions. Lynne asked him to mark out on the floor a first position where he could stand, followed by positions marking the other people involved in the project. His spacing indicated relative distances in relationships, illustrated on the next page.

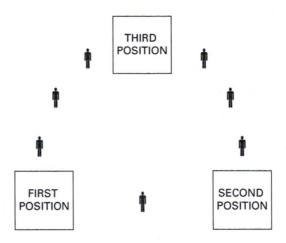

Mapping out where John placed his stakeholders, Lynne guided him to stand in each of the positions that he had marked on the floor and, in each place, to tell her what he noticed. As he stepped into the shoes of each of the people involved, he became aware of what might be happening for each person, how each related to and perceived the others (including himself) and how that person might be feeling.

When he finally stepped back into the first position with his newfound insights, John was amazed at the difference. Suddenly he felt optimistic about the project again, and knew what he wanted to do to make things happen. He listed his action plan immediately and rushed off to get started. Within 10 days, with the cooperation of the others involved, he had achieved two milestones in the project. Six months later, as scheduled, the initiative was successfully launched and the project team applauded.

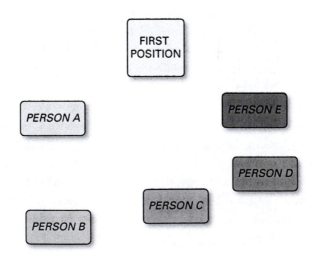

Anchors

Anchors are reminders identified after a coachee has reached a desired state for performance, so that the state may be recalled at will when required. For example, an anchor for recalling a state of confidence before public speaking could be visual, say picturing a symbol, or kinaesthetic, such as crossing the fingers, or rooted in one of the other VAK types.

As a temporary crutch, an anchor can be helpful. However, it is more effective to resolve the underlying block than mask it with an artificially accessed state, which sometimes delivers an impression of people who are 'uncomfortable in their own skin'. Again, I believe that this is because conflicting messages are emitted by the conscious and unconscious minds. David Grove's Clean Language and Emergent Knowledge, explored in Chapters 27 and 28 respectively, are highly effective ways of resolving such unconscious disorders and negate the need for any artificial remedies.

Logical levels

Logical levels was developed by Robert Dilts and encourages exploration of the different perspectives of spirituality/purpose, identity/mission, beliefs and values, capabilities/strategies, behaviours and environment. This is another effective way of helping a subject gain new insight about a situation.

Timeline

Timeline asks the coachee to pace out an imaginary line representing the coachee's life in terms of past present and future. Physically moving up and down the line gives access to resources and frees up blocks that may have accumulated in the past. It is effective at delivering new perspectives and insights and provides some access to the unconscious mind by taking the subject into the metaphor of the line, which can result in the dissolution of knots and blocks accumulated over the years and a clearer sense of how to move forward.

NLP at work

Deni Lyall is a coach with broad experience and training in several fields including NLP. She recounted to me how she had used NLP techniques in coaching a senior engineering manager at a defence company, who was excessively nervous about the technical presentations that he had to deliver to senior managers and at conferences.

Firstly, to establish trust, Deni used the mirroring and matching techniques described above. Next, the meta model proved useful as Nick tended to use generalizations and distortions when describing his inability to control his nerves. Through the meta questions, Nick became aware of how much of the problem he was creating himself. For example, he realized that participants who asked awkward questions were not out to humiliate him – they may have been inarticulate or simply having a bad day. Nick began to believe that he could do something about the situation and that he was in control.

After continuing the coaching through various NLP techniques, Deni sought to embed Nick's new thinking by walking him through the logical levels, from envisioning his next presentation room, through to his new capabilities and finally to his new beliefs and values. After this he was evidently calmer and his language had become more positive and solution focused, around how to make things work instead of what might go wrong. Over his next three presentations, Nick received some excellent feedback and found he was able to handle the tough questions confidently.

Conclusion

NLP sets out some interesting theories about how the brain and emotions work. The processes can be useful in raising awareness and helping people get clear on their patterns of behaviour. Caution must be exercised by the coach (or coaching style manager) not to become distracted by linguistic patterns and physical movements (as this can result in incongruence and a failure to listen and respond empathetically) and not to make judgements about the subject's beliefs or statements.

As is the case with most psychological interventions, no scientific testing of NLP has taken place, nor results measured. There are evangelists of NLP who elevate the practice to quasi-religious status, practitioners who attempt to manipulate people with the techniques and then again, many congruent, intelligent and highly effective coaches who use the techniques creatively, rationally and with excellent results.

Systemic Coaching

SUMMARY

- Systems in families, teams and communities
- Knock-on effect of change
- Social, financial, structural, intellectual and societal capital
- Repetition of childhood behaviour
- Coaching the organization
- Systems theory, cybernetics, family systems theory, complexity theory and chaos theory
- Systemic Coaching in the public sector

Systems in families, teams and communities

We are all part of a system of relationships: the family we grew up with, the one we may have since created, our teams at work, the wider community we live in and the world of which that community forms a part. Systemic Coaching looks at the influences these relationships may have on our thoughts, emotions and behaviour. Ghosts of past relationships intermingling with current ones give rise to assumptions, reflexes and actions that may affect our later progress through life. Our physical bodies are also recognized as forming part of our system and Systemic Coaching is said to be effective in healing because it treats all parts as interrelating.

Knock-on effect of change

Systemic Coaching postulates that we can change our patterns. In any system, if one part alters, then there is a knock-on effect with all the other parts; therefore it must be possible for us to bring about change in others, in relationship to us, by changing ourselves. One of the technique's influences is quantum physics, which states that when the state of one part of a system is known, information about the state of the other parts may be deduced without direct interaction. Systemic Coaching applies this to human and organizational relationships.

For example, an organization's value lies not only in its financial achievements but in areas such as its IT systems and hierarchy (structural capital), relationships between individuals and departments (social capital), retention of knowledge skills and experience (intellectual capital), and its impact on the wider community and sustainability (societal capital):

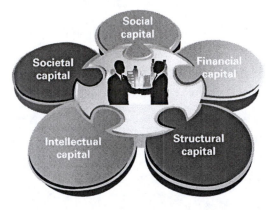

All of these interlink and the effectiveness of one is affected by the performance of all.

Repetition of childhood behaviour

An example in an individual coachee might be a situation where a woman is transferring emotions she habitually experienced in childhood onto her current relationships, treating her reports as children (perhaps being over-bearing or micromanaging) or relating to her peers in the way that her own siblings interreacted, say by shouting, harbouring jealousy or being territorial. The behaviour that occurred in

the childhood relationships might be inappropriate in the workplace, yet people projecting this type of transference are often unaware of the effect that they have on those around them.

The systemic coach will start with diagnostics, to assess how well the system is functioning at present, then set some goals, then coach on strategies to achieve the goals. The process can be applied to individuals, teams or whole organizations. The system can include the emotional one in an individual's mind, the colleagues who work around him, and the organization as a whole.

To take an individual example, it is accepted that stress triggers hormones that can produce irrational behaviour and physical symptoms as well. Sometimes a simple exploration of the nature of the stress using the systemic model described above – its causes, the reactions and situations generated, reframing the situation in a more positive light, and setting some goals or strategies – may help to alleviate the symptoms associated with the stress, both mental and physical.

Coaching the organization

Similarly, in the use of Systemic Coaching for a whole organization, an exploration of the reactions and situations generated by a team or between a set of teams can be conducted through focus groups and one-to-one coaching. This can include an examination of the practical systems in place as well as the relational ones. One of the core principles of coaching in general is to create awareness (Whitmore, 2009), which in itself generates both the desire to change and the knowledge of how to accomplish the changes. The systemic approach will produce new awareness and motivation to change.

In common with other coaching related practices, Systemic Coaching treats people as complete, resourceful beings with all the knowledge they need. The coaching helps people to set in motion self-directed learning, to activate their inner resources and plan ahead for future growth.

Sometimes we behave in ways which we do not understand. Certain behaviour may be caused by entanglements from the past, so that we play roles such as the victim, the bully or the people-pleaser, arising from situations like the following:

- Anger at perceived childhood betrayal, which may make us suspicious and resentful of others.

- An over-controlling authority figure, which may result in bullying leaders or co-dependent relationships.
- An over-critical parent, which, by reducing our own sense of identity, compels us to live by someone else's standards and values.

Any of the childhood situations above can result in an adult who either bullies others, or is resentful, bitter and believes him or herself to be a victim of circumstances, or is constantly seeking approval from others. Indeed, some personalities will exhibit all three types of behaviour at different times and in different situations.

Systems theory, cybernetics, family systems theory, complexity theory and chaos theory

The foundations of Systemic Coaching lie in systems theory, which itself draws on a wide range of knowledge, including cybernetics, family systems theory, complexity theory and chaos theory. One of the founders of the systems approach was the biologist Ludwig von Bertalanffy, who postulated that the world consists of interdependent and hierarchical systems all interacting with their surrounding environment and each other. To employ these theories in coaching, it is necessary to bring all parts of a person's situation, life and work into focus using coaching's customary open and non-judgemental questioning techniques. From this exploration, the coachee will discover new knowledge about how the various parts function together, the relationships between them and how to improve them.

One of the proofs of this theory is the way we tend to behave differently in different groups; some will bring out the best in us and some the worst. In some we may find ourselves playing the role of victim or bully, and in others we may be the well-balanced and rational adult. It is the system around us which is dictating our state and this is what Systemic Coaching enables us to recognize, making it an efficient tool for whole system as well as individual change.

Systemic Coaching in the public sector

Mandy Gutsell, a leading practitioner of Systemic Coaching, described to me how she used the technique when working with four departments in a public sector organization over a period of 12 months. There was some conflict within the team and a high turnover of staff, so Mandy was asked to coach managers from all four departments to open the channels of communication and provide recommendations for the team.

She began the programme by asking each department of seven people to complete an Enneagram profile (which is described in Chapter 48) in order to assess their strengths and challenges regarding their roles within the team. Then all the participants had three individual coaching sessions to explore their areas for development, followed by half-day group sessions for each department.

Eventually strengths and weaknesses began to emerge. For example, one group identified that they tended to be high on vision and direction but did not give enough time to observation and self-reflection. Another was high on observation but lower on vision and direction. Each department chose the person highest in these skills to spend time mentoring and coaching their peers in the other departments.

During the first of three group days, attended by all four departments, the roles were further explored through Worldwork (Mindell, 2000: www.aamindell.net), a process based on 'deep democracy', where each voice and feeling must be represented in order for the team to know itself and resolve its issues. The goal is not to create a conflict-free environment: the method trusts that conflict signals the diversity that might be necessary to create an honest and open team. People were encouraged to move around in the room and voice a 'role/position' from which they wanted to speak. Others would then step forward and contribute content and personal material.

While the teams were interacting, Mandy began to notice a 'ghost role' of the former manager of the team, who had left the organization about six months before. Even though this person was no longer physically present, he continued to have an impact on the current system. People spoke of him with emotion and respect, and there was a sense of needing to acknowledge him publicly. Then some participants shared feelings of conflict around their relationship with the new manager, in terms of resisting his new ideas because they were different to those of the former manager.

Over the months that followed, this did not result in complete acceptance of the new manager's way, but it did created a more open dialogue where what had previously been unspoken could now be discussed. It also created a space for the staff to acknowledge the former manager while, at the same time, acknowledging the new manager's skills and personality.

In another one of the half-day coaching sessions, a department began to develop competitiveness around work for tenders. Some of the staff felt that more time should be given to the clinical focus of the organization's child-centred work and less on the bids for new work. However, as the newer team members had stronger business backgrounds, they seemed to be gaining higher status in the department. This in turn led some staff who had worked for the organization over a number of years to feel pressured into spending time on competing for bids at the expense of their core duties.

Mandy felt it was important here to consider the concept of 'attractors'. An attractor represents the complex system of influences that cause system properties to gravitate towards particular values. These may show up in the ways a group talk together, defensiveness, energy levels and, in this case, competitiveness around the tenders, which had become an 'emergent property' of the system.

The dynamics were such that at meetings, staff with strong business backgrounds were gaining credit, while those whose experience was more clinical were beginning to feel less valued. There seemed to be a lot of blame emerging. However, using the systemic model, Mandy asked questions around:

- How useful are each of these behavioural patterns in terms of the client's goals?
- What are the assumptions, rules and feedback loops that elicit these behaviours?
- What changes could be made to elicit different, more useful behaviours? (Cavanagh, 2006)

As a result, a balance was achieved at the meetings between clinical content and monetary value. It was decided that each tender should be assigned to two members, one from business and the other with a clinical background. The two sides began to appreciate each other's viewpoint and skills.

The same department used the 'Communicube' as a structure for exploring the complex system that included attractors, roles, tensions, impact of other departments, external pressures from agencies and the meaning of 'team'. The Communicube was devised by Dr John Casson and is a transparent, open, five-level container. Light reflects off the shelves, which are each printed with a grid of 25 squares. These grids float within the structure like a series of transparent chess boards, one above the other. When objects such as buttons and stones are placed in the grid squares, they may be reflected by the other shelves. The Communicube appears like a floating world, holding within it the tension of opposite polarities and related objects. Viewed from above, the whole is instantly visible, a mandala containing disparate elements yet integrated in one world. It provides a stable, integrative container, holding dissociated fragments, separated on different levels yet in association with each other, within the whole.

Working with this Communicube helped the department to gain perspective on how other parts of the system affected them and created more empathy, not only within their department but with other departments as well. In addition, within the Communicube's structure, there is a central square through which all the diagonals pass, providing a powerful, integrative 'pull' like an 'attractor' in chaos theory. The department changed the meaning of this central square a number of times before coming to a consensus that it defined it as 'the leading edge of the child-centred work'. This emphasized what they held in common despite their differences.

Mandy finds that by taking the systems theory perspective, coaches are able work with individuals outside of their relationship system. This may in fact reduce the possibility for overall change, as the changing coachee has an impact on the larger system, which may in turn support the change or resist it in order to maintain the status quo. Her focus as a relationship systems coach is to design an alliance with the larger system so that the individual and the systems can be synergistic.

33 Transactional Analysis and the OK Corral

SUMMARY

- Social transactions
- The states of parent, child and adult
- Changing behaviour
- Franklyn Ernst's OK Corral

Social transactions

Transaction analysis was conceived by psychologist Eric Berne, famous for his 1960s best-seller, *Games People Play*. The name refers to the social interactions, or what Berne termed 'transactions', that take place between people:

> 'The unit of social intercourse is called a transaction. If two or more people encounter each other … sooner or later one of them will speak, or give some other indication of acknowledging the presence of the others. This is called transactional stimulus. Another person will then say or do something which is in some way related to the stimulus, and that is called the transactional response.' (Berne, 1964)

The states of parent, child and adult

During the course of working with hundreds of patients in the 1950s, Berne noticed a familiar pattern occurring. At any one time, most of his patients tended to be in one of three states, all of which existed alongside each other. He defined these states as parent, child and adult.

The parent state occurs when people are reproducing behaviours or attitudes that they have absorbed from their own parents or early role models. Babies are programmed to learn by reproducing what they see and experience from the people around them; some of the patterns absorbed are useful in later life and others less so. If you have ever heard yourself speak, and then realized (possibly with dismay) 'That's what my mother/father used to say', then you were having an Eric Berne 'Parent' moment. Reproduced parent transactions can be useful in affording discipline and responsibility; too much can result in over-control, bullying and finger wagging. Words like 'always', 'never', 'for once and for all', might be used.

The child state is a reproduction of the reaction we had to the transaction with our own parents. Berne came to realize that babies require interaction (or transactions) with other humans from birth in order to develop, and that if no positive transactions are available, they prefer negative transactions to no transactions at all. This is why negative behaviour is assimilated as much as positive. The negative behaviour exhibited in child transactions might be sad, despairing, throwing temper tantrums, giggling and speaking in baby talk. The language might involve the use of words like 'I'm gonna', 'things never go right for me', 'the best ever'.

The adult state is the label Berne gave to the times when we are interacting 'in the moment' without repeating a pattern from the past. This is the healthy way of living, free of the baggage of prejudice, painful memories and 'knee jerk' reactions. These types of transactions are straightforward, attentive, non-threatening and non-threatened, and engender tempered language such as 'I see' (rather than a contradiction), 'possibly' (rather than never), 'probably' (not definitely), 'disappointing' (not 'devastating'), 'I think' and 'I believe' (taking responsibility, instead of 'you are', 'it is always', 'it never'). The language of coaching strives to elicit all of these adult qualities and encourages coachees to take responsibility, discard prejudice and view each situation from a clean slate instead of falling back on previous behaviour patterns.

Changing behaviour

Human beings, whether babies or children, tend to absorb and reproduce all of the transactions they experience. As we grow older, we can make choices between which behaviours we reproduce, but it is not always easily to distinguish a pattern of behaviour set in place by childhood experience from that which is an untainted approach. Ancient patterns are sometimes bewildering to ourselves and for those around us. An example of such a pattern is the statement 'Men/women always leave me', which sets up an unconscious pattern of choosing only those partners who will leave. Another is 'I never do anything right', which results in people sabotaging their own success.

A useful aspect of Transactional Analysis in terms of coaching's solution focused approach is its underlying philosophy that everyone has the ability to change; our behaviour patterns are not innate character traits but mere habits that can be mastered and reprogrammed once recognized.

Berne's original work has been developed by a number of psychologists, in particular Ian Stewart and Vann Joines, and Thomas Harris MD, who wrote the best-seller *I'm OK, You're OK* in the 1960s. Taking Berne's three transactional states, Parent – Child – Adult, a stage further, Harris identified four positions people can take in their relationship to each other which result in either effective or ineffective communication.

His theories were neatly expressed in a quadrant which Franklyn Ernst devised and called the OK Corral.

Franklyn Ernst's OK Corral

> **I am not OK – You are OK:** This is Berne's Child state, when people feel 'small'; a new employee might feel incompetent, or someone with a fear of authority might find that he or she becomes tongue-tied when speaking to the boss (or headmaster, magistrate, professor etc). This state of mind might result in frustration, tantrums or simply not achieving very much through fear and refusal to take responsibility.

I am OK – You are not OK: This state of mind can produce bullying, at home or at work. It is the equivalent of Berne's parent position. It might mean taking too much responsibility for another person's results, which goes against the coaching way of thinking.

I am not OK – You are not OK: This is the worst possible result, when people are behaving from either or both of Berne's parent and child states. Everyone gives up and we might hear words like 'This is hopeless', 'She goes or I go', 'We'll never get anywhere'. The equivalent phrases expressed during childhood might have been 'I'm not playing any more' from the child or 'The conversation is closed' from an adult. It is the easiest way out of a difficult situation and the least productive for everyone concerned.

I am OK – You are OK: This is Berne's adult state, where both people in the transaction take responsibility and make some effort. Each might be saying, 'I am capable and confident and I believe you are capable and confident. Together we can do great things'. This is the peer to peer stance which underlies good coaching, rather than a master–pupil type of relationship.

The ideas set out above can be highly productive when used in coaching or leadership work. Explaining the squares in the quadrant to a frustrated manager and asking questions about his or her position in different situations and with different people can be revelationary to that manager, and may enable a choice to be made about future positions, instead of following the primitive patterns formed in childhood. The manager could be asked to shade the diagram in to identify the various positions, which may change at different times and in different situations:

Equally, the coach can ask coachees about their position in relationships with reports and how they believe their reports relate to them. The diagram can form a rich basis for a whole coaching session and has proved to be an effective instrument for bringing about real change.

360-degree feedback

SUMMARY

- The process
- Pitfalls
- Coaching the results
- Alternatives

360-degree feedback is a process used by many organizations today to provide managers with feedback on how they are viewed by the different categories of people they come into contact with in the course of their work, for example the managers they report to, the staff who report to them, and their colleagues, customers and clients.

The feedback is usually delivered anonymously and participants are asked to fill in a series of tick-boxes (often online) and to provide individual comments about various aspects of the subject's performance, typically around their skills, abilities, attitudes and behaviours.

Sometimes the subjects can choose the participants and at others the participants are selected for them.

The process

The subject will receive a detailed report, which quite often includes pie charts and diagrams similar to the one shown on the next page, which shows that the respondents who took part in the survey were selected from the subject's peer group, direct reports, clients and his manager. The chart seems to show a person who is popular and productive. There is perhaps some scope for development on leadership and decision-making. A question that he might ask himself is whether he sacrifices some authority and avoids hard

360-degree feedback chart

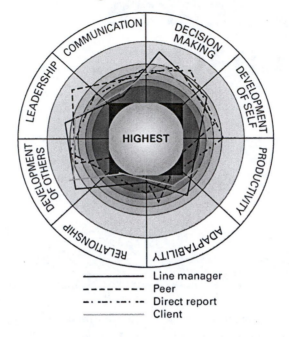

```
————————    Line manager
- - - - - - -    Peer
-·--·-·--·--    Direct report
〰〰〰〰〰    Client
```

decisions because of a wish to be liked. A coach in this situation might offer this insight as a suggestion if the subject does not come up with it himself.

The way a coach would handle delivering such a report is to ask insight-creating questions, such as:

- What have you learned from this?
- How important is this aspect to you?
- What impact does this have on your work/life?
- How would you like it to be?
- Where do you shine?
- What aspects you would most like to change?
- What would you like this survey to show if it was done again in six months time?
- How could you achieve that?

If any of the comments have had a negative impact on John, it will help to explore his feelings and reactions thoroughly so that he can see past any initial anger or fear created by the survey.

The process can be helpful in the case of a manager who does not realize he or she is a bully, perhaps, or to identify the areas to work on during a forthcoming coaching programme. It is particularly useful when a whole tier of management is out of touch with how it is viewed by the rest of the organization.

It is important that the questions in the survey are designed to take into account employment law issues such as sexism and ageism (which is illegal since legislation passed in 2006). Respondents should also be made aware of such legislation in terms of their responses.

Pitfalls

The pitfalls of this type of survey are that:

- Respondents are not always honest in case their identities are guessed.
- Sometimes their identities are guessed or, at worst, wrongly presumed.
- Personal grudges, jealousy or ambitions can influence a respondent's comments.
- Negative feedback can be meaningless without knowing where it comes from.
- People tend to hear criticism louder than praise and can become demoralized by the process.
- The process does not adhere to the openness and transparency advocated in coaching.

Coaching the results

Any type of survey where some members of staff are asked to give feedback about other people in the business must be managed with great care, for example the recipient should be coached through the results rather than just handed a report. I have personally worked with a manager whose confidence was so shattered by her 360-degree feedback that she was unable to return to work for a week, in spite of having previously been an apparently successful and popular manager for many years. She later discovered that some of the most injurious comments had been intended to refer to a different manager altogether – but, astonishingly, this was not made clear when she was given the results. She says that she may never regain her confidence.

Another unwelcome side effect is that some managers hide behind the process of written feedback, particularly when it is available on a regular basis, rather than confront a colleague, boss or report with their grievances. I worked with a senior manager of a multinational who intensely resented the fact that some scathing comments from his own line manager had gone the rounds of HR and various directors before he had even seen them. To add to his sense of injustice, his manager had never raised any of the criticisms listed with him directly; in fact, the situation was quite the reverse and he had thought himself highly regarded and doing a good job.

Surveys such as these fly directly in the face of the principles of coaching, namely building self-belief, enabling self-directed learning and creating a 'blame free culture'. Nevertheless, they have taken a firm hold in many of the companies whose stated aim is to create a coaching culture, so coaches need to know how to handle their effects.

In situations such as I have described, the guideline to follow would be to get the individuals involved talking – coach them on how to have a non-confrontational, inoffensive conversation, offer to facilitate a meeting, or give them some training in coaching skills and concepts. Find a way to get the conflicts out into the open, off paper, and into the discussion arena.

A 360-degree survey run throughout an organization will be more acceptable to staff if it is run from top down rather than bottom up, so that people have the opportunity to appraise their own leaders rather than just being appraised; an additional advantage of this is that the senior leaders may obtain new insight into their own qualities, skills and behaviour.

Sadly, it is probably true that the more an organization's managers can deal with the results of a 360 in a 'grown up' way, the less likely they are to require the information. So where there are managers who show substantial room for improvement in their leadership, communication and performance skills, the survey is more likely to have a detrimental effect, creating fear, depression and defensiveness. On the other hand, managers who score highly in the areas mentioned are likely to welcome some adverse feedback as a helping hand towards even higher achievements.

What a 360 can reveal is information about the culture of the organization as much as the performance of any particular manager. Some organizations operate in a way that limits performance. For example, I once worked in a company where the sales and marketing combined division put most of its energies into proving that the products delivered by the creative/R&D division were unsaleable. This concept was identified in an astute book written by Anthony Jay (creator of political satire 'Yes Minister') in the 1970s, called *Corporation Man*, based on his experiences of working at the BBC.

Alternatives

An alternative to the 360's focus on passing judgements about individuals is Richard Barrett's Cultural Transformation Tools explored in Chapter 40. CTT surveys ask questions about what values an organization currently exhibits and what the participants would like to see instead. The results provide useful yardsticks against which an organization's leaders can measure their performance without pointing the finger at any one individual.

The culture of an organization can bring out the best in its people, enabling them to take risks, stretch their imaginations, support future leaders and discover hidden resources within themselves, or it can direct their energies into watching their backs and undermining colleagues regarded as threats or competition. The results of individual 360-degree surveys when studied as a whole will show up strains that tend to surface throughout the organization.

35 The Reuven Bar-On Emotional Quotient inventory (BarOn EQ-i)

SUMMARY

- History
- The five elements
- Validity safeguards
- Emotional intelligence in the IT department

History

Reuven Bar-On is the American clinical psychologist often credited with having originally coined the term 'EQ', representing 'Emotional Quotient', during his doctoral studies in the 1980s to refer to a type of intelligence that is different to IQ, the Intelligence Quotient model popularized during the middle of the last century.

In the workplace, two of the key applications of EQ are in management and leadership skills and relate to motivation and teamwork, while IQ would cover knowledge, skill and experience. In the public arena, Daniel Goleman's work is more well-known due to the publication of his best-seller, *Emotional Intelligence*, although Goleman recognizes BarOn's contribution to the field. There is some controversy over who in fact coined the term EQ, and its popular usage probably started with a *Time Magazine* headline in the 1980s.

The BarOn Emotional Quotient inventory (BarOn EQ-i) can be divided into two main parts. The first part is the theory of emotional intelligence and is sometimes referred to as the BarOn conceptual model; the second provides a means for measuring it and is known as the BarOn psychometric model.

The five elements

The inventory assesses EQ through a series of questions, similar in structure to an IQ test, comprising 133 short statements. Participants are asked to mark their preferences on a scale from 'very seldom or not true of me' (1) to 'very often true of me or true of me' (5). Many of the questions are similar but asked from a slightly different perspective, which helps to self-correct answers that may be consciously striving towards a desired image rather than the true personality of the participant.

Participants are graded both on an overall score and a score for each of the following sections:

- **Intrapersonal** deals with one's understanding of oneself, for example self-esteem, self-knowledge, confidence and self-actualization.
- **Interpersonal** is about the effect we have on others and measures aspects such as empathy, social responsibility and the ability to manage relationships.
- **Stress management** looks at our tolerance to stress and to what extent we are able to control our impulses when under stress.
- **Adaptability** is concerned with how flexible we are when faced with changes and challenges, how well we are able to distinguish between reality and our own perceptions, and our ability to come up with solutions.
- **General mood** measures our ability to be optimistic and happy.

Validity safeguards

A pitfall with such a test is the possibility that people will skew their answers to impress, or to fit a particular job specification. To rectify this, four validity indicators are included which look at how many responses have been missed out, occurrences of inconsistencies and tendencies towards over-positive or over-negative responses to the questions. The resulting built-in correction factor reduces the likelihood of the distortions mentioned above and hopefully increases the accuracy of the results.

As one might expect, high scores indicate a person who functions well in terms of relationships and social exchanges, while low scores suggest some difficulties which might include a distorted perception of reality, an inability to solve problems, low stress tolerance and difficulty with controlling impulses when under stress.

However, as with any psychometric tool, it is worth taking into account that people who are suited to one type of work may require different emotional skills to those suited to another. For example, put a highly successful sales director who enjoys socializing and competitive situations into a job where she has to manage a team of IT engineers, and she may very soon start exhibiting a lower tolerance to stress and difficulty controlling her frustration with their different way of thinking. Similarly, put an IT executive in charge of a team of sales people and both sides will be complaining before long.

My personal view is that Bar-On's tests give their best value when used as a tool for increasing self-awareness rather than for managers to learn about current or potential staff. There is no right or wrong social behaviour, only behaviour that is appropriate to the environment. In Chapter 11 I describe a successful IT director who scored low on an emotional intelligence test which all the managers in his organization had been forced to take. His team of IT engineers were thriving under his style of communication, which they shared, yet he was given a coach to try to 'improve' his EQ score.

Another caution to be aware of is a practice I have come across not infrequently in today's widespread use of psychometric tools – people are asked to complete the process, then simply handed the results and expected to get on with correcting any behaviour that the test has highlighted as limiting. Such tests should only ever be conducted with the pre- and post-support of a coach or similar practitioner, who can ensure that the experience is a productive and stimulating learning curve rather than a blow to confidence. Used in this way, Bar-On EQ-i can be a revealing and productive measure in management in the workplace today.

Bar-On also devised a correlating 360-degree feedback model, called the EQ-360, and a youth version of the original inventory called The EQ-i:YV (BarOn Emotional Quotient Inventory Youth Version) for ages seven to eighteen. He currently spends his time writing and speaking about emotional intelligence.

Emotional intelligence in the IT department

Leadership development expert and founder of the MOE Foundation described in Chapter 13, Darren Robson, provided the following case history which offers some insight into the practical applications of the Reuven Bar-On EQi tool, with a 'real life' example of how it can be useful for an individual's ongoing development and a caveat about the need to provide the individual undertaking it with sufficient support.

Peter (not his real name) had worked as an IT manager in a pharmaceuticals supplier for 28 years. The company culture was fast-paced, with a lot of fire-fighting and little or no time spent on developing people, and the hierarchy dictated that people receive promotions based on length of service rather than their competency or inclination. Peter was at this point 18 months into a new role as IT Lead, which was taking him out of his personal comfort zone and natural preference for small, stable, familiar groups, towards being part of a broader stakeholder community. He felt challenged on a number of levels and was becoming labelled as 'difficult to deal with'.

When Darren first saw Peter's EQi results before they met, shown on the next page, he felt concerned at the overall low score and the fact that a number of areas highlighted the potential need for further development. However, through discussion it became apparent that the 'difficult' label was unfairly placed. It was simply that Peter was a very detailed and factual type of person, preferring to have data and information in front of him before providing recommendations or conclusions. His approach appeared to be at odds with the more senior leaders, who tended towards a 'gut' reaction and relied on their intuition. As a result, they would place Peter 'on the spot' when he was unprepared, a position that rendered him unable to provide the requested information.

An additional barrier was that the organization was reluctant to support or fund any development for Peter. They wanted the EQi to be a 'one-hit wonder': to get the results, give him the feedback and let him get on with it. Darren managed to put in place two face-to-face EQi working sessions and a series of ad hoc telephone check-ins. Peter's own point of view was that he did not feel the need to work too much on his personal development; he just wanted to make it through to retirement in five years' time.

From the outset they agreed to identify two or three practical things that Peter could work on within the limited amount of time available. The strengths that Peter felt made up his winning strategy included:

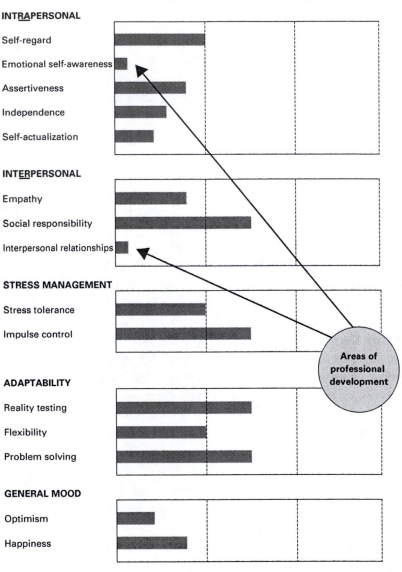

- **Impulse control**: under pressure, Peter kept his cool and was able to keep a clear perspective in difficult circumstances – a useful set of skills in a 'fire-fighting' environment.
- **Reality testing**: Peter felt that his ability to read the environment and understand the required response meant that he was able to find IT-related solutions that met people's needs.

The areas of focus to help him perform at his best, in his current role and within the organizational context, included:

- **Emotional self-awareness**: being aware of his internal voice and considering what impact this had upon his behaviour and the way he came across to others.

- **Interpersonal relationships**: if he was to maintain his current role, it was evident to Peter that he would need to stretch out of his IT comfort zone and take the time to get to know others across the organization.

However, the story ended here because Peter's organization refused to provide ongoing support and development for him. Darren and Peter continued to check in with each other on an informal basis for six months, but Darren's own learning from this was never again to provide EQi feedback unless it forms part of a broader coaching and development programme. It is important from the outset to ensure that there is the right level of commitment and engagement from the organization. In Peter's case there was a clear threat to his future role because his capability was being questioned, as well as developmental requirements evident in his profile which indicated that focused support could have helped him to grow to the next level. However, the help that Darren might have given was limited by the organization's expectation of the 'silver bullet' fast result without considering the need for a longer-term solution. Today Darren contracts with organizations upfront to ensure that the right buy-in and commitment to support their people exists. If not he refuses to undertake the work.

This case history underlines the importance of how any development tool such as EQi is handled, including 360-degree feedback, MBTI and any other process which aims to tell people something that they do not already know about themselves. At worst, I have seen an executive's confidence destroyed by unsupported feedback, and trust destroyed in another situation – and in both of these cases I was brought in solely to deal with the fallout. In addition there is always the danger that an impressionable person may live up to any detrimental labels that are pinned upon them.

36 Thomas-Kilmann Conflict Mode Instrument

SUMMARY

- Dealing with conflict
- Using the TKI
- Pitfalls of using the TKI
- The conflict continuum
- The TKI at work

Dealing with conflict

Conflict is part of human nature and, when managed effectively, can be a spur to new discoveries, achievements and ways of moving forward. The extremes of the conflict continuum, identified by Thomas and Kilmann as competing (assertive) and accommodating (passive), can be damaging to relationships inside organizations and in life in general.

The Thomas-Kilmann Conflict Mode Instrument (TKI) was devised by Kenneth W Thomas and Ralph H Kilmann in 1974, following on from the development of a number of models for dealing with conflict, including the Mouton and Blake axes, during the 1960s. TKI has since become possibly the most prevalent of all the models and identifies five styles of dealing with conflict:

- *Competing.* The proverb 'All's fair in love and war' comes to mind. 'Competing' represents the attitude of someone who will do anything to achieve his ends, such as trampling on the ideas of others, bullying, or stealing credit for achievements. This is the extreme end of conflict, the battle zone. Life can be quite stressful if you have to work alongside, or for, someone in this state of mind. This is a major concern in business today because, as well as the question of how the performance of the bully's team is affected, organizations are worried about being sued by stressed employees because of this type of behaviour.

- *Avoiding.* Avoiding the issue can be productive or otherwise, depending on the situation. The least productive type of avoidance arises from the fear of dealing with a problem. This may go hand in hand with a 'competing' tendency; someone who finds that she regularly ends up in a shouting match with people who have different views will often avoid such situations altogether, because the consequences are as upsetting to the aggressor as to those on the receiving end.

  On the other hand, some discussions are best deferred to a more suitable time. For example, a team that is facing a redistribution of roles is not likely to be open to the spirit of collaboration the day after valued colleagues have been made redundant. The key here is to be aware of the different levels of avoidance and able to identify one's own true intentions, so that the decision of whether to intervene or wait is a conscious one.

- *Accommodating.* In the TKI model, 'accommodating' means taking the path of least resistance, often at the sacrifice of one's own position. This trait comes up regularly in one-to-one coaching, with managers who have difficulty in speaking up at meetings and find themselves consenting to decisions they do not agree with. Accommodating behaviour in this sense may also masquerade as selflessness or generosity, even to the perpetrator himself. One of the ways this tool is useful is in helping people identify the true motives behind their behaviour.

  Although such passive behaviour may afford a quiet life, it is clearly not a productive method of getting the best out of the human capital in an organization. Quiet people have good ideas too, and as well as working on their own assertiveness, they need a team leader who will ensure that everyone finds a way of being heard.

- *Collaborating.* Collaborating is a much more enjoyable and productive way of working. In this phase, people will put their intellect and energy into creating a situation where views can be shared and mutually suitable solutions found. During collaboration, there is a tendency for new ideas to be created and this illustrates conflict at its best – two minds coming from different knowledge, attitudes and experience, working together to create something better than either could alone.

- *Compromising.* Compromising is the adult way to settle differences. It may not be possible, perhaps due to different values or reasons outside of the control of the parties concerned, to reach a collaborative way forward. In that case, both parties can show respect for the other by cheerfully working out what they can cede while retaining any aspects that they feel are crucial to the end result.

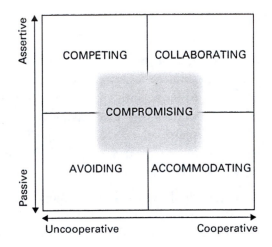

Using the TKI

The instrument can be used with individuals as an awareness-creating tool, or with groups of people to bring some clarity on how they can best work together.

The process consists of answering a series of multiple-choice questions, for example:

- I try to find a compromise solution;
- I sometimes sacrifice my own wishes for the wishes of the other person;
- I am very often concerned with satisfying all our wishes;
- There are times when I let others take responsibility for solving the problem;

- I propose a middle ground; and

- I press to get my points made.

The results are interpreted through a facilitator qualified in the instrument. Some users find prescribed multiple-choice questions frustrating, if none of the answers accurately expresses their attitudes. However, the overall results can deliver to users a clearer picture of how they react in situations of conflict, and awareness is half the battle towards resolution.

Pitfalls of using the TKI

As with all tools which attempt to define personality, there are pitfalls to look out for, when the process can run contrary to the coaching ethos:

- The resulting categorization may act as a label that the person then unconsciously starts to fit herself into, thereby limiting his or her own potential. This is a particular danger with young staff, whose confidence in their working styles is not yet fully formed. For example, if I am told that I have a tendency to bully, on the one hand I may make efforts to curb it, but when I lapse I may say 'it's my nature, I can't help it', and make less effort. The other extreme, of someone being told he or she is not assertive enough, may have the more drastic effect of reducing confidence and rendering the person even less assertive than before.

- People are not always honest in their responses, for a number of reasons, among which might be:

  - When there is not enough trust present for them to believe that confidentiality will be maintained.

  - When they are trying to impress the boss. They may ask themselves, 'what type of person would best succeed in the career path I want to take?' and attempt to masquerade as that type when responding to the questions. Whether it is possible to fool the model in this way is debatable; however it will certainly skew the results, particularly in a group survey.

  - When they are worried about what the facilitator will think of them.

  - The model is quite black and white in its definitions of 'good' and 'bad' behaviour, and does not take into account context; for example, there are times when a competitive edge is of benefit to a business and it can form part of the strength of great leadership.

Coaching cultures are by no means conflict-free zones. There was a great deal of conflict on a daily basis at Virgin, which is the best example of a coaching culture I have ever come across and where I worked at board level for 10 years. Meetings were often excited, angry and passionate events. From this experience, I can add two more classifications to the existing models, and they are simply 'healthy conflict' and 'unhealthy conflict'.

The conflict continuum

- 'Healthy conflict' requires an atmosphere of complete trust in which people can safely speak their minds, argue and even have a short-lived shouting match from time to time: they need to know that job prospects will not be damaged by disagreeing with the boss or making the occasional mistake; that people will not be bullied or humiliated; that people will be listened to and supported in taking risks. This type of atmosphere builds strong and sustainable relationships.
- 'Unhealthy conflict' is what occurs in an atmosphere of fear and features the type of rows that cause lasting damage to the fabric of

relationships. The result of this is resignation, the sack or, outside of the office, divorce.

Conflict is nothing to be afraid of and its energy can be harnessed for the good of the individual, team, organization or family. The Kilmann model can be helpful in creating awareness on what type of conflict is being demonstrated and how the energy can be harnessed to productive purposes.

The TKI at work

Denise Taylor is an occupational psychologist who finds the TKI a useful tool for helping clients to understand how to handle conflict, how people's different styles affect personal and group dynamics and how to select the most appropriate style of behaviour in a situation where conflict arises.

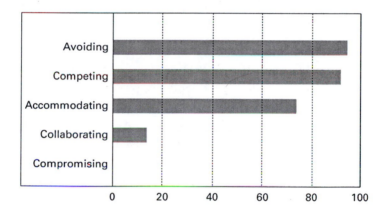

The above graph shows the score for one of Denise's clients, Natalie (whose name has been changed), compared to a sample of 8,000 people who had already taken the assessment. Natalie wanted to help improve her relationships with her colleagues. As can be seen in the graph, her way of dealing with conflict was predominately one of extremes: she tended either to avoid it completely or to take a challenging and competitive approach to others.

Clients often ask if their approach is wrong and what the right approach might be. Coaches can only reply that 'it depends', as different approaches suit different situations. At times a collaborative approach works best while in other situations we may need to be more accommodating or competing.

However, what we can be sure of is that a conscious choice about which mode to use will be more effective than responding impulsively.

The way in which we relate to others is very much a result of the situation in which we find ourselves. Natalie worked in the City, where a competitive approach is expected, so she needed to be able to demonstrate some competitive qualities to perform effectively in her organization.

During the coaching, Natalie talked about her relationship with her co-workers and how difficult she found it to be herself at work. Denise helped her to develop a plan for the future:

1 Natalie was to be vigilant for the next conflict situation and note the approach she took to it.

2 Later she would review how effectively she had dealt with the situation and reflect on the effect that alternative styles would have had on it.

3 She would then review this with Denise during the next coaching session.

Over four sessions, Natalie moved from not considering how to deal with conflict at all, to being much more flexible in her approach. This had a positive effect on her relationships with her colleagues.

Another client of Denise's, whom we will call Simon, was a newly-promoted manager who felt taken advantage of by the people he worked with. He was in his first management job following a career as a trainer and, with a coaching qualification himself, he felt that a collaborative style was the best approach. However, he soon discovered that both sides in a relationship have to want this and that one cannot collaborate on one's own. Simon told Denise that his colleagues did not meet him part-way and he felt that he was losing his authority.

The assessment confirmed that *collaboration* was his preferred style, while his score on *competing* was low. Through feedback and coaching he came to understand more about the range of styles available to him and how to be more flexible in his own approach. It was not an easy personal journey for him and at times he did not achieve his desired goals, but he found himself able to move forward one step at a time.

Denise also worked with a highly effective salesman called Neil (not his real name), who had failed in a bid for promotion to sales manager. He was looking for ways to understand more about himself in order to increase his chances of being successful at the next assessment.

Neil was highly competitive and determined to win but, while this was an effective style for him when the competition was sales people from other companies, it was less appropriate in a leadership role where he had to be the one to motivate the team. His confrontational style would not have gone down well at the interview nor in the group exercise that formed part of the assessment.

Coaching with Neil helped him to develop more flexibility in handling conflict and to try out different approaches with staff. Again, it was not easy for him. He had to work hard at becoming open to different styles, but his high sense of goal-orientation helped him to make significant improvements.

The TKI is a short and simple questionnaire which, through a coaching discussion, can raise awareness and thus help clients expand their repertoires for dealing with conflict. To use the TKI practitioners can register with OPP Ltd and no qualifications are required.

37 Marshall Rosenberg's 'Non-Violent Communication'

SUMMARY

- Exploring conflict
- Finding the compromise

Exploring conflict

Rosenberg (2003) presented some effective frameworks for exploring conflict, recognizing it and healing it. He identified that at the root of a conflict is often a difference in people's needs, and that these needs may go unrecognized not only by one's perceived antagonist, but by oneself. Some useful questions for a coach or coaching manager to ask could be based on the ones below:

- What are your needs in the situation?
- In what ways are your needs not being met?
  - How does that feel?
- In what ways are your needs being met?
  - How does that feel?
- What sort of behaviour are your needs causing in you?
- What sort of behaviour are your needs causing in other people?
- What effect are your needs having on the situation?
- What other needs might you have which are not so obvious?

- What are other people's needs in the situation?
- How could everyone's needs be met? What compromises are possible?
- What strategies could ensure that everyone's needs are met?
- What have you learned from looking at your needs and others'?

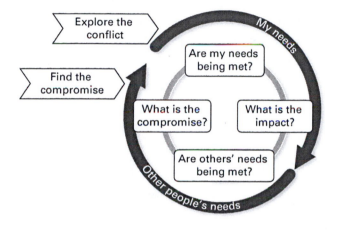

Finding the compromise

It is impossible to control every situation but what does lie within one's power is the choice about how to respond to it.

Inflammatory language is subjective, critical and judgemental, eg:

'You made me feel awful!'

'It's all your fault!'

Such language is likely to make any difficult situation worse.

Deflammatory language, however, reduces tension and calms people down. It is objective, neutral and involves a lot of permission, eg:

'When I heard you say [xxx] I felt [yyy]. Could we talk about it please?'

Conflict is sometimes exacerbated because one or both of the parties does not actually want to resolve the situation; their motives (whether consciously recognized or not) are to win the point, make the other person feel bad or to take out their own negative feelings on someone else.

It is possible to make people do things in many ways, including through the fear of punishment or the hope for a reward – or purely because they want to. People perform better when their reason is the latter, hence the need to motivate people rather than simply bully or reward them:

> 'The objective of getting what we want from people or getting them to do what we want threatens the autonomy of people ... whenever people feel they are not free to choose, they are likely to resist. Through threat or application of punishment, or the promise of giving a reward, we try to influence someone to do something – whether that be a task or behaviour. Both reward and punishment are control over others; in that respect, reward comes out of the same thinking as punishment.' (Rosenberg, 2003)

Situational Leadership

38

SUMMARY

- Origination by Blanchard and Hersey: the original quadrants
- Blanchard's revised quadrants
- Delivering all types of leadership in a coaching style
- Situational Leadership and Japanese hierarchy

Origination by Blanchard and Hersey: the original quadrants

Fifty years ago the world was a far more authoritarian place than it is now. On the whole, people did what their parents told them to, then what their teachers said and, eventually, they followed a boss's instructions at work. Politicians, policemen and the clergy were regarded as figures of authority and treated with respect. But with the social revolution of the 1960s, all this started to change.

The first Situational Leadership model was created by Ken Blanchard and Paul Hersey back in 1969. It identified that different situations require different types of management in order to raise the motivation of the workforce. No-one had worried much about motivation before this because, after the 1930s depression and a war, if a job could be found at all it would be held onto for life if possible.

The 1960s led to a time of prosperity where education and health care were free to everyone and jobs were plentiful. To entice the right calibre of employee, businesses had to start thinking about how to keep their staff happy.

The original Situational Leadership model comprised four quadrants listed below and is still in use in organizations and promoted by Paul Hersey:

Style	Situation	Type of Employee
1 TELLING	The leader gives directions and instructions; the employee is low on experience and ability in regard to the task	Trainee
2 SELLING	The leader still directs but starts to get buy-in from the employee by giving space for the employee to take ownership of the task	Team member
3 PARTICIPATING	The employee has gained some confidence and is encouraged to manage the work and use the leader as a sounding board and support; decision-making is shared	Supervisor/ manager
4 DELEGATING	The employee knows the job possibly better than the leader by now and can be left alone to get on with it	Department head

Blanchard's revised quadrants

During the 1980s, Ken Blanchard renamed the quadrants, calling his model 'Situational Leadership II', and amicably agreeing with Paul Hersey that each could promote his own model. Blanchard's quadrants contained the following labels, with the same meanings attributed as before:

STYLE
1. DIRECTING
2. COACHING
3. SUPPORTING
4. DELEGATING

This change was made to reflect Blanchard's belief that people enter a task with a high level of commitment which drops once they have met some challenges, with the result that their initial enthusiasm is curbed. The term 'coaching' is used here because it relates to a sports coach, who would be concerned not only with technique but with the athlete's motivation and persistence.

Some confusion has arisen from the use of the word 'coaching' in Blanchard's new model, as it has come to have a different meaning today than the one originally intended. When it is understood that this quadrant refers to coaching in a conventional sports coaching style, we can then infer that a performance coaching style in the modern sense of the word might be applied to all four quadrants in both models. Performance coaching is not merely a set of skills, nor is it about asking questions all the time. It is a mindset, a behaviour and an attitude, which encompasses treating people with respect and believing in their ability to raise the bar on their own knowledge, skills, experience and performance. This is described in more detail in Chapter 10, 'Coaching in leadership'. Therefore all four of the quadrants can and must be delivered in a coaching style for successful modern leadership to flourish.

Delivering all types of leadership in a coaching style

The fundamental principle of the Situational Leadership model is that there is a time and a place for all types of leadership. When someone runs into the room shouting 'Fire!', a good leader (or any sane human being for that matter) will not stop to ask how people feel about the fire.

When the situation calls for it (hence the use of the term 'situational'), it is not only acceptable but desirable to:

- direct people with clearly stated expectations, or straight answers, and tell them what to do;
- guide people towards a solution by demonstrating, encouraging, supporting and asking them to draw on their own resources;
- ask people for their own solutions and recognize their achievements; and
- leave people alone to get on with it once they know what they are doing.

In any of these situations, unacceptable behaviour would be that which demeans people, reduces their confidence, or attempts to manipulate them into making a decision that they do not understand.

The situations are flexible and interchangeable. There may be times when a very senior and experienced person needs direction, even from those below. If this is done in a coaching style, the leader will not feel threatened or demeaned. Similarly, there are times when a beginner has grasped something more quickly than usual and will take great pleasure in being allowed to run with it.

A key attitude in any of the quadrants is to remain solution-focused throughout, as this will shrink the difficulties and generate higher energy to deal with them. When working with any model it is important to remember that the model is a tool not a master, and a framework not a constraint. People should always trust their own intuition over and above any model they may have been taught.

Since his best-seller *The One Minute Manager* (Blanchard, 1981), Ken Blanchard has built a highly successful business empire and written many books about leadership.

Professor Paul Hersey founded the Center for Leadership Studies and continues to lecture on the original Situational Leadership model. He is a renowned speaker on management, has authored many articles and books on the subject and is a consultant to industrial, government, and military organizations.

Situational Leadership and Japanese hierarchy

Paula Sugawara of Tokyo Coaching Services coaches and trains managers in Japan, where today's leaders face the very real problem of how to move away from micro-managing and forward towards modern methods of delegation. The names have been changed in this account of a coaching intervention where Paula used Situational Leadership to coach a manager who faced such challenges.

Takashi was a junior level manager in the Tokyo office of a global investment bank. Although a high performer in a specialist field, there were issues about his relationships with his team members and direct reports. More specifically, he wanted a higher level of communication with his team, to improve his relationship with a senior team member and to manage the development of an underperformer.

Paula frequently coaches Japanese managers who believe that they have to know all the answers, who are task-focused and who spend their time giving orders; in short, 'micro-managing' their reports. Emotional intelligence is not a priority, which often results in boss/subordinate relationship with limited communication and a fear that prevents the report from seeking help or advice from his or her managers.

This was an accurate description of Takashi's current style of leadership, so communication skills became a priority at the start of the coaching and Paula helped him to learn the basic coaching techniques of asking open questions, giving his team members more responsibility and supporting them in goal-setting.

The first step was to establish to what extent Takashi felt he could trust his team to make decisions. Did he believe in their ability to do their job? Was he able to connect with them on a personal level? Asking questions of this nature helped Takashi realize that he was not confident about the team's abilities because he had never given them the opportunity to show what they could do.

At this point Paula introduced Takashi to the Situational Leadership model and addressed how it might help him to work with his team. She asked him to consider the different learning levels of each team member and, to his surprise, Takashi that there was a substantial difference between even the junior members, whom he had previously regarded as being much the same. He began to realize that each person would need a different approach in order to be their best and that Situational Leadership techniques could be of help in achieving that.

One of Takashi's biggest challenges in terms of relationship was a veteran manager called Shoichi. In non-Japanese companies, where promotion is awarded on performance and ability, it is not uncommon for managers to be younger or less experienced than the people who report to them. But for some Japanese executives who are used to the traditional seniority system, where rank is based on years of service or age, this can prove difficult to accept. This was the exact problem facing Takashi, who had a team member who was older, had been with the firm for longer and who was frustrated that he had been passed over for promotion in favour of Takashi.

Paula shifted Takashi's focus towards the positive contributions that this veteran might make to the team, rather than the negative view of how to control the executive or neutralize the effect of his resentment. They brainstormed ways of harnessing his skills into a specific role.

In terms of Situational Leadership, Takashi identified Shoichi as an S4 type: 'experienced and able to operate independently'. Accordingly, Takashi adopted the approach of delegating and creating a function for the executive by making him a mentor and trainer to some of the younger members of the team. As well as the advantage to the organization of reaping the benefit of Shoichi's knowledge, this would give him a sense of purpose, and of making a meaningful contribution, that might offset his current frustration.

As Shoichi grew into his new role, Takashi noticed a change in his own attitude. He began to regard the veteran not only as a contributor to the team but as a source of support to himself. Conversely, Shoichi now enjoyed a position of greater respect from others and was able to alleviate some of Takashi's work burden. Their relationship became much more positive than it had been before.

Another area for coaching was Takashi's relationship with the underperforming member of his team. Jiro refused to acknowledge his weaknesses and maintained that he was performing well. Takashi faced the challenge of providing developmental feedback without demotivating his team member. He found their meetings frustrating in the face of Jiro's attitude, which sometimes amounted to boastfulness, and at times felt himself becoming over-emotional.

The focus of the coaching conversations was how Takashi could remain objective and unemotional during discussions with Jiro, but still be firm in giving his feedback. Paula approached this by encouraging Takashi to take a more positive view of Jiro. He admitted that he had allowed his emotions to colour his judgement and that there might be something to be gained by stepping back, focusing on Jiro's strong points and giving him the benefit of the doubt in some areas.

Once Takashi was able to do this, Jiro's own stance started to shift. He began to open up about his areas for improvement and their relationship moved away from 'stand-off' towards collaborative and conciliatory. Jiro began to feel that Takashi was on his side and was finally able to ask for the support and input that he needed.

In all of these areas, some simple coaching techniques and the framework of Situational Leadership had brought about a major shift in the mindset of this Japanese manager, had helped him to transform two potentially negative elements into positive ones and had brought about a greater level of rapport and communication within his team.

39 Kouzes and Posner: The Leadership Challenge

SUMMARY

- Development by Kouzes and Posner
- The five elements

Development by Kouzes and Posner

The concept of the Leadership Challenge was formed in the United States in 1983 by Jim Kouzes and Barry Posner who started to research the essential qualities of a good leader.

Surveys were conducted with middle and senior level managers in private and public sector organizations, to discover what they had learned about techniques, strategies, behaviours and achieving one's personal best. A series of open questions was asked without any pre-conceptions of what the answers might be.

It might have been expected that the responses would favour topics such as strategy, planning, organizational ability and how to direct and control staff. However, this was not by any means the case. From the replies, Kouzes and Posner categorized the top requisites for dynamic and inspiring leadership, which they named the 'Leadership Challenge model'. These comprised the elements shown on the next page:

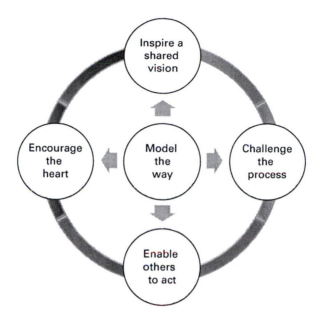

The five elements

The above patterns of behaviour can be described more fully as follows:

Model the way

Effective leaders establish patterns of behaviour and become role models, demonstrating principles of how to behave towards others in the workplace, whether reports, peers, bosses or customers. This is the most effective way of training future leaders for two reasons: firstly, because humans are designed to learn from copying others and, secondly, because the safest way to succeed in an organization is assumed to be by imitating the behaviour of the boss. If a receptionist is rude to a visitor, it is a fair indication that the CEO is equally rude to the staff on a regular basis, because behaviours seep through organizations as if by osmosis. Leaders must model the behaviour they wish to see in their staff.

'You must be the change you want to see in the world.' (Ghandi)

In addition, effective leaders look at the big goals and chunk them down into smaller steps, which are less frightening and confusing to a workforce, particularly one faced with uncertainty. Leaders like this simplify the way forward, unravelling bureaucracy and creating opportunities for others to experience recognition and reward for victories along the way.

Inspire a shared vision

Inspiring leaders are passionate about their visions for the future, motivating others by their sheer enthusiasm. If leaders are authentic and congruent in their beliefs, behaviour and actions, then people will trust them. The phrase 'the ring of truth' says it all: whatever words may be spoken, whatever values listed or visions described, people can sense when leaders are not walking the talk and if that happens, nothing will induce workers to buy in to what they are hearing.

Challenge the process

Effective leaders are constantly searching, evaluating and looking for ways to change or do things better, and encourage their people to do the same. However, this cannot work in a culture where people look for scapegoats when things go wrong. Mistakes must be viewed as part of the learning process along the way to success, otherwise the organization will stagnate because people are afraid to take action or admit their mistakes.

Sir Richard Branson created just such a learning culture at Virgin, which is explored in Chapter 6. His attitude was as if he were standing at the start of a maze, where every mistake was celebrated as another dead end eliminated, leaving us one step nearer to the goal on the other side. Even today, the Virgin website quotes: 'We trust [people] to make the right decisions, and the odd mistake is tolerated.'

Enable others to act

Good leaders are fun to work for. They support people and challenge them to stretch themselves and to discover unrealized potential. They ensure that their words are designed to build people's confidence, even when something difficult has to be said. They treat everyone with respect.

Encourage the heart

Successful leaders recognize the achievements of others and reward their people. Many surveys have shown that satisfaction outweighs financial rewards for the majority of workers, and the fastest way to satisfaction is often simply to hear that one has made a difference, whether this comes in the form of thanks, an employee of the year award or a simple 'Thank you'. Sincere recognition is a wonderful motivator. As Bob Nelson said, 'You get what you reward' (Nelson, 2005) and the best rewards are not always the material ones.

The Kouzes and Posner model is a well thought through and accurate reflection of the diverse strands which make up the kind of leader people enjoy following. All the elements described above need to be present, and the leadership will not be truly effective if any of the categories is wanting.

The model was way ahead of its time. The workplace remained authoritarian throughout the 50s and 60s, and in the 70s, when Branson introduced his liberal leadership style into the workplace, it was viewed as exceptional and probably not as a style of leadership at all. However, it is now what would be described as a 'coaching style of management' and the result for the organization, if the leaders get it right, will be the emergence of 'a coaching culture'.

40 Cultural Transformation Tools

SUMMARY

- Origination by Richard Barratt
- The Seven Levels of Consciousness
- Identifying values
- Building a values-driven organization in IT services

Origination by Richard Barratt

The Cultural Transformation Tools® were developed by Richard Barratt, a Yorkshireman now based in the United States, as part of his innovative work in the field of values-based leadership. The foundation of the tools is Barratt's 'Seven Levels of Consciousness' model.

The Seven Levels of Consciousness

Inspired by Maslow's 'hierarchy of needs' (shown in Chapter 1), the Seven Levels of Consciousness model adds an inverted top tier that encourages examination of the complex issues and aspirations in business and life today.

Unlike most evaluating tools, such as 360-degree feedback (which requires workers to rate the behaviour and performance of their peers, reports and seniors and is described in Chapter 34), CTT measures the values of individuals and organizations, rather than their performance. The underlying principle is that the values espoused by an organization can be meaningful only if they reflect the true values of its workers:

'Organisational transformation begins with the personal transformation of the leadership.' (Richard Barratt)

The vision and mission statements of an organization reflect its 'what' and 'why', while it is the values that provide the 'how' – how people think, how they perform and how they behave towards each other, the organization and its customers.

The Seven Levels of Consciousness

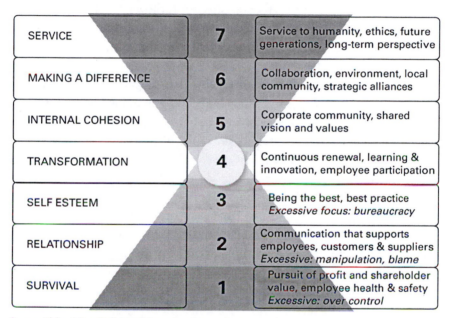

SERVICE	7	Service to humanity, ethics, future generations, long-term perspective
MAKING A DIFFERENCE	6	Collaboration, environment, local community, strategic alliances
INTERNAL COHESION	5	Corporate community, shared vision and values
TRANSFORMATION	4	Continuous renewal, learning & innovation, employee participation
SELF ESTEEM	3	Being the best, best practice *Excessive focus: bureaucracy*
RELATIONSHIP	2	Communication that supports employees, customers & suppliers *Excessive: manipulation, blame*
SURVIVAL	1	Pursuit of profit and shareholder value, employee health & safety *Excessive: over control*

© 2004 Richard Barrett & Associates www.valuescentre.com

Identifying values

The tools consist of online surveys where people are asked to choose their top 10 personal values, then the top 10 values that their organization exhibits at present, then the values they would like to see the organization espouse. The list of values is provided by CTT and can be altered to suit the organization. The surveys are conducted through a licensed CTT practitioner and can be completed by individuals or up to a staggering 35,000 participants, producing new insights for all those involved: for example, individuals gain new perspectives and ideas for change while senior managers might learn what their workforce really thinks about the organization and what changes might be beneficial.

The values offered in the survey may be positive or otherwise; in the case of the latter they are labelled *limiting* rather than *negative*. Reports are prepared at CTT's head office, based on the results, and these can be custom-designed to provide specific information by any desired demographic, such as employees in one location, directors, female workers under 40, etc.

Measurement is a key factor in CTT and Barratt quotes the phrase, 'If you can't measure it you can't manage it'. For example, if the limiting value 'bureaucracy' is frequently returned across a wide number of participants, a further survey can be run asking people to estimate what percentage of profit is lost (or how much absenteeism/staff turnover etc is caused) by this bureaucracy. Although not technically accurate, the resulting patterns can form a convincing enough trend to make the organization's finance controllers take note and take action.

One of the great advantages of CTT is that the surveys do not ask the participants to point a finger at individual colleagues. This is where processes such as 360-degree feedback fly in the face of coaching culture values because they do not adhere to the coaching principles of openness and transparency and they invite judgement and blame. With CTT, participants are firstly asked to look inside and question their own attitudes and behaviours before considering those of their colleagues. There is no place here for 'behind the back' criticism, but if the results from a team reporting to one particular manager regularly show up a specific limiting value, such as 'bullying', then the manager is more likely to recognize that he or she needs to change without the rancour that a specific comment from an unidentifiable source may give rise to. Equally, when completing 360-degree surveys, participants tend to be either too lenient, for fear of being identified, or over-critical, and they may have a personal axe to grind against the person being appraised. I would find it hard to evaluate criticism without knowing who had offered it.

Individuals undertaking the surveys are likely to recognize significant insights, such as which values they have to leave at home when they come to work in the morning, and how that affects their lives and work. Organizational cultures are no more than habits acquired over a period of years, and the first step in changing the way people treat each other at work is to acknowledge detrimental habits and institute new ones.

On the next page is an example of a survey result, which would be sent to the licensed CTT practitioner accompanied by an explanatory report. This is a survey completed by an individual and the practitioner will coach the participant through the results, identifying insights and actions along the way. If the survey was commissioned by an organization's leaders for whole sections of its workforce to complete, the diagram will show the collective

Survey result example

Jane Smith

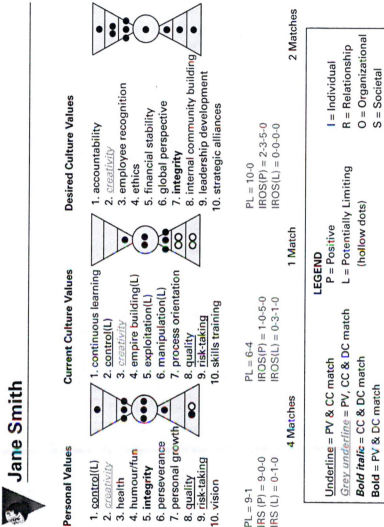

Personal Values

1. control(L)
2. *creativity*
3. health
4. humour/fun
5. **integrity**
6. perseverance
7. personal growth
8. quality
9. risk-taking
10. vision

PL = 9-1
IRS (P) = 9-0-0
IRS (L) = 0-1-0

4 Matches

Current Culture Values

1. continuous learning
2. control(L)
3. *creativity*
4. empire building(L)
5. exploitation(L)
6. manipulation(L)
7. process orientation
8. quality
9. risk-taking
10. skills training

PL = 6-4
IROS(P) = 1-0-5-0
IROS(L) = 0-3-1-0

1 Match

Desired Culture Values

1. accountability
2. *creativity*
3. employee recognition
4. ethics
5. financial stability
6. global perspective
7. **integrity**
8. internal community building
9. leadership development
10. strategic alliances

PL = 10-0
IROS(P) = 2-3-5-0
IROS(L) = 0-0-0-0

2 Matches

LEGEND

Underline = PV & CC match   P = Positive   I = Individual

Grey underline = PV, CC & DC match   L = Potentially Limiting   R = Relationship

Bold italic = CC & DC match   (hollow dots)   O = Organizational

Bold = PV & DC match   S = Societal

results and the practitioner will coach the leaders through what might be some unexpected and startling information, towards identifying ways of changing habits and culture.

The results pictured show that this worker's own values are not reflected in those of the organization. Some other key pointers which emerge are that she regards herself as too controlling at times, and that control, empire-building, manipulation and exploitation are common in the organization where she has to spend her working hours. Contrasting this with the desired values, which include ethics, integrity and internal community building, it seems that there is a great deal of work to be done by the organization if this individual is to be retained.

Reproduced below is a paper survey that I devised from the Cultural Transformation Tools. This is useful for coaching clients and groups to stimulate reflection on their place and attitudes in life. It can be used as an alternative to the 'wheel of life' tools, which asks people direct questions about their work, life, health etc.

VALUES QUESTIONNAIRE

Select values from the following list and mark them in the margins. Add more values if you wish:

- 10 personal values (mark with a P).
- 10 values that represent the current culture of your organization (mark with a C)
- 10 values that represent the desired culture of your organization (mark with a D)

	Accountability		Diversity		Job security
	Achievement		Ease with uncertainty		Leadership development
	Ambition		Efficiency		Mentoring
	Balance (home/work)		Empire building		Openness
	Being liked		Health & Safety		Personal growth
	Bureaucracy		Environmental awareness		Philanthropy
	Caution		Excellence		Profit
	Clarity		Exploitation		Recognition
	Commitment		Financial stability		Reliability
	Competition		Flat structure		Respect
	Conflict resolution		Global perspective		Self belief
	Conformity		Hierarchy		Short term thinking
	Continuous learning		Humility		Status
	Control		Fun		Team cohesion
	Courage		Information hoarding		Tradition
	Creativity		Information sharing		Trust
	Customer satisfaction		Innovation		Vision

Matches P-C		Matches C-D		Matches P-D		Matches P-C-D	

In recent years, Richard Barratt's focus has turned towards the greater global picture, and he has used the CTT surveys on whole countries to work towards bringing about whole system change in business and the way the world works.

Building a values-driven organization in IT services

Several years ago Niran Jiang and Alex Feher utilized the Cultural Transformation Tools with one of the largest, and fastest growing wholly-owned IT services company in the Asia Pacific region. At the time, Niran and Alex were partners with Sir John Whitmore in the Institute of Human Excellence in Sydney.

The project began with one-on-one interviews with all the senior managers in which a range of issues were identified, including structural impediments, hidden/limiting values, resource misalignment, change weariness, inconsistent management language, rocky communication and minimal collaborations. Three key areas of focus for change were identified:

- Develop values-based leadership capability as a foundation to activate culture change in the organization.
- Shift senior managers' focus from managing results to managing people, and broaden their performance management spectrum to include the intangibles.
- Balance individual excellence with teamwork excellence and create a shared culture identity and organizational cohesion.

An organizational development programme was designed and delivered, which included the following three stages:

Stage I: Leadership values assessment

The objective of this was to understand the performance drivers and barriers of each senior manager for their individual leadership development. The values-based leadership tool described earlier in this chapter was used to provide a diagnosis of the values profile of each individual and the individual's team. Through this assessment, each manager was able to identify his or her leadership development areas, focus and pathways.

Niran and Alex made sure that a confidential environment was created in order to give the managers control of their own assessments, briefing and development process. They were each assured that there would be no reporting back to their own managers, which significantly increased the buy-in and the ownership for the program, and gave all the participants a sense of being 'in the driver's seat'.

Stage II: Leadership retreat

A two-day offsite retreat for leadership training and team building was conducted to link the individual development process with the group work, where individual strengths were explored and built upon within the leadership team context. A consistent leadership framework, language and measurement system was established to activate the development of the team.

Group vision, goals and action plans were created to be worked towards over the next 12 months, and almost all of them stated that the managers were experiencing authentic connections with each other, and a real sense of being a team, for the first time.

Stage III: Tailored leadership coaching

Each manager had the option to elect ongoing 12 sessions of individual coaching on a volunteer basis, paid for out of his or her own budget. The coaching programme was tailored for each individual based on that person's assessment results and developmental goals.

The individual coaching sessions were combined with a group training session. In the middle of their coaching programme, a two-day Inner Game (following the principles of Tim Gallwey's 'Inner Game' techniques described in Chapter 41) session was delivered for the management group to build their people management capabilities and skills. Sport was used as a learning metaphor on the programme for communication, teamwork and management via coaching.

Key qualitative results of the initial programme

Most senior managers at the company gained confidence and self-belief in their capacity to lead and manage people by example, with increased self-knowledge and authenticity. They developed a robust sense of meaning and purpose in their work. Through this intervention, the managers were equipped with models, techniques and skills with which to understand and guide the processes of staff, team and organizational development and transformation. They strengthened and consolidated relationships, and built trust, openness and integrity within their teams, creating high level of performance and enjoyment at work.

There was significant increase in the morale and motivation level across the whole organization. One impact of the new leadership competencies was a sense of increased concern and caring for staff, which directly led to better customer care and higher staff retention. The organization as a whole developed the capacity to prepare its staff and teams to embrace change rather than fear it. The positive change in leadership and culture led to increased customer retention, revenue growth and substantial cost savings.

Key quantitative results of the programme

At the start of the programme, a full-scale Gallup workplace engagement survey was conducted for the whole organization. This same study was repeated 12 months later. During this period of time, the leadership programme was the only external organizational development programme used by this company.

The Gallup study showed a statistically significant improvement throughout the workplace. There were substantial increases in the area of people management capability, especially improvements in 'recognition', 'cares about me', 'opinion count' and 'best friend'.

Market analysts identified the company as a significant contender to become the leading non-multinational IT services organization in the Asia Pacific region and it grew rapidly in terms of finance, customers and locations. Profits came in at above the target level and client retention was excellent. Management team collaboration started to occur at all levels.

41 The Inner Game

SUMMARY

- Timothy Gallwey's background
- The inner opponent
- The Work Triangle
- Non-judgemental awareness
- Self-directed learning
- The Inner Game in team building

Timothy Gallwey's background

In 1971 Harvard graduate Timothy Gallwey took a sabbatical to captain the Harvard tennis team. One day he noticed that when he briefly left the court, a student who had been stuck with a technical problem had improved by the time he returned. He began to realize that people could teach themselves better while working alone than through conventional sports coaching.

Gallwey started to develop methods to enhance this process and named it 'self-directed learning', developing a series of questions and instructions which were aimed at raising the student's awareness of what was happening with the ball, the racket and the student's own body.

The inner opponent

Gallwey theorized that in every player there is a 'Self 1' and a 'Self 2'. Self 1 provides a running commentary on everything that Self 2 does – and the commentary tends to be critical. Self 1 not only reminds Self 2 of the baggage of previous failure, but creates the tension and fear that may beset people when confronted by challenge. In fact, it is Self 1 that creates the worst of the challenge, while throwing all the blame onto Self 2, with inner dialogue like 'You really blew that; you'll never be any good.'

Gallwey found a way of getting round Self 1's interference with instructions like 'focus on the seams of the ball', instead of 'try to hit it in the centre of the racket'. He discovered that directing the student's attention towards something inconsequential in terms of successful playing was a way of shutting out the nagging voice of Self 2. His pupils' techniques improved dramatically.

I witnessed this principle in action on a demonstration by Gallwey at the Queen's Club in London. The volunteer had no experience of tennis at all. Gallwey asked her to say 'bounce' when the ball bounced and 'hit' when it came into contact with the racket of either opponent. The resulting volley lasted for several minutes until Gallwey himself brought it to an end – and she never missed a ball. Because her focus was absorbed in noticing when the ball bounced or hit her racket, the chattering of Self 1 was silenced and her instincts, intuition and unconscious mind were given full play.

This was a visual exercise and Gallwey has also found that listening to the sound the ball makes, and feeling one's grip on the racket, are effective in silencing Self 1 and improving focus. This relates to the VAK (Visual, Auditory and Kinaesthetic) preferences defined by psychologists as early as the 1920s.

We have all experienced times when we were 'in the zone' – for example, a moment when we played the perfect shot, or wrote the right lines, won a deal or played an instrument. The interference of Self 2's critical voice is silenced during these times. The techniques that Gallwey developed help people attain that state. He realized that the real obstacles to playing well lie in the player:

'The opponent within one's own head is more formidable than the one the other side of the net.' (W Timothy Gallwey)

He summed up the effect of Self 1's interference in the theory:

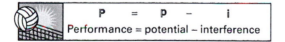

P = p – i
Performance = potential – interference

This bears a similarity to coaching techniques of identifying limiting beliefs (explored in Chapter 4) and Nancy Kline's questions about limiting assumptions (explored in Chapter 42).

After setting out these theories in the best-seller *The Inner Game of Tennis*, Gallwey published four more books applying the Inner Game to golf, skiing, music and *The Inner Game of Work*, written after business managers had started to pick up on the techniques and ask how they could be applied in the workplace. His theories were also discovered by Sir John Whitmore, who developed the principles into performance coaching, applied first in sport and later at work (Whitmore, 2009).

Gallwey's first corporate Inner Game assignment was at AT&T, where he was asked to improve courtesy levels in customer service. He agreed to take on the challenge on the condition that he did not have to mention the word 'courtesy'! The customer's voice became the tennis ball, and operators were asked to identify its tone – for example, loud, soft, angry or nervous – and recognize the tones in their own voices. They started to measure these qualities on a scale of 1–10. The process worked on a number of levels, not only improving the relationships between operators and customers, but providing the operators with a more enjoyable workplace, because what they were doing seemed like a game.

The Work Triangle

One of Gallwey's illuminating models is 'The Work Triangle':

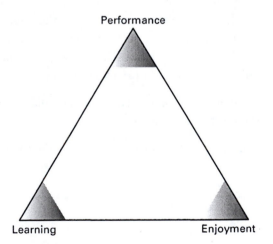

When working under pressure for extended periods, people dream of giving it all up and spending the rest of their lives lying on a beach. However, when holiday time arrives and they are finally at liberty to do exactly that, within a few days restlessness sets in and they are planning sightseeing trips or sporting activities. The Work Triangle illustrates the innate human need to balance the attractions of learning and enjoyment in order to feel contented, satisfied and perform at one's best.

An essential part of the Inner Game process is to identify what Gallwey termed the 'critical variables' – the elements of any situation which matter, as opposed to those that don't. The critical variables are not always the obvious ones and defining them can produce some valuable insights as well as providing guidance on how to move forward.

Non-judgemental awareness

Another core principle of the Inner Game is non-judgemental awareness; simply asking questions to obtain clarity about what is happening in any situation, physically, mentally and emotionally. It is reminiscent of the ancient philosophy of mindfulness, which is also gaining credence in the workplace today and is explored in Chapter 44. For example, if one's neck starts to ache during a long drive, paying attention to what needs to be adjusted – whether position or tension – will ease the pain. An emotional application might be when person A feels angry or resentful at person B. Simply by recognizing these emotions, person A will be able to function alongside the anger without being overwhelmed by it. I have found this particularly useful for clients working in situations where they cannot do much about someone else's behaviour, for example having a boss who is a bully.

Self-directed learning

Although Gallwey's work has contributed on a fundamental level to the field of coaching, these days he is concerned that sometimes the coach's own performance becomes the coach's focal point, instead of that of the client. He stresses the necessity for the coach to step back and allow people to learn for themselves, whether they be managers, sports players or children. The key is 'self-directed learning', which is achieved by keeping the focus on the coachee, not the coach:

> 'In sports, I had to learn how to teach less, so that more could be learned. The same holds true for a coach in business.' (W Timothy Gallwey)

The Inner Game in team building

Inner Game coach Matt Somers finds that Gallwey's techniques can make a real difference in work situations. He recently worked with a government-funded business development agency tasked, in part, with awarding grants to start-up and fledgling businesses to promote sales growth, IT usage, staff development and so on. The business advisers had individual targets for the numbers of clients to be seen and the level of service take-up. At the time Matt was consulted, things were not going well and that quarter's targets were likely to be missed.

Early discussions with some of the advisers revealed that while they had no problem securing appointments with prospective clients, too few of those appointments resulted in signing up for the service. Training had been provided and, although the advisers felt they had picked up some useful techniques, it had not taken them far enough.

Matt decided that his first task was to see whether Inner Game principles could explain what was going on.

Performance = potential − interference

Gallwey's simple formula for defining the Inner Game neatly captured what was happening to the business development advisers. Between their *potential* to achieve results and the actual results they were posting, there was *interference*.

The advisers all had the potential to achieve what was needed, of this there was no doubt. They had been recruited through a well-constructed assessment centre, had appropriate backgrounds and experience, and had been given the necessary training. Nothing needed to be added to the potential, but interference had to be reduced.

At a workshop Matt asked the advisers to consider two sources of interference – external and internal – and to list examples of each. Among other things, they came up with:

EXTERNAL	INTERNAL
• Poor management	• Trying too hard
• Poor relationships	• Negative thoughts
• Policy and procedures	• Self-doubt

It was clear that the external factors would need attention over the longer term and that senior management were already aware of some of the issues. However, it seemed there were some 'quick wins' to be had if the advisers' minds could be refocused away from the sources of internal interference and towards something far more useful instead.

Critical variables

A variable is anything that changes during or between activities. A *critical variable* is one that can have an impact on the outcome. The weather might vary over the course of a day in which an adviser makes four client visits, but that is unlikely to make much difference to his success rate. However, the level of interest shown by the client might equally vary between appointments and this could have a massive impact on the chances of success.

An Inner Game approach to coaching has coach and coachee work together to find the critical variables in a given situation and then choose one to focus upon. Gallwey's findings on the tennis court and in the workplace were that if people were able simply to focus, notice and concentrate on the critical variables – the things that made a difference – performance improvement would take care of itself. This is because a mind that is focused on these details is too busy to pay attention to the self-doubt and negative beliefs that otherwise vie for its attention.

By now Matt's task was becoming clear. He had to work with the group to find one critical variable focus on first, trust in their potential to be great business development advisers and leave them to get on with it.

Matt also felt that he needed to keep the adviser's managers off their backs because these managers were providing a source of interference rather than a means of focus. The managers feared the targets would not be reached and the consequences if that happened. Their apprehension was driving them to micro-manage the advisers and command that they 'try harder'. Unfortunately, trying harder rarely produces a sustainable result, just more anxiety, frustration and exhaustion – more internal interference, in other words.

Matt resolved to teach the managers some basic coaching skills and insist that they allow their advisers to experience three things:

1 **Awareness:** If the advisers could become more present in client interviews, simply more aware of how the client was responding, they would naturally find useful things upon which to focus.

2 **Choice:** The advisers needed to know that they were in control of deciding which aspects of their own performance they wanted to

change and that they were responsible for the outcome. If the managers dictated what they thought needed changing, the advisers would be simply following instructions and there would be no sense of motivation or empowerment.

3 **Trust:** The advisers needed to be believed in. They wanted reassurance that their managers recognized their potential and trusted them to figure out a way to solve the problem.

Playing the Inner Game

After some discussion, it was decided that the advisers should split into two groups. The first group (used as control) was asked to carry on as normal. They would have their usual targets and be asked to do what they had always done. The second (experimental) group was told that they would have no conversion targets at all for a week, because Matt wanted them to find out as much as they could about *how clients show interest*. This had been identified by the advisers as the most important critical variable.

Freed from the interference of worrying about targets and trying hard, the advisers began to tune into their clients and recognize how they showed interest. As the advisers learned more, they were able to identify when they were over-explaining a point or getting too technical.

Armed with this awareness, they quickly and automatically changed tack and became more client-focused, asking more questions and listening more attentively – real and lasting change that came as a result of simply replacing interference with an appropriate point of focus.

In the end

During the week there was a marked take-up of the services the advisers offered, so much so that the following week the control group were asked to take part in the experiment too. The quarterly target was achieved with ease and customer feedback improved dramatically as well.

Of course, the targets were always there, they had never gone away. What changed was the realization that in order to achieve targets people need to be allowed to find their own ways of doing so.

Matt points out that although Gallwey has never written a coaching manual, his ideas can be found within most models and coaching approaches. Coaching people to master their Inner Game requires us to give up the need for control and move away from an overly directive, instructional communication style. Instead we need to develop the ability to ask provocative coaching questions that create a climate of awareness, choice and trust. In such climates, the critical variables in any situation become apparent and we can then focus on them and make natural changes and improvements.

The Inner Game teaches us that learning and doing are not separate things, and we know there has never been a greater need for our people to learn from their daily experiences. In the words of Peter Block, writing in the foreword to Gallwey's *The Inner Game of Work*: 'High performers are simply those people that learn faster.'

42 Nancy Kline's Thinking Environment

SUMMARY

- Origins of the Thinking Environment
- The 10 components of a Thinking Environment
- The Thinking Session
- The Incisive Question™
- The power of listening
- The Thinking Partnership in action

Origins of the Thinking Environment

The origins of the Thinking Environment are steeped in one observation and one question. The observation is: 'The quality of everything we do depends on the quality of the thinking we do first', a statement that has powerful implications. The consequent question is: 'What does it take for people to help each other to think well for themselves?' (Kline, 1999, 2009)

Nancy Kline was articulating this observation and asking the question more than two decades ago, after she had founded a school in her native United States. When she put the question to people, she noticed that the answer tended not to be about IQ, education, or experience. It turned out that the single most important factor in the quality of someone's thinking was the way people were being treated by those around them. Nancy went on to identify 10 ways that were most dependable in this regard, and these became known as the 10 components of a Thinking Environment:

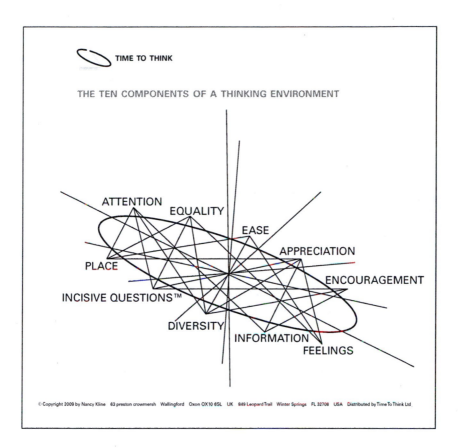

The 10 components of a Thinking Environment

The components are:

1 **Attention**: Listening with palpable respect and without interruption.

2 **Equality**: Treating each other as thinking peers; Giving equal turns and attention; Keeping agreements and boundaries.

3 **Ease**: Offering freedom from internal rush or urgency.

4 **Appreciation**: Offering genuine acknowledgement of a person's qualities; Practicing a 5:1 ratio of appreciation to criticism.

5 **Encouragement**: Giving courage to go to the cutting edge of ideas by moving beyond internal competition.

6 **Feelings**: Allowing sufficient emotional release to restore thinking.

7 **Information:** Supplying the facts; Dismantling denial.

8 **Diversity:** Welcoming divergent thinking and diverse group identities.

9 **Incisive Questions**™: Removing assumptions that limit our ability to think for ourselves clearly and creatively.

10 **Place:** Creating a physical environment that says back to people, 'You matter'.

The Thinking Session

A Thinking Environment can exist between two people – a Thinking Partnership, comprising Thinker (coachee) and Partner (coach) – or in a group, at a think tank or any other type of meeting.

To me, the most important factor of the Thinking Environment described above is the quality of attention in the listening. The type of listening that Nancy encourages is not inactive. She describes it as profound attention bestowed on the Thinker by the Partner and that, for an effective session, this attention needs to be an equal balance of three streams:

'In the first stream the Partner's attention is on the content of what the Thinker is saying.

In the second stream their attention is on their response to what the Thinker is saying.

In the third stream their attention is on the creation of a Thinking Environment for the Thinker.' (Kline, 1999)

Her theories are supported by practical structures that enable the Thinker to work through issues, gain some clarity and find a way forward.

The Thinking Session takes place in three parts, starting with a simple question: 'What would you like to think about and what are your thoughts?'

The Thinker, who we will call 'he', is then able to talk through his situation at will. The key here lies in two elements: the quality of attention given by the Partner, who we will call she, and the Thinker's knowledge that he will not be interrupted. Therefore it is important that a 'contracting' process takes place prior to the conversation, where the Partner explains the process and promises not to interrupt, so that the Thinker knows he will be allowed adequate time to voice his thoughts. Eventually, the Thinker is likely to reach a point where it seems everything has been said. He will pause and the Thinking Partner can then ask: 'What more do you think, or feel or want to say?'

The phrase 'what more' acknowledges and honours what has gone before, while encouraging further thinking, and the Thinker may be surprised at how many different thoughts come to mind. Because he is in the Thinking Environment created by the Partner, he has the leisure to express and explore these thoughts, and it is a fact that we often find out what we think by talking out loud.

'What more?' questions can be asked repeatedly until the Thinker has nothing further to reveal. At this point he is ready to identify his true goals and the Partner can facilitate this by asking: 'What more do you want to achieve in this session?'

This is likely to trigger a whole new set of thoughts, and the Partner can encourage the Thinker to marshal these into a short, concise goal which will be easy to remember, which aligns with the EXACT goal-setting process described in Chapter 24.

Then the Partner can help him identify what is holding him back by asking: 'What are you assuming that is stopping you from xxx?'

This question can be asked repeatedly until the Thinker has identified all of his limiting assumptions.

The Incisive Question

At this point it is time for what Nancy terms an 'Incisive Question'™, for example: 'If you knew you would be listened to, what would you say, and to whom?'

Some similar questions might be:

- What assumption are you making that is getting in the way?
- If you knew you were to become the boss, what problem would you solve first and how?
- If you knew you are vital to this organization's success, how would you approach your work?
- If things could be exactly right for you, how would they have to change?

The Thinking Environment is highly effective in group work and meetings. One of the techniques here is the 'Thinking Round', which ensures everyone has a chance to say all they want to. As is the case with the Thinking Partnership, it is the contracting at the start of the meeting which brings the value.

'To be interrupted is not good.

To get lucky and not be interrupted is better.

But to know you will not be interrupted allows you truly to think for yourself.'
(Nancy Kline)

The principles of the Thinking Environment bear similarities to coaching, which was being developed during the same time period. Both are fundamentally about respecting people, caring for their welfare and development, and building relationships grounded in trust. Some of the processes parallel tools used in coaching, such as Clean Language, which is explored in Chapter 28, and the limiting beliefs explored in Chapter 4.

One difference to coaching is that Kline does not recommend reflecting the Thinker's words back, a coaching technique explored in Chapter 19. Having experienced being coached by Nancy Kline at a demonstration, I found myself wishing that she would interrupt with the usual coaching interventions of clarifying, reflecting and questioning. However, I eventually identified that the root of my need was to create a distraction so that I could avoid facing some difficult issues! When presented nothing other than 'What more?' from Nancy, I was forced to face these issues and, as a result, reached an unexpected breakthrough. Having said that, I would not dismiss the interventionist coaching techniques from the coach's skill set, as they can be effective in creating rapport and helping to focus the mind in a variety of situations.

The power of listening

Kline's work highlights the effectiveness of giving people 'a good listening to' (my words, not hers). There is much debate among coaches, especially those in training, as to the most effective questions to ask, what supplementary techniques will lead to new insights for the client, what structures to use and how to 'dance' with the client in the coaching conversation. If we are not careful, the end result can be a coach who gallops all over clients like an enthusiastic pony, focusing on being a star performer and begetter of solutions instead of concentrating on the coachee's own experience.

When it comes to her own life, Kline walks the talk. Her courses take place in a stunning riverside environment and include not only comfortable surroundings but excellent lunches! All the other nine principles of the Thinking Environment are respected too, particularly in terms of listening and authentic appreciation, and she relates how she and her husband regularly provide each other with thinking time at home.

The biggest takeaway for me from the time I spent studying with Nancy is a reinforcement of the power of listening, giving quality attention, and contracting to do so at the start, so that my coachees, or 'Thinkers', have to focus only on their own thought processes without any distractions.

The Thinking Partnership in action

Ruth McCarthy, a Time to Think coach and consultant, uses the techniques with clients like Sarah (not her real name), who at the time of their work together was preparing her degree exhibition at a London art college. With only three months to go, she felt stuck, unmotivated to complete the work and unable to face her head of department.

Ruth explained the process and principles behind the Thinking Environment, establishing the contract for their work together, and then began with the first question: 'What do you want to think about, and what are your thoughts?'

Sarah thought and spoke for quite some time about her schooling, the poor A-level results she had obtained despite excellent GCSEs, her inability to get on with her current studies and a sense of personal failure.

When she came to a halt, instead of summarizing or asking a question as most coaches would, Ruth waited. It was vital not to interrupt at a moment when a clear new idea might be emerging. Only when Sarah said 'That's enough for now', did Ruth pose her second question: 'What more do you think, or feel, or want to say?' This affirming question honoured all the work done so far and encouraged deeper thinking.

It led to a flood of new concerns and doubts about how Sarah was seen by her peer group and tutors, and she spoke of a deep-seated fear of having to show her work in public.

Still Ruth did nothing to interrupt Sarah's thinking process, asking only 'What more?'

Sarah revealed just how strong was her fear and how much it held her back. She said she felt 'paralysed by her own inaction'.

When Sarah had finally confirmed that she had finished expressing all her current thoughts, Ruth moved on to Part Two of the process, aimed at identifying Sarah's goal, and asked: 'What more do you want to achieve in this session?' By asking for more, Ruth was acknowledging what had already been achieved during the session alongside a specific request to nudge her thoughts towards a solution-focused outcome, which is in line with all types of coaching. At this point they were 40 minutes into a 90-minute session.

Initially Sarah ran through possible ways of finishing her exhibition work, and then said 'I want to apply myself to finishing – I know it's so important, why can't I do it?'

Part of the process is to encourage the Thinker to express the goal concisely in a way that is easy to remember. Sarah confirmed that her further goal was 'Applying myself to finishing my exhibition'.

They moved on to Part Three of the Thinking Session and Ruth asked Sarah the first assumption question: 'What are you assuming that is stopping you from applying yourself to finishing your exhibition?'

This triggered a whole series of assumptions that Sarah's peer group would not respect her work, and how that might make her feel even more useless.

Ruth continued to explore this area by asking several times, 'What else are you assuming that stops you from applying yourself to finishing?' until Sarah came to a halt.

The next step was to identify the chief assumption, so Ruth asked Sarah, 'Out of those assumptions, or any others that spring to mind, which is the one most stopping you from applying yourself to finishing?'

Ruth was careful to use Sarah's exact words when repeating back the goal. Words contain a universe of meanings and if we use our words instead of the Thinker's, then the Thinker will have to navigate through a new universe to retrieve the original meaning.

Sarah examined her assumptions until suddenly she said very firmly: 'I'm assuming that my work will be worse than everyone else's, and they'll think I'm stupid.'

Ruth took this as the chief assumption and, again using Sarah's words, tested it with the question: 'Do you think it is true that your work will be worse than everyone else's and they'll think you're stupid?'

Sarah hesitated, visibly struggling, and then replied: 'I know deep down that my work can't be worse than everyone else's, it just feels like it will be.'

Ruth asked for reasons and Sarah listed hastiness, lack of preparation and previous failures, but it was obvious that she was not convinced. There seemed to be a contradiction in that although the three criteria of logic, information and positive philosophical choice did not support the chief assumption, Sarah retained a strong sense of belief that it was true.

So Ruth asked an 'invitation question': 'Given that the assumption that your work will be worse than everyone else's and they'll think you're stupid is stopping you from applying yourself to finishing your exhibition, what do you credibly need to assume in order to apply yourself and finish it?' It was a necessarily long phrase, containing all Sarah's key words, which would resonate much more deeply with her than a paraphrase or Ruth's own words.

In fact Sarah asked for the question to be repeated before replying: 'I'd have to assume that my work is as good as anyone else's and that I have enough time.'

Now they were able to move on to the Incisive Question: 'If you knew that your work is as good as anyone else's and you have enough time, how would you apply yourself to finishing the exhibition?'

Sarah's face cleared and she answered without hesitation: 'I'd ring my tutor today when I leave you, and go and see him, and get this sorted out.' Her voice strengthened: 'Then I'd get my portfolio together and work out what I can use and what pieces I need to start from scratch. And then I'd look at the weeks, and slot in the time I need for each piece...' Her voice tailed off and she looked at Ruth expectantly.

Ruth simply came back with the same question, slightly differently phrased (which aligns with the iterative questions of David Grove, described in Chapter 29):

'If you knew that your work is as good as anyone else's and you have enough time, how else would you apply yourself to finishing?'

'I'd ask my sister to help with this – she'd do it without annoying me. And I'll take my computer out of my room; I waste so much time on it.'

Ruth offered the Incisive Question again but this time Sarah replied 'That's enough I think. Now I just want to ring my tutor!' She sat quietly for a moment and then said: 'This is amazing – I really feel excited about doing this. I can't believe it!' Ruth invited Sarah to write down her Incisive Question and to create an action plan, which Sarah found herself able to do without any difficulty. Finally Ruth offered an appreciation of a quality she had noticed during the session and shared how much she appreciated her honesty and wry humour.

Three months later Ruth received an e-mail from Sarah informing her that the exhibition had been a great success, that her overall result was a 2:2 – not as good as she had hoped when she started the course, but a great deal better than she had feared in at the time of their meeting. And she added: 'Something changed for me during that session – I suddenly knew I could do it. Isn't it amazing how much our assumptions can hold us back?'

43 Appreciative Inquiry

SUMMARY

- Origins of Appreciative Inquiry
- The four stages of Discovery, Dream, Design and Destiny
- Appreciative Inquiry in the United Arab Emirates

Origins of Appreciative Inquiry

Appreciative Inquiry is an organizational change methodology developed by David Cooperrider, Professor of Organizational Behaviour at Case Western Reserve University in Ohio.

AI, as it is commonly known, appears to have its roots in the changes in psychology, which came about during the 1950s. Previously, psychologists such as Freud and Jung focused on what was wrong with people and how to fix it. The solution focus shift that occurred around the middle of the last century, piloted by psychologists such as Maslow and Perls, moved attention from the problem to the potential for excellence. This is explored in more detail in Chapter 1.

AI can be used with individuals, organizations (as above) or even countries. The questions asked and exercises undertaken assume the subjects to have all the resources and talent required to identify and be their best. The AI processes are designed to uncover and tap into possibly hidden knowledge that will result in self-correction and a natural, organic progression to the subjects fulfil their inherent potential. This description fits coaching too, which is why AI fits well into the coach's toolbox.

The four stages of Discovery, Dream, Design and Destiny

Appreciative Inquiry progresses through four key stages, which correspond to the standard coaching GROW model, albeit in a slightly different order:

DISCOVERY:	Looking at the best of what is working at the moment
DREAM:	Envisioning the best that could happen
DESIGN:	Working out how to achieve the vision
DESTINY:	Allowing this achievement to emerge naturally, collaboratively and by using existing resources

The 'Discovery' stage aligns with the coaching exploration of Reality described in Chapter 23 on the GROW model. In the case of an individual, this could comprise extensive questions about what is happening at the moment, what impact it is having, who else is involved, how much, how many and what has happened up to now. An organization might run a series of surveys and interviews with its staff and directors, plus focus groups and workshops to ascertain where the workforce is at present.

DISCOVERY QUESTIONS

- What impact it is having?
- Who else is involved?
- How much?
- How many?
- What has happened up to now?
- How important is each aspect?
- What are the qualities and special gifts that you bring?
- What gives life to the organization?
- Recall a time you were excited to be part of this organization

The 'Dream' stage matches the Goal stage of the GROW model. An individual would be asked questions that throw the focus forward to the perfect desired state, exploring what might be described as 'future reality'.

DREAM QUESTIONS

- What is the world calling this organization to become?
- What would success look like?
- What will you see, hear, feel?
- What will be different?
- What do you really want?
- What is the best that could happen?
- What kinds of partnerships might you wish for?

To complete this stage, an organization could continue with surveys, interviews and workshops, giving permission to and encouraging people to speak their minds about how they would like the organization to be, what values they would like to see it exhibit, what changes they would like to see in place and what the organization might achieve.

In both cases the more tangible and measurable the answers, the more motivating the vision will be to the people involved.

'Design' is the GROW model's Options phase. By this time people will be feeling quite energetic and keen to make changes, whether as individuals or employees. The nature of this phase is to 'think outside the box' and come up with all the changes that could possibly happen, however ambitious they seem. People brainstorm how to achieve their vision, what systems need to be changed or put in place, what attitudes might change and how these outcomes could be achieved.

DESIGN QUESTIONS

- How will you do it?
- What could you do?
- Who could help?
- What are your options?
- What systems might support the vision?
- What processes, structures and relationships do you need to create or change to make the vision a reality?

The final stage, eloquently termed 'Destiny', reflects the Will section of the GROW model. In this phase, the individual or group will work out a plan to which they can commit. In the case of an organization, this stage will involve the overhaul and pulling together of systems, departments and individuals to achieve the vision. It is vital at this stage that people's ideas are explored, supported and validated, and that they are given ownership of carrying out the plans.

DESTINY QUESTIONS

- What will you do?
- In what time frame?
- What resources will you allocate?
- What roles will people play?

It is interesting that in both the AI and the GROW models, the word 'actions' is not used for this stage, although taking action is what is required here. Both the terms 'destiny' and 'will' (signifying commitment towards action) are aspirational rather than simply about practical steps. There has to be a sense of being on the right path to achieve the vision, and in this attitude, pitfalls, adjustments and challenges that show up along the way can be handled without loss of enthusiasm or conviction. The new vision must be allowed to unfold in its own way, integrating surprises and ideas that crop up along the way, and calling upon existing resources, particularly the various individuals within the organization.

It is essential that the lines of questioning throughout the process are positively framed. Rather than asking about the problems that exist and how to troubleshoot them, ask people to describe what they would like to see in place. Everyone in the organization should take part; the questions do not have to be asked by an army of consultants, as a series of questions can be designed by a facilitator and delivered by various levels of staff throughout the organization.

The 'miracle question' of solution focused brief therapy, developed by Steve de Shazer and Milton Erickson and described in Chapter 1, is a good model for an AI question.

Appreciative Inquiry treats an organization as a phenomenon to be celebrated, in all its diverse and conflicting glory, rather than as a problem to be solved. Every individual working there is regarded as having something of value to contribute to the whole. An artist viewing a landscape in order to paint it does not look for the faults in the landscape but for the best aspects that he or she could portray. Similarly, AI searches for all that is valuable and special about an organization and its individuals, whatever form that may take. Out of recognizing and giving voice to these elements will evolve the means to change.

A case history which David Cooperrider has recorded concerns an organization with a chronic sexual harassment problem. After two years of training, the problem was becoming worse not better and employees reported that they felt even less able to communicate with the opposite sex than before the remedies had started.

Cooperrider's approach was to start by asking the simple question 'What do you really want to do?'.

Predictably, the first response told him what the organization wanted to stop doing: 'We want to dramatically cut the incidence of sexual harassment.'

Cooperrider countered with: 'What would that look like?'

The reply came back: 'What we really want is to be a model of positive, cross-gender working relationships!'

This demonstrates how the focus was shifted from problem to goal, or the 'Dream' phase of AI.

> 'What distinguishes AI is that every carefully crafted question is positive. Knowing and changing are a simultaneous moment. The thrill of discovery becomes the thrill of creating. As people throughout a system connect in serious study into qualities, examples, and analysis of the positive core – each appreciating and everyone being appreciated – hope grows and community expands.' (Cooperrider, 2008)

Appreciative Inquiry in the United Arab Emirates

Michael Daly is an international coach and mentor. He combined a number of methodologies including Appreciative Inquiry to work with a company in the United Arab Emirates (UAE). The company had been formed during the 1980s as a wholly-owned subsidiary of a regional trading organization. Initially successful, it had gradually lost market share until in 2005 it posted its first negative profit statement. The owners decided that the situation called for a basic examination of its business model and strategy. Instead of commissioning a typical business turnaround consultant, the owners decided to try corporate coaching to produce a sustainable change in business performance.

Methodology

Michael was careful to try to understand the company without being adversely affected by its past performance. It is generally better to accept what one has as the starting point without delving too far into previous problems which can lead to apportioning blame and having low expectations of future performance.

The senior executives were given a number of psychometric tests to improve their awareness of themselves and their colleagues. The systems used to achieve this included Belbin team roles, DISC profiles and Apter motivational styles. Each executive was asked to share the results, which initially met with some reluctance, but the reports helped everyone to understand why they needed to tailor their communications with certain individuals and explained some of the past problems and personnel conflicts.

The Belbin system allowed 360-degree feedback and the Apter system allowed 180-degree feedback, which helped the executives appreciate the impact their style was having on the motivation of their teams.

Each executive was then asked to complete a subjective assessment of the company's performance using a simple balance wheel chart. The assessments were carried out independently and anonymously with the results being displayed at a joint meeting. There was a reasonable amount of variation in the assessments which averaged out to produce the profile shown below:

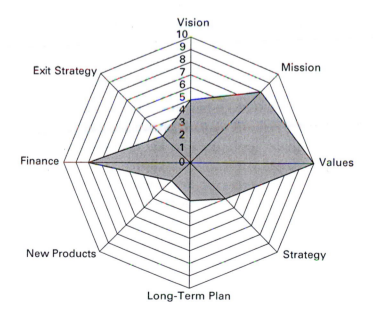

The overall assessment suggested that although the organization exhibited strong corporate values and, thanks to the parent organization was financially strong, it lacked vision and hence direction.

The next technique Michael used was Appreciative Inquiry. This helped everyone understand that the company was good at some things and that these should be concentrated on to provide some much needed motivation. Most of the executives had received a typical Western business management education, which focuses to a large extent on identifying and then solving problems. A significant focus on problems can give the impression there are only problems and that this is a 'problem organization'. This type of negative feedback can be very demotivating and does not fit well within a coaching culture.

As Michael is based in the United Kingdom, the logistics of coaching an organization a few thousand miles away had to be thought through. The project was divided into phases with the first phase comprising the psychometric tests, which took place in the UAE over the space of a week. During this time the tests were completed and feedback given during a series of one-to-one and group sessions.

Over the following two months the implications of the psychometric tests were considered during a once per week conference call.

Phase two comprised the Appreciative Inquiry section, for which Michael again spent a week in the UAE, and which was followed up with the regular weekly conference call.

Phase three was the change implementation and monitoring phase, which also involved visits to the UAE and weekly conference calls.

Outcome

The outcome from the psychometric tests, including the 360- and 180-degree feedback, was an acknowledgement that the organization still employed an old-fashioned command, control and coerce management style. This produced demotivated employees who did not feel they were allowed to contribute to corporate tactics and certainly not to corporate strategy.

It was also at this point the executives realized that Michael was not there to provide them with answers, like the type of consultant they were used to, but instead would help them to find their own answers through coaching questions. He did, however, suggest that they did some background reading and recommended *The Art of War* and *36 Stratagems* by Sun Tzu.

Coaching

Michael began by using an NLP technique called 'value elicitation' to enable the executives to articulate their corporate values and define the type of organization they wanted. The background reading they had completed suggested that they had been managing rather than providing leadership; they decided they would like to have leadership at all levels of the organization as well.

From the mass of results and feedback Michael facilitated them in identifying three main goals and the strategies they would use to implement them. It was at this point that the first change in approach occurred, when they decided to delegate the tactical plan and actions to more junior staff. This freed the executives to concentrate on strategy and to start putting into place new commercial agreements with suppliers and customers.

Subsequent coaching sessions concentrated on moving towards the strategic goals and ensuring that the tactical plans were aligned with those goals.

Results

Through corporate coaching, an organization that had been performing badly for years turned itself around. Managers became leaders, new markets were entered, individuals worked as team members, absenteeism disappeared and hierarchical structures were dismantled. Sales and profits increased to a point that the return on investment for corporate coaching was greater than 10 times within the first year.

The company continued to grow and some of its strategies were adopted by its parent organization. Individual executives continued to receive one-to-one coaching and became keen to introduce a coaching culture into the whole organization. As part of succession planning, a mixture of coaching and mentoring was used to develop future executive leaders. New goals were developed in consultation with all the employees and increasingly with customers.

44 Mindfulness

SUMMARY

- History of mindfulness
- Relaxation exercises
- Mindfulness in Yoga and other practices
- Mindfulness in conflict
- Mindfulness questions
- Mindfulness at work

History of mindfulness

'The secret of health for both mind and body is not to mourn for the past, worry about the future, or anticipate troubles, but to live in the present moment wisely and earnestly'
—Buddha

The practice of mindfulness has its roots in ancient disciplines, such as the Buddhist principle of 'calm acceptance', and is now becoming part of the Western set of tools for managing mental and physical state. Mindfulness has been combined with cognitive behavioural coaching, stress reduction, meditation and yoga to name just a few areas, and there are claims that it can help with health disorders and bring about cures. It is a simple technique that can be applied at any moment in any situation for clarity, understanding, relaxation and comfort.

Relaxation exercises

The essence of mindfulness is to take notice of what his happening internally and externally at any given moment. The key is not to make any judgement about what is found there.

For example, the following mindful meditation can provide a quick path to relaxation:

- Sit comfortably straight in a chair with your feet flat on the ground and your hands in your lap. Preferably do not lean against the back of the chair.

- Notice your breathing, how you bring the air into your body and how you let it out.

- Notice what thoughts come to your mind: there will always be thoughts – that is what minds do. Do not make any judgement about what comes to mind, just bring your attention back to your breath.

- Do a body scan, again without making any judgement, and notice where there is tension, pain, or a good feeling. How do your feet feel in contact with the ground, your thighs in contact with the chair?

- Continually notice when your thoughts stray and bring them back to your breath and your body.

Only five minutes of this simple meditation can produce changes to the mental and physical state, and the process can be continued for as long as required.

One of the reasons for the recent rise in popularity of mindfulness is that it satisfies the criteria of our times that techniques have to be fast and easy. Not many of today's pressured executives, professionals, spouses or parents have the time or energy for concentrated application. It is particularly pertinent during this time of recession, where people have to accept situations that cannot be changed. Permitting oneself to experience life in the moment without making any judgement brings a remarkable level of comfort, serenity and even a sense of happiness in the face of unchangeable adversity.

Mindfulness in yoga and other practices

Another useful application of mindfulness is during the practice of physical exercise like walking, yoga, swimming or going to the gym. My personal experience of this is that, having practised yoga for 30 years, I can now stretch to levels not reached for two decades. It has stepped up the enjoyment of my daily practice too.

Mindfulness in conflict

A Mindful approach is useful in corporate coaching, for example with coachees who feel trapped in relationships with colleagues or bosses with whom they have nothing in common; it helps people to manage their relationships with people who have different values, behaviours and styles of communication, particularly bullies or manipulative managers. Noticing the feelings of frustration, rage, impotence and anxiety which may arise during a meeting with such a person, without passing judgement on those feelings (for example, 'It's not fair,' or 'I should be able to handle this'), can enable people to function alongside their emotional storm without being overwhelmed by it. There is no guilt, no 'should' or 'must' in mindfulness, just an acceptance that 'it is what it is'. The key is simply to notice emotions as they arise and, without trying to change them, without deciding whether they are helpful or unhelpful, without judging oneself as a better or worse person, just refocusing the mind on the current situation and allowing those emotions to exist or pass.

Most of us in the developed world today are fixated in the past or the future. Mindfulness anchors us in the present, allowing us to appreciate the moment or grieve for whatever discomfort we are suffering.

Mindfulness questions

Some coaching questions to promote mindfulness in a coachee are:

- How is this affecting you?
- What are you experiencing in your body?
- What are you seeing?
- What are you hearing?
- What are you feeling?
- To what extent?

Another aspect of where mindfulness can be useful is the need that people have to be in control, rooted in our earliest heritage of living in caves, where control over one's environment meant the difference between life and death. Fighting a political battle at work can trigger emotional echoes of those prehistoric battles, eliciting panic feelings of 'fight or flight' in the hypothalamus area of the brain which sets off the production of adrenalin. If we simply recognize that feeling and acknowledge it, we may find that we can function as normal alongside it instead of being engulfed. Similarly, it is possible to recognize desires without being controlled by them.

We tend to focus on what we have categorized as good – for example being loved, being right, being financially secure – and if we notice what is happening at all we are tempted to change what we are conditioned to judge as bad – fear, anger, anxiety. We often live for years with the mantra, 'If I can just get this I will be happy', but no sooner is 'this' achieved than there is another 'this' on the horizon, whether it be money, job, partner, family, expertise or whatever else can be hankered after. The practice of mindfulness helps to bring about calm, an enjoyment of the present and an appreciation of what we have now, enabling us to rise to challenges more calmly and keep a healthy sense of perspective in our lives.

Mindfulness at work

One of the leading exponents of mindfulness in the United Kingdom is Liz Hall, the Editor of *Coaching at Work* magazine. She tells me that she recently worked with a client whom we will call Marie (not her real name), a manager in the public sector. Marie came to coaching at a time of widespread uncertainty in her organization. She was unsure whether she would still have a job further down the line and wanted to explore potential alternative options for her future.

It soon became apparent that Marie was not only finding it hard to cope at work, but at home as well. She was having trouble sleeping and had recently experienced a panic attack. She described feeling like a 'bundle of nerves' and struggled to maintain harmonious relationships with colleagues and family members. Performing well at work was very important to her, yet at a time when arguably the spotlight was more on her performance than ever, she was, in her words, 'making a pig's ear out of everything' – messing things up.

Liz noticed that Marie sounded breathless as she recounted her story, and that her facial features looked pinched. Before attempting to explore future plans, which might overwhelm rather than inspire Marie, Liz felt that it was important to move her into a more resourceful state.

As a 'mindful coach', mindfulness underpins all the work that Liz does, helping her to be more emotionally intelligent, creative and able to read data from herself and from others. Her mindfulness practice underlies all that she does and is, rendering her more present and able to attune to others. She does not always work with it explicitly or call it mindfulness. Sometimes the practice can manifest through working on emotional intelligence, stress management or resilience, for example. As a matter of course she frequently shares with clients her own insights and what she may have noticed about them, always careful to do it with as little judgement and attachment to outcome as she can muster.

In this case, it felt appropriate to share with Marie how her story, and the way she was 'being', impacted on Liz. Attending mindfully to what was arising in her own field of experience in the moment, Liz shared that she was feeling panicky and contracted in her stomach. Her shoulders had become hunched and she felt somewhat paralyzed. Liz asked whether that was how Marie was feeling. Marie nodded and her eyes filled with tears.

Liz suggested a breathing exercise to help to shift Marie from this state and led her through an 'awareness of breath' mindfulness practice for about five minutes, first encouraging her to relax her shoulders and jaw, move her head from side to side, straighten her back (but not arch it), and to feel her feet on the floor. She invited Marie to approach the practice with curiosity, non-judgement and compassion. Compassion is a core component of mindfulness, yet we often seem to find it hard to be kind towards ourselves.

After the practice, Liz invited Marie to share what was going on in her body at that point. Marie said her breathing seemed deeper and slower and that there was less contraction in her stomach. Then Liz employed a model called FEEL, which she developed specifically for working with mindfulness in coaching.

Liz invited her to turn towards the contraction. What did it look like? What did it feel like? Did it have a shape, a colour, a form, a name; how big was it, and so on?

Marie described a large 'gloopy mustard-coloured mass with blurry edges', 'screwed into her insides'. It did not have a name.

Liz asked what emotions Marie could find there and Marie replied that there was fear all over her body, not just in her stomach.

Liz invited her to shine a spotlight onto this fear, and to sit with it rather than reject it, embracing it gently like a baby. More tears followed.

And then Liz asked Marie if she wanted to let the fear go. Marie responded that she was not ready, because the fear was keeping her safe, so Liz let that be and reminded Marie to be compassionate towards herself in the future.

A fluid model for bringing in mindfulness

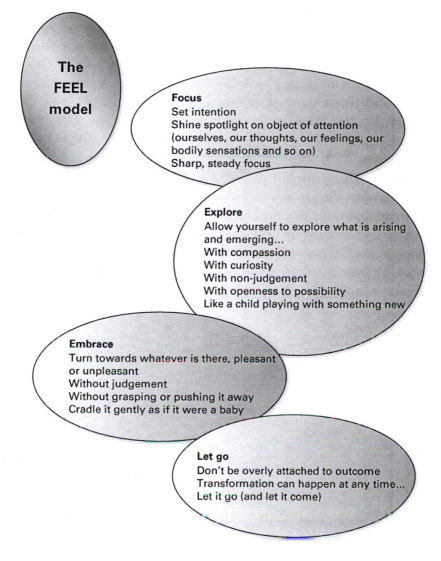

The FEEL model

Focus
Set intention
Shine spotlight on object of attention
(ourselves, our thoughts, our feelings, our
bodily sensations and so on)
Sharp, steady focus

Explore
Allow yourself to explore what is arising
and emerging...
With compassion
With curiosity
With non-judgement
With openness to possibility
Like a child playing with something new

Embrace
Turn towards whatever is there, pleasant
or unpleasant
Without judgement
Without grasping or pushing it away
Cradle it gently as if it were a baby

Let go
Don't be overly attached to outcome
Transformation can happen at any time...
Let it go (and let it come)

Liz instigated a 'landing' practice before starting each session, in order to leave any baggage that might distract Marie behind, such as a hectic journey on public transport. This helped Marie to be more grounded in her own senses so that she could start each session in a creative, resourceful state.

Over subsequent sessions, Marie and Liz worked with more mindfulness practices, both within the sessions and as 'homework'. Marie reported that she was sleeping more soundly and getting on better with her colleagues, but still not as well as she would have liked with her husband.

One of the practices used during the sessions was the 'loving kindness meditation' (also known as the 'befriending meditation'), in which one extends loving kindness to oneself, a loved one, someone neutral, someone disliked, and the whole of humanity, in that order. Marie initially struggled with the first, but gradually started to find it easier, particularly when she imagined herself as a child. She said she had stopped 'beating myself up with a stick'. And the fear gradually subsided.

Marie reported being much more able to see the bigger picture at work, to think strategically and to come up with more creative solutions to issues as they arose.

Liz invited her to explore possible future career options, some of which Marie found exciting, but it soon became clear that her attitude had changed. She reported that she now felt more able to 'ride it out' and see what happened next in her current position, that she was continuing to include mindfulness in her life, especially the short breathing practices, and that she no longer has panic attacks. She said that she was finding it easier to get along and stay calm with those around her, including her husband.

45

Elizabeth Kubler Ross's Change Curve six stage model

SUMMARY

- The six stages of the Change Curve
- Development from grief counselling
- Uses in coaching
- Application to organizational change

The six stages of the Change Curve

One of the greatest challenges that face corporate workers today is constant and unwanted change through mergers, acquisitions, redundancies, frequent changes of staff at every level, new systems and changes in policy.

The Change Curve was devised by Elizabeth Kubler Ross (1926–2004) a Swiss psychiatrist who worked extensively with the bereaved and dying and was a key founder in the hospice movement. She noticed a pattern of reaction to news of impending death, which went through stages of denial, anger, bargaining, depression and finally acceptance.

A number of variations on Kubler Ross's original stages have taken their place in corporate management training, and a reasonable representation of the corporate model is shown in Figure 45.1.

One of Kubler Ross's theories was that the key element needed to deal with change is time, but managers today rarely have that luxury. I recently worked with 20 managers from a major financial institution who, on being

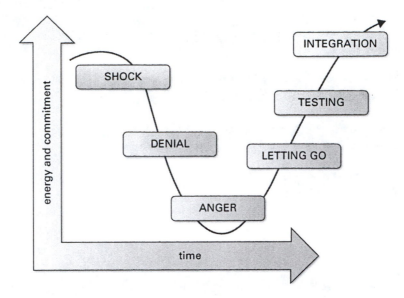

asked where they were on the Change Curve, said that they went through the whole curve every day and expected to continue that way for the next two years.

Looking at the model can alleviate some of the stress when people realize that emotions of anger and despair are normal human reactions, that they are not alone in these feelings and that there is hope that in time they will pass.

The coach can contribute firstly by asking coachees to consider whereabouts they are in the six stages and secondly by asking where they would like to be. This will create new perspectives and give people the realization that they have a choice, if not in the situation itself, at least about their own reaction to it. This will in turn give them a sense of control, raising their energy and shrinking problems.

Bruce Tuckman's 'forming, storming, norming and performing' team development model

46

SUMMARY

- The four elements of team development
- Addition of 'adjourning'
- Additions of 'mourning' and 'dorming'
- Recommendations for teams and team leaders

The four elements of team development

Creating and maintaining cohesive teams is a challenge in today's world of cyclonic corporate change, where relationships are made and changed through global mergers, demergers, portfolio careers, cost cutting redundancies and a widespread lack of ability in organizations to nurture and retain their home grown talent.

Addition of 'adjourning'

Over the past 40 years, Bruce Tuckman's classic model has provided insights and guidance to managers and team members. Tuckman created the model in 1965 and a decade later added a fifth element, *adjourning*, to describe the disengagement of a team after its project is completed. The model was part of a growing awareness of the extent to which the success of a business depends upon the relationships between its people.

Tuckman's stages of group development

Additions of 'mourning' and 'dorming'

Facilitators sometimes add two further stages: 'mourning' for the sense of loss and regrouping that has to take place when a member leaves the team, and 'dorming', which means the team is stagnating and needs new challenges.

Recommendations for teams and team leaders

Tuckman first published the FSNP model in an article for the *Psychological Bulletin*. He has continued to develop many aspects of organizational psychology without much reference to this early model and, at the time of writing, is a professor at the Ohio State University, yet the FSNP model has gained increasing momentum purely on the strength of its own elegance and usefulness.

The model describes how the team members first come together, welcoming, polite and not a little wary, how they may experience conflict while establishing their positions, how the boundaries are eventually and sometimes tortuously established and, if all goes well, how the team reaches a place of stability where it can perform to the best of its combined abilities.

The stages Dr Tuckman identified are set out below, accompanied by guidance on how the team leader can best guide the team through each stage.

Stage	Behaviour
Forming	
Each member of the team focuses on the leader, accepting only the leader's guidance and authority and maintaining a polite but distant relationship with the others. During this stage the leader must be seen to be open with information and ready to answer questions. Boundaries, strengths and weaknesses will be tested, including those of the leader. There may be baggage from the way people have been treated in the past, which could result in some clinging to the old ways if their experience was positive, or suspicion and apathy if not.	*Time invested by the leader and the team members in listening to and empathizing with the others will pay off substantially further down the line. Expectations and job descriptions should be clearly laid out and the leader should role model the behaviour he or she would like to see the team exhibit.*

(Continued)

Stage	Behaviour
Storming	
This is a difficult time for all. Team members are more concerned with the impression they are making than the project in hand, wanting to earn respect, battling feelings of inadequacy, wondering who will support or undermine them, and above all wishing to prove to the leader their value to the team. There is a danger of factions forming and some members becoming isolated.	*Each member should focus on delivering as much sincere positive feedback to the others as they can, working towards stable relationships where suggestions will be viewed as contributions rather than criticisms. Let go of the small stuff. Encourage people to do things in their own way wherever possible, so that they can choose the way which suits their own learning and performing styles (as explored in Chapter 49). This will result in higher efficiency and more enjoyment in the task.*
Norming	
If the team can reach the Norming stage they are probably home and dry. Sadly, there are teams which have been stuck in the Storming stage for many years, in businesses which are successful but being slowly undermined by the tension. The Norming stage, when achieved, is an exciting time for all. Big decisions can be made and implemented, new ideas turned into reality, risks taken and failure seen as simply another step along the pathway to success. Roles and relationships are now established, freeing people up to concentrate on exercising the talents that got them into the team in the first place.	*Leaders should use a coaching style and trust the team to manage its tasks and work out its own solutions. A team at the Norming stage will have much to offer in terms of experience and ideas which, if accessed, can save leaders time and energy, leaving them free to focus on the wider horizon, such as broadening the scope through strategic partnerships and succession planning.*

Stage	Behaviour
Performing	
The team is now a powerful engine running with all cogs turning. Plenty of healthy conflict, of the type that does not damage the fabric of the relationships (explored in Chapter 36), is interspersed with fun and humour. Successes almost seem to create themselves. The leader and team members have learned to give their best then get out of one another's way.	*The leader and team members should recognize the contributions of others and ensure that credit is awarded where due. This applies as much to team members validating the leader as the other way round. If anyone is left feeling that their contribution is not being recognized, the resentment may be carried through to the next project and Storming will be proportionately harder to overcome in the future.*
Adjourning	
The 'adjourning' stage is about bringing a sense of closure to a team whose project is completed. If the team successfully negotiated the first four stages, there may be some bonding between members and a sense of loss at disbanding those relationships. People will also be looking back to the beginning, noticing how far they have come and measuring what their contribution has been to the whole. The way in which this is handled can have a profound effect on the next team each member joins; if an organization is constantly forming and reforming teams as people move around the international executive circuit or develop new projects, a collective cultural memory may come into being, influencing existing team players and absorbed by newcomers to the organization.	*Adjourning is a time for thank-yous, recognition of individual achievements, reflection on how far the team has come and the turning points along the way, and consideration of what its members can take forward from the team to the future. Ensure that all the stakeholders outside of the team are aware of collective and individual achievements and that no-one's contribution has been ignored.*

The Myers-Briggs Type Indicator (MBTI®)

SUMMARY

- Jung's archetypes
- Development by Isabel Myers and Katherine Briggs
- The 16 personality types
- The difference between extraversion and introversion
- MBTI in team development

Jung's archetypes

Personality typing has existed for thousands of years, including Greek archetypes and the Enneagram described in Chapter 48. The originator of the techniques used in the workplace today was Carl Gustav Jung, who identified two areas of consciousness, which could be sub-divided into two more:

Perceiving:		Judging:	
Sensation	Intuition	Thinking	Feeling

These are in turn modified by two attitude types: extraversion and introversion. The resulting eight categories are:

Extraverted Sensation	Introverted Sensation
Extraverted Thinking	Introverted Thinking
Extraverted Feeling	Introverted Feeling
Extraverted Intuition	Introverted Intuition

Development by Isabel Myers and Katherine Briggs

The Myers-Briggs Type Indicator® (known as MBTI®) is an assessment instrument based on the work of Jung and developed by mother and daughter psychologists Isabel Myers (1897–1980) and Katharine Cook Briggs (1875–1968), some 60 years ago.

The MBTI® asks the client to answer a series of 'forced-choice' questions, where each choice identifies one of four paired traits. The test takes about 20 minutes, and at the end the client is presented with a precise, multi-dimensional summary of her or his personality, classifying it into types based on four bi-polar dimensions:

1 Extraversion-Introversion (E-I)
   Energizes either from being with people (E) or
   being solitary (I)

2 Sensing-Intuition (S-N)
   Gathers information directly through data and detail (S) or
   indirectly through relationships and possibilities (N)

3 Thinking-Feeling (T-F)
   Makes decisions using objective logic (T) or
   using subjective feeling (F)

4 Judging-Perceiving (J-P)
   Likes to plan and organize in order to know what lies ahead (J) or
   prefers flexibility and being open to options (P)

The 16 personality types

Cross-referencing these four categories results in 16 personality types. For each question, the client chooses his or her strongest preference. This is called the dominant function. The next strongest preference is called the auxiliary function, the next the tertiary and the fourth, which is the least strong, may be called the inferior function. The traits people show to the outside world can be very different to the alignment of their inner worlds. MBTI® helps to clarify the gap and ease the contradictions that people experience in their inner and outer lives.

The 16 personality types

	sensing	←→	intuitive		
judging ←→ perceiving ←→ judging	ISTJ	ISFJ	INFJ	INTJ	introvert
	ISTP	ISFP	INFP	INTP	↕
	ESTP	ESFP	ENFP	ENTP	extravert
	ESTJ	ESFJ	ENFJ	ENTJ	
	thinking	←→ feeling ←→	thinking		

Where MBTI differs from some personality tests is that it does not portray some traits as more desirable than others. The cross-referencing of the questioning system mirrors the positive approach that we use in coaching, regarding all traits as valid and enabling subjects to identify which emerge most strongly without imposing any judgement or comparison with other people.

The tool can enable people to recognize a part of their psychological makeup that they might never have understood before. For example, imagine a man who lives a life largely surrounded by people, perhaps as the CEO of an organization, regularly chairing meetings and speaking in public. It seems, to himself and to others, that he is excelling at something that comes naturally to him and which he enjoys, yet he finds himself regularly suffering extreme exhaustion which only time spent alone can alleviate. Seeing that others in his position seem to revel in being surrounded by people and not need this time alone, he might feel that he is failing somehow in comparison to his peers.

The difference between extraversion and introversion

The MBTI® definition of the difference between an extravert and an introvert, based on the work of Jung, is that the former recharge energy through being with people, while the latter recharge by being alone. So the test may reveal to our CEO that, in spite of his talent with people, at heart he is an introvert so needs time alone to recharge his batteries. He can then give himself permission to build this into his schedule, while continuing to exercise his talent as a leader.

> 'Each person seems to be energized more by either the external world (extraversion) or the internal world (introversion).' (Jung, 1961)

Used in this way, MBTI® can be an enlightening transformational tool. However, a key part of MBTI® is that preferences can and do change and new ones may emerge. It is crucial that participants understand that they hold the power of choice in terms of which traits to develop or reduce, so that the results do not introduce labels that become self-limiting beliefs (as described in Chapter 4). It is hard enough to break down these patterns without having them reinforced, which would go against the whole ethos of coaching in terms of enabling people to fulfil their potential.

For example, in the case of our public leader above, if the test had been administered at an early stage in his life, before he developed his leadership skills, he might never have aimed for the public stage, believing that he was not 'that type' of person. A further risk is that, once aware of the reason for his exhaustion, this leader may find it more difficult to summon up the energy required for the assertiveness that his current public role requires.

Executives today often describe themselves to me by way of introduction as, say, an INTP, or ESTJ, and it is sometimes offered as a means of justifying or excusing a way of behaviour, a 'this is the way I am made, so there is no point in trying to change' attitude. This use of MBTI® runs against the intentions of the model, yet it happens with surprising frequency and could arguably be seen as the organizational version of 'I'm a Virgo so I'm tidy' horoscope personality typing.

Despite its popularity, there has been no quantifiable research to show whether the results of MBTI® testing are beneficial or otherwise to its participants, and this is the case with most psychometric tools. A good deal of the effect of the tool, whether positive or otherwise, is dictated by how the delivery of the results is handled. Ideally this will be supported by a coach who will facilitate the participant in gaining constructive learning from the process. Some coaches use the results to guide them in choosing what questions to ask during sessions.

There is a risk from the organization's point of view that candidates may fake their answers to appear more suited to a certain job. Participants may well feel they have something to gain by answering the questions in a way that will result in the profile most likely to win them a job or promotion.

Whatever the pros and cons, as this tool is almost universally used in large organizations, it makes sense for coaches to become familiar with it in order to facilitate executives through the process in a way that will deliver the maximum possible benefit.

MBTI in team development

Carolyn Pickin, a management development coach, used MBTI to underpin a programme for a group of managers who worked shifts and were underperforming as a team. Conflict was on the increase both between the managers and the people who reported to them, there were personality clashes, and communication across the shifts was inconsistent. Unsurprisingly, these managers had received very little development during their time at the company.

Carolyn worked with them over a period of 10 months, providing a combination of one-to-one coaching, and training in key management skills, initially focusing on their inter-team communication, the conflict and the communication issues. She selected MBTI as a tool which is easy to understand, which provides clear information to individuals about their own personality types and because it uses positives for all the results.

First of all the managers completed the questionnaire online. Before reviewing the results with the team, Carolyn provided a brief overview to ensure that everyone understood its purpose and how MBTI had been developed, in order to strengthen its credibility. She stressed that there were no right or wrong answers and that preferences can change over time.

To demonstrate each bi-polar dimension she led a variety of exercises, which the participants completed in small pre-prepared groups. For example, to show the differences between extraversion and introversion, the managers were asked to produce a group poster depicting their perfect weekend. To create this, they were divided into groups according to the results of their online assessments, so all the 'E' individuals were in one group and the 'I's in another.

The completed posters were put up on the walls, and the managers asked if they could see any differences. These were not hard to spot, as the extraversion group featured lots of family and friends at group activities such as barbecues and parties, while the introversion group's poster depicted more solitary pursuits such as walking and mountaineering.

Carolyn mined the results further by asking how they had all gone about completing the task. The extraversion group recalled that they started drawing straight away and talked over each other in their enthusiasm to get their ideas and thoughts onto the flipchart. The introversion group, on the other hand, realized that they had reflected quietly at first to think through the task, before discussing how they would approach it and nominating one person to be 'the scribe'.

An understanding began to dawn among the managers of why they approached things differently at work, and that no one's way was wrong or right. They realized that each method brought its own strengths to the team and that the key was to understand how to utilize these for the benefit of the whole. And each became aware of why his or her relationship seemed easier with some managers than with others.

Exercises were completed for the other MBTI dimensions and the managers' understanding of why the team was not working well together grew.

The next step was to identify some personal actions to enable each to work with the different personality types within the team. For this, Carolyn coached each manager individually, encouraging them to talk about how they felt about their profiles and what that meant not only in terms of their work situation but in their home life as well. She shared with them that managers who show a preference for extraversion are said to become tired if they work in isolation, and are re-energized by family and social activities. Conversely, managers who tend towards introversion are believed to find all day meetings tiring and need some quiet time before engaging in family activities at home.

They were asked to consider the impact that their preferences had on the people who reported to them, and this led to ideas for ways of developing their relationships with specific team members. The sessions resulted in individual action plans to manage the variety of preferences, alleviate inter-team conflict and to raise the level of consistency in communications across the board.

The MBTI results were referred to when the managers completed other assessments and were generally found to match the results from other tools, which raised the credibility of the processes as well as highlighting areas for ongoing development. The tool proved to be an effective way of helping the individuals to recognize their own needs, understand their impact on others and to achieve their full potential as a team.

48 The Enneagram

SUMMARY

- Ancient history
- The nine types
- Differentiating core values from personality traits
- Manifestation of types

Ancient history

The Enneagram (pronounced any-a-gram and sometimes referred to as 'Enneagon') has its origins in ancient philosophy, possibly as far back as 4,000 years ago. Derived from the Greek 'ennea' meaning 'nine' and 'gram' meaning 'point', the name refers to a nine-point circle depicting nine personality styles. The whole combines archetypal spiritual wisdom with modern psychology, uniting the work of Jung and the Greek philosophers, including Islamic Sufism, the esoteric Russian Gurdjieff and South American psychologists along the way. Today, people from cultures all over the world are able to relate to the psychological and spiritual values which are represented in the universal reach of the Enneagram.

The nine types

The nine points of the Enneagram vary in name according to different sources, but are broadly the same in meaning. I have chosen to use the ones designated by the Enneagram Institute.

As the Enneagram has been passed down the ages through different sources, there is no one correct set of questions. An effective Enneagram exercise asks many questions, some quite similar but coming from slightly different angles, and is thus able to identify the subject's core values and personality traits.

The nine points of the Enneagram

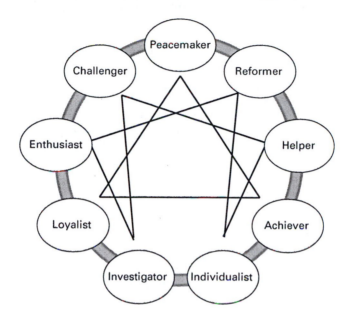

Each type ranges along a continuum from a positive manifestation to one where the traits are excessive and become limiting, as described on the next page.

Differentiating core values from personality traits

The Enneagram seeks to enable people to differentiate their core values from personality traits which they may have developed as a way of surviving the challenges of life. For example, a woman who is a type 3 Achiever may need constant affirmation from others that she is of value and worthy of respect. She may appear to be confident and, indeed, many such people are successful in life precisely because they have been driven to excel by this deep-seated need to meet their perceptions or the expectations of others. Such a woman may not even be consciously aware that she is living her life to impress. One result of this might be that she chooses a partner who 'ticks all the boxes' in terms of what she thinks the world views as an ideal mate, yet such a partner may not actually fulfil the deepest needs of the woman herself.

	Type	Positive	Limiting
1	THE REFORMER	Rational, determined, disciplined, idealistic and a perfectionist	Controlling, domineering, critical
2	THE HELPER	Emotionally demonstrative, caring, sympathetic, with a desire to please	Sycophantic, easily led, a self-styled martyr
3	THE ACHIEVER	Success oriented, focused on excellence, image conscious, outwardly confident	Ruthless with self and others, willing to sacrifice values to win or to be popular
4	THE INDIVIDUALIST	Introverted, sensitive, withdrawn, original, creative, true to oneself	Self obsessed, selfish
5	THE INVESTIGATOR	Deep thinking, cerebral, passionate about ideas	Secretive, cynical, isolated, obsessive
6	THE LOYALIST	Committed, trustworthy, responsible, faithful	Suspicious, anxious, misguided, afraid
7	THE ENTHUSIAST	Versatile, busy, energetic, passionate, fun loving	Short attention span, scatty, not finishing, unreliable
8	THE CHALLENGER	Confident, persuasive, decisive, strong, brave, enjoys taking risks	Aggressive, confrontational, rash
9	THE PEACEMAKER	Amiable, balanced, inspires confidence, impartial	Self-effacing, complacent, downtrodden

Manifestation of types

Most people show a leaning towards one main type and are potentially influenced by two lesser types. It is easy to mistake one's type. For example, a Loyalist 6 who exhibits authoritarian anger might be misidentified as a Challenger 8. No-one manifests their primary type all the time. For example, 9s, the Peacemakers, may indeed be aggressive sometimes, but they will eventually return to peacemaking as a sort of 'home base' and the anger itself will arise from different causes to that of an 8, whose anger will in turn derive differently from a 6.

When we are functioning from our core values, we are at our most powerful and whatever the challenges we face there is a sense of ease in making decisions, coping and triumphing. However, without realizing it, we sometimes function from our 'strategic' personality which may have been created in childhood or to deal with later challenges.

People sometimes live their whole lives according to the values of, say, a domineering parent, choosing jobs and partners which conflict with core values they may have lost sight of along the way. Studying the Enneagram and asking well-devised questions can reveal such anomalies and set the subject on a journey of self-discovery which will lead them towards a more fulfilling and effective life.

It is common for people to feel that there is a unique 'pathway' for them in life – if they could only find it! When people encounter a work situation, project or relationship with which they feel completely at one, they might use terms like, 'It was meant to happen', or 'This is what I was born for'. It is at these times that outside circumstances have coincided with the core nature. Life feels inspiring, even magnificent, yet has a certainty that makes every step a simple one. Nothing feels like hardship during these times, whether there is a scarcity of material comforts, long working hours, or any other sacrifice to be made.

The Enneagram is at once immensely complicated and beautifully simple. As with all systems that attempt to define personality types, it is crucial that tests are not done in a way that will limit people's own belief in their abilities. The system is designed to enable transformation and should always be explored with this in mind.

49 Kolb's learning styles

SUMMARY

- Background
- The learning styles quadrants
- The four preferences
- Learning styles at work

Background

David Kolb's Experiential Learning Theory (ELT) developed over many years and reached a wider audience with the publication of his book *Experiential Learning: Experience as the Source of Learning and Development* in 1984. This seminal work has been acknowledged as a primary influence for later methods, most notably Honey and Mumford's.

The learning styles quadrants

The basis of the learning styles identified by Kolb lies in two continuums: how we think and feel about something, versus how we watch or take action.

THE PERCEPTION CONTINUUM

FEELING	THINKING
Concrete	Abstract
Experience	conceptualization

THE PROCESSING CONTINUUM

DOING	WATCHING
Active	Reflective
Experimentation	observation

Kolb theorized that it is impossible to carry out both perception and processing at the same time, and one's learning style is defined by how that conflict is resolved. The first continuum ranges from people who prefer to think and analyze data before engaging with a task, through to those who base their approach on an emotional response, gut feeling or intuition. The second continuum ranges from people who like to observe before acting, to those who prefer to jump straight in. Somewhere between these scales lies everyone's preferred learning style.

The combination of the intersecting axes produces four types of learning style:

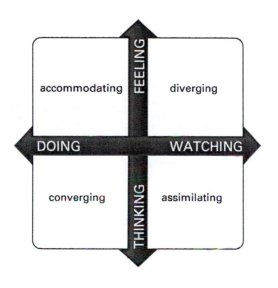

Kolb believed that the ideal learning process incorporated all of the styles, notwithstanding that some would be more pronounced than others.

Honey and Mumford have always credited Kolb as the basis of their own work, which took the learning styles theory into more workplace friendly use and terminology. Their Learning Styles Questionnaire (LSQ) is widely used in business today and can be downloaded from the internet: www. peterhoney.com.

The four preferences

The results identify the individual's preferences across the four types, which are labelled as:

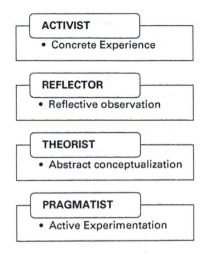

A discussion about the experience of completing the questionnaire, the results and any interpretations will draw out greater depth of understanding of the preferences and the individual's best learning environment. This identifies the kind of learning options they will naturally gravitate towards, as well as those they may avoid or not think about.

Learning styles at work

Amanda Bouch is a learning and change facilitator who relies on Kolb's Learning Cycle and Learning Preferences to ensure that she is working with clients in the way that will be most in line with their learning styles and therefore most productive for them. She implements this either by asking the coachee to complete a questionnaire or by introducing relevant questions early on, in the 'getting to know you' phase.

Clare (whose name has been changed to protect confidentiality) was an executive who found management meetings a challenge: she frequently found herself getting wound up by discussions, especially when there was opposition to her point of view. She wanted to manage her behaviour in and contribution both to these meetings and in general with senior managers.

Clare began by describing what she had tried to do about the situation, giving examples of a couple of different tactics she had experimented with. This indicated to Amanda that Clare had a strong preference for *Concrete Experience*.

Amanda followed up with an open question about learning: 'If you needed to use networking to make contacts for your work, how would you go about it?'

Clare replied that she would find and attend some networking groups, and do general research online or among colleagues to get tips. This response fell mostly into the categories of *Concrete Experience* and *Active Experimentation*.

In answer to a question about when the issue of her behaviour occurs, Clare said that the problem only occurred at work. When there were disagreements with friends and family she was able to find ways of handling the situation. Amanda deduced from this that Clare had not learned from the differences between two situations. So she asked Clare to reflect on her experiences with friends and family in order to develop her thinking about what worked well, and then to apply that to the work situation.

Amanda used *Active Experimentation* questions to elicit a description from Clare of some non-work discussions and to identify the behaviours she used, the impact on herself, on others, and the consequences or outcomes of behaving that way. They talked through several examples until patterns of behaviour started to emerge.

Moving on to *Assimilating*, Amanda asked Clare what she noticed about the arguments and discussions that had a positive outcome. Interestingly, the process of *reflection* had encouraged her to slow down somewhat and now she took her time to think through her behaviour patterns; this resulted in a real 'aha!' moment as she concluded that *her responses depended upon the level of* her interest in the other person's point of view. With friends and family that was higher, which meant that she asked more questions, which *in turn* gave her more information and helped her express her viewpoint in terms that the other person would appreciate. Amanda helped Clare to develop these insights further so that Clare *would be able to apply the same pattern to her management meetings, and she left the session with* some clear actions to carry out at the next management meeting.

Clare's action plan was soundly based on behaviours she now knew herself to be capable of, and her motivation to try them out was high. Amanda tested this in the *Converging* phase of the session, by role-playing a management meeting and having her experience what it would be like to adopt the new behaviours. The session closed with a plan of how Clare would prepare for the next management meeting.

At the next session, she was keen to report on how the meeting had gone and happy to take part in a reflective process, checking, adapting and confirming her conclusions based on this experience and reconfirming her commitment to continue to adopt the new behaviours.

Within three months her relationship with her manager had improved dramatically and they were working well together. In addition, the management team now valued her contributions and respected her opinions on operational management issues.

DISC

50

SUMMARY

- The four types
- William Moulton Marston's instigation of behavioural science
- Comparison with Jung's archetypes and MBTI personality types

The four types

DISC is a personality inventory tool that divides people into four types. Versions of the tool proliferate and the labels vary across all of them. Below is a common representation.

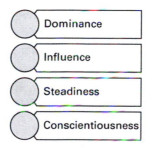

William Moulton Marston's instigation of behavioural science

DISC is based on the work of William Moulton Marston, who is regarded as the originator of behavioural science after publication of his book *Emotions of Normal People* in 1928. Marston did not himself devise any inventories, but his work has been used as a basis for the hundreds devised by various organizations to explore the behaviour of teams in the workplace. There exist many variations in the terms used, mainly to update them from the perspective of the modern workplace, for example the fourth category was named 'compliance' in Marston's original list, and the third 'submission'.

People are assumed to be a composite of all four types, usually exhibiting one type strongly, with a second or third type to a lesser extent. The tool is normally administered through a questionnaire, where marks are awarded for each section to show how the propensities lie. The traits of the four areas are:

Dominance: Individuals who score highly in this area tend to be driven, task focused and energetic, focusing on goals rather than people. They may be high achievers but sometimes create unacceptable levels of stress in the teams they lead. They are often decisive, determined and brave. The key to dealing with such people is to be well prepared, backing up suggestions with facts and figures and making sure that you have answers to hand. A 'dominant' type may respect decisiveness in others and can be fearful of loss of status or position. They may be competitive to the point where they see people who might be able to combine strengths in a strategic alliance as a threat.

Influence: Influencers are intuitive people who are likely to be highly emotional intelligent with well-developed communication skills and magnetic personalities. They lead by inspiring, earning commitment and loyalty, and tend to be very motivating managers. The way to work best with influencers is to be open, authentic and win their trust. Influencers thrive on positive feedback and approval from above and below in the workplace hierarchy. They may be slack about timekeeping and detail. In excess, influencers can allow their hearts to rule their heads and may have difficulty keeping boundaries in place.

Steadiness: People who score highly in this area are likely to be calm, reliable, capable and known for their persistence and ability to make things happen. They can become pedantic or over-controlling, particularly in legal or accountancy type roles, where they are often found in positions of responsibility for setting rules and monitoring compliance. They may be resistant to change. They are excellent at implementing the visions dreamed up by the influencers and the strategies put in place by target-focused dominators. To get along well with a steady person, it is advisable to stick to the facts and not display too much emotion. Steady types like to know where they stand.

Conscientiousness: Conscientious style people make hard workers and are essential for carrying out the administrative, repetitive and mundane tasks in the organization. They need to know what is going to happen and be well primed in methods and expectations. In excess, conscientious people can slow things down by going into too much detail, and frustrate others by being unable to see the bigger picture. To work well with conscientious people, prepare them, inform them and avoid surprises. They are perfectionists, who can become over-cautious and plagued by fear of failure. They value loyalty and consistency.

Comparison with Jung's archetypes and MBTI personality types

It is possible to make comparisons with MBTI (explored in Chapter 47) and the work on personality types undertaken by Carl Jung also described in that chapter, but there is no direct overlay. Jung's work, and the MBTI system derived from it, relate more to thinking styles, while DISC is about the way people behave. Comparison to Jung's work can be attempted by laying out the four types in a grid:

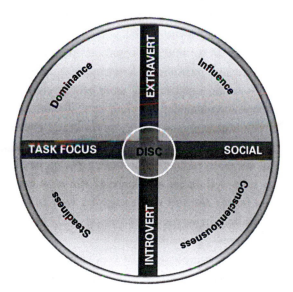

The value in DISC lies in its ability to help people understand more about themselves, about others, and about how they impact on others.

For the coach asked to help a manager interpret the results of such a questionnaire, it is important to treat the categories as a reflection of the present situation, not a prescription. People can and do change their behaviour, and a belief reinforced that someone is weak in one area of the quadrant might have a limiting effect in the future.

It is possible that someone showing the traits of, say, Dominance or Conscientiousness, is merely exhibiting behaviour learned from role models like parents, teachers or managers. If new behaviour is learned, then that person may uncover a latent talent for influencing. The coach's role here is to broaden perspective, explore and help the coachee to build confidence.

A coaching manager's role in this situation might be to support such a team member in taking risks to develop new skills, without judgement or blame, and with plenty of recognition for achievements.

DISC in team building

Fiona Kerr runs a coaching and management development consultancy and uses DISC to underpin her work. She facilitated a team-building exercise with a group of private client relationship managers, portfolio managers and support staff. The team leader, Philip (whose name has been changed), had reported to Fiona in a previous job.

To place the exercise in context, the organization had recently undergone a period of change from a partnership environment, in which professionals worked as individuals and support staff were neither challenged about their lack of development nor rewarded for their contribution to a client-focused business model that required teamwork, meritocracy, execution and integrity. Performance management and team leadership were relatively new challenges for all the team managers including Philip, but he embraced the change and was regarded as an advocate of the new business model. As such, he was keen for his team to work together well and wanted to get the best out of its members in terms of achieving goals and objectives, while avoiding conflict wherever possible.

This new team was a combination of two separate teams, including the two previous team leaders, one of whom (and we will call him Gavin) had to relinquish his position. Philip felt slightly threatened by this and was keen to bring the new team together as it seemed to him that the individuals were not working collectively but to their individual agendas.

Fiona suggested using DISC to help the team get to know and understand each other on a deeper level, by identifying each member's own DISC style, enabling them to identify the styles of the others, and understand how they impacted on each other.

The four types are described in detail earlier in this chapter.

- *Dominance*: relating to control, power and assertiveness, focusing on goals rather than people.
- *Influence:* relating to social situations and communication.
- *Steadiness:* relating to patience, persistence and thoughtfulness.
- *Conscientiousness:* relating to structure and organization.

Philip's category turned out to be 'Dominance', which surprised him initially. He believed he tended more towards 'Influence/Steadiness' – a good team ambassador with lots of ideas who is aware of all his team members and their feelings. However, the characteristics of Dominance suggest that such individuals create unacceptable levels of stress within their teams and this was certainly true in Philip's case. He needed autonomy to lead his team, make the decisions and to feel that he could challenge the team to prove his ability. But it was also important for him to feel he was making connections with his colleagues and gaining recognition for his efforts.

One of the biggest challenges for Fiona in terms of working with Philip was his tendency to want to solve the problem on his own, without any support and, as the Dominance style suggests, to be in control.

Gavin's profile emerged as Steadiness, with Influence as his next strongest attribute. He could be resistant to change if he did not think it was a good idea and at times was blunt and tactless, uncaring of whom he upset, unlike Philip, who liked to please everyone. This was one of Philip's major issues with Gavin.

Philip's challenge was to change Gavin's mindset and behaviour to fit into the team.

Fiona encouraged him to show Gavin how his work and input would benefit the team but, more importantly, to set clear and specific expectations for him.

Another key member of Philip's team was Kay, again not her real name. Her profile type was 'Conscientiousness', with 'Steadiness' as her next highest style. Conscientiousness style people need to know what is going to happen and be well primed in methods and expectations; they can slow things down by going into too much detail and are perfectionists who can become over-cautious and plagued by fear of failure.

Kay enjoyed working on her own and was meticulous in her approach. What she disliked was being hurried or having to work to a deadline. Philip found this a challenge because although both he and Kay were task-focused, he liked tasks to be completed quickly.

Before his appointment as team leader, Philip and Kay had been peers who worked well together because their styles complemented each other. Kay found the change in roles difficult to cope with as in the past she had depended on Philip.

There were three other key people in Philip's team: Emma, who provided administration support; Nigel, who, like Kay, Philip and Gavin, was a relationship manager; and Kenny, who provided technical support. Again their names have been changed.

Kenny's DISC profile was 'Steadiness' while the rest were all 'Conscientiousness'. Both Nigel and Emma were quite shy and did not like conflict. They found Gavin difficult to work with and, at times, felt bullied by his manner and approach. Kenny did not like change at all; he lacked confidence and was reluctant to make decisions on his own.

Philip's first reaction on seeing their profiles was to wonder how this team could ever hope to work together!

However, there was some encouragement to be drawn from the idea that someone may show the traits of, say, Dominance or Conscientiousness, because they are exhibiting behaviour learned from a role model. This was indeed the case for Philip, particularly as he had only ever worked for the one company. However, if new behaviour is acquired through, for example, training in coaching skills, then that person may uncover a different style altogether as his true nature.

Therefore, Fiona encouraged Philip to ask himself continuously: 'What help and support do I need to improve team dynamics and work collectively as one?' Her role in this situation was to support him in developing new skills, in understanding his team's individual traits, their strengths and weaknesses, likes and dislikes and to put in place both personal and team action plans.

This was achieved through a series of team meetings where each member was encouraged to express his or her views and feelings. This built trust and rapport through open and transparent communication. Philip was careful to reward and praise the team where appropriate and he dealt with any issues or challenges at monthly one-to-one meetings.

He found that an understanding of the different characteristics and traits of his team members helped him to meet his overall objective of having them work together as one. He asked for their input when decisions were required, and they came to respect him as a trusted leader who engages people and empowers them through ownership and accountability.

Being given the opportunity to lead was both a challenging and rewarding time for Philip, but by using direct and honest communication, he was able to ensure that the team 'gelled' together and drew on individual strengths.

51

Johari Window

SUMMARY

- Development by Joseph Luft and Harry Ingham
- The four quadrants
- Dangers of public feedback
- Respecting boundaries

Development by Joseph Luft and Harry Ingham

Since being developed by American psychologists Joseph Luft and Harry Ingham in the 1950s, the Johari Window model has become increasingly relevant in modern business, where the focus of training and development has shifted from skills and knowledge to relationships and team building.

The Johari Window model

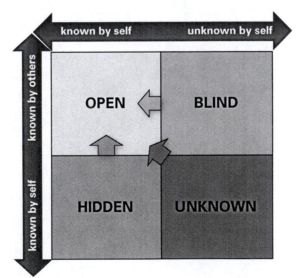

The model derives its name from a combination of the first names of its founders: Joseph and Harry. It is designed to increase awareness of oneself and others in a work situation and is designed to be used with groups.

The four quadrants

The **OPEN** area represents what is known about the subject by herself and others. It represents ease of communication, free expression and strong relationships because all parties have agreed on what goes in here.

The **BLIND** area identifies what others know about the subject that she does not know about herself and will contain information supplied by those who come into contact with her at work. It is intended to open the subject's eyes to strengths and weaknesses which she may not have recognized.

The **HIDDEN** area is an exploration of elements which the subject consciously hides from those who work around her; things she knows about herself but chooses not to let others know. These could include emotions like fear, resentment and self-doubt, some of which are best kept confidential, and the subject may also find some factors which can be moved into the open area.

The **UNKNOWN** area is there to elicit new information of which neither the subject nor those around her may be aware; this is a place for discovering new talents and developing the confidence to exploit them. So this part of the exploration can be particularly useful for younger, less experienced workers. It may also provide an awareness of what might stand between the subject and her full potential, such as fear, self-doubt or misalignment of her talents in relationship to her role.

Ideally, as much information as possible will be moved into the open area through this process. This is the healthy place where relationships work instinctively, ideas can be developed in conjunction with the team and potential conflict can be resolved in an honest and trusting environment.

Dangers of public feedback

There is a need for caution when using this model because of the danger of crushing confidence and reducing an executive's effectiveness in the workplace. One of the generally accepted guidelines for negative feedback, as described in Chapter 25, is that it should only ever be given in private, but the Johari Window flouts this rule.

It is vital that people undertaking this exercise as the subject of it are in control of how much information they receive and from whom, and that their personal boundaries are respected. Some people have grown up in a culture where criticism is the norm, while others have not been so exposed to it. Added to this, either culture might produce an over-sensitivity to criticism. There are international differences too. Allowing for exceptions, I have found British managers to be less open to 'improving' feedback while German managers cannot get enough of it.

Putting workers on the defensive, however well meaning, rarely results in a happy team. Humans have an inbuilt need to control their environment, which derives from living in caves millions of years ago and being vulnerable to weather and wild animals. Not having control was a matter of life or death and it can sometimes feel just as uncomfortable when the 'fight or flight' mechanism is triggered by a work situation that feels out of one's control. No-one should be forced to receive feedback in front of others, and some people find even public positive feedback embarrassing. If people do volunteer to receive it, they should be encouraged to regulate the process themselves. This reflects the core principle of coaching, 'self-directed learning', where coachees are enabled to make their own discoveries.

A coaching method for applying this quadrant might be to show it to a coachee during a confidential one-to-one session, and ask the coachee questions about each section. It is quite likely that some elements from the last three boxes will find their way into the Open box during the process. The coachee might solicit one to one feedback from team members of his choosing, possibly not in a formal way, to populate the 'blind' box.

The model can also be used by a group in relation to other groups. Here the danger of crushing individuals is reduced, but we need to be mindful of the possibility of raising territorial boundaries and a sense that teams are being pitched against each other – it is almost impossible to prevent this from developing into a competition where the focus is on scoring points over the other teams. However, if a positive tone is firmly set and a reasonable amount of trust exists between the teams, the exercise can be fun and bond the teams more strongly.

The window shown above represents each box in equal sizes. The proportions can be varied according to the ratio of each box pertaining to the person. For example, the quadrant of a long-serving team member might look like this, because a relationship may have been established where all parties know the person well:

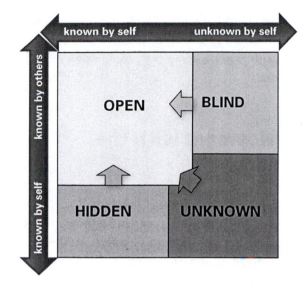

Or a beginner's quadrant might look like this because he or she has only just begun to explore latent potential and has a lot to learn:

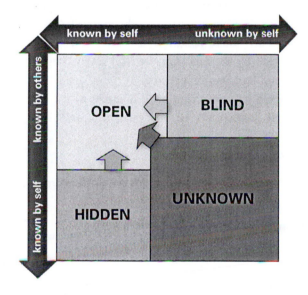

The Johari Window was one of the first models of its kind and many modifications have been developed since. It bears some relationship to Transactional Analysis (explored in Chapter 33), Tuckman's team building model (explored in Chapter 46), and Hersey and Blanchard's Situational Leadership model (explored in Chapter 38).

The key to working with the Johari Window is for a facilitator to manage the process, steering it away from becoming a list of complaints, resentment or envy, and towards positive awareness, recognition of strengths and inspiration for the team.

Team development with the Johari Window

Executive development consultant Christina Bachini uses the Johari Window model as a feedback tool to expand self-awareness and awareness of others. When there is a lack of trust, direction, hidden agendas or conflict she finds that the model creates opportunities for discovery and change.

She recalls an example of how she used the model to help a team of senior executive sales managers in a well-known telecommunications organization. The MD felt frustrated, having inherited a team that did not function cohesively, people were leaving unexpectedly and there was poor communication, a lack of direction and too much gossip. Meetings had become a war zone of point-scoring, tasks were falling through the cracks and individuals took ownership only when personally affected by the outcome. The situation was not helped by the fact that the MD was younger than most of his team members and had less experience.

Christina started by consulting each member of the team, including the MD, about their perception of the situation and their objectives for success.

The main issues that emerged were:

- lack of team cohesion or agreement about the common mission and vision;
- lack of open, honest communication, with everyone blaming someone else;
- a controlling, young MD who micro-managed people more senior, creating a dynamic of secrecy and resentment;
- team meetings being disrupted by point-scoring and turf wars;
- overlapping areas had not been agreed, leading to conflict; and
- one member was made a scapegoat.

There was an overall lack of trust, credibility and integrity. Team members complained openly about the hidden agendas of others, their irritations and areas of conflict, but there was no platform for dealing with the issues or for tackling people who were not felt to be pulling their weight.

The scapegoat had become a focus of the irritation and Christina could not fully understand what he had done to create so much tension.

The objectives became:

- build a collaborative team capable of meeting the organization's expectations;
- develop a structure for dealing with differences and conflict; and
- develop team members' trust in, and credibility with, each other and their stakeholders.

For the next stage of the process a two-day event was held. Christina introduced the Johari Window on day two, after some groundwork on the rules of engagement had been established.

Each person received three cards on which they were to write feedback for each of the arena positions, with the suggestion that the more courageous they could be in giving feedback, the more successful the exercise would be.

They were advised that the response to feedback must be simply 'thank you', except when someone wanted to ask for more clarification, and that this was not a time for discussions or defensiveness – they had to let the feedback settle before responding.

While the group completed their cards, Christina placed a large, physical representation of the Johari Window in the centre of the floor and labelled each window pane.

Members of the team were anxious both about what they might hear and what they would have to disclose to others. Christina supported them in being honest in their feedback, so that it would be meaningful. Her personal outcome was to create a safe place where they could establish trust, plus a shared vision and mission that they would all be happy to work towards.

Step 1: Self-disclosure

Each person in turn went into the open arena and shared with the whole group something that was important to the person speaking, but which they believed the others did not know.

Examples of self-disclosure were:

- 'I find balancing my home life and my love for this job really hard to manage.'

- 'I'm scared that we will have blood and guts all over the floor and this team will be torn apart.'
- 'I am really excited that finally we are going to address the underlying issues that are getting in the way of this team being really successful.'

Step 2: Blind spot

For this stage, Person 1 sat on the blind spot chair and invited a team member into the window to hear what Person 1 had written about that member, for example 'I think you have a blind spot about the fear you create in me and, I believe, others when you are angry about something, and I avoid telling you what is really happening.'

The team member said 'thank you', took the card and moved out of the window.

Person 1 then chose a second team member to step into the window and, again, gave his feedback. When all of Person 1's blind spots had been delivered, he left the window.

Everyone was required to invite people of their choice into each window. The blind spots which emerged included:

- 'I feel you are micro-managing me and this inhibits my creativity and commitment.'
- 'When you leave your empty coffee cup on my desk, I get really annoyed and feel disrespected. You seem to have no awareness of how this affects me and others in the team.'

As all 12 members of the team entered the blind spot area, it became clear that the MD was receiving feedback about his style of management and its effect. In addition, the scapegoat was called into the window many times to receive feedback based on gossip and hearsay, and it was this that was causing as much of the situation as what he was actually doing. For example, he had a habit of leaving coffee cups on the desks of one or two people, who had gossiped about it to others, and now everyone was complaining about the coffee cups whether it had happened to them or not.

We spent some time unpicking the information and eventually it became clear that the new MD felt somewhat insecure in his position because he was so much younger than the others. He had also assumed (wrongly) that two of the people who had applied for his position were being unhelpful on purpose. Happily, he discovered that they were in fact very supportive of him in his role, but needed him to trust their judgement more.

Step 3: Hidden agenda

In the first round of addressing the hidden agendas within the group, Person 1 revealed something he knew that he had withheld from a fellow team member, for example 'although we have agreed to do X, I think my idea of Y is much better and I have been avoiding doing what you want by ignoring your requests. Now it is in the open, I want to have a discussion about it'.

The team began to realize that unspoken agendas were having a very powerful, negative impact.

In the second round, Person 1 challenged colleagues about hidden agendas he believed that they might have, like 'I notice that you spend a lot of time engaging with the new boss and I think you want to become his favourite. Your "brown nosing" really irritates me'.

Then the whole group discussed together what had been shared and looked for a way forward to keep the dialogue open and ongoing. What emerged was the recognition that they were not a cohesive team because:

- Each member was working on his or her own.
- The MD realized that he had set objectives for each member of the team without reference to his own. He saw that his own objectives were not aligned with those he had set for the team, in that his own goals were dependent on the team achieving theirs, but even if they accomplished the objectives he had set for them, the result would fall short.
- Communication and trust were non-existent.
- The unspoken, underlying issues were influencing the team.

Everyone now mapped out the feedback they had received, updated their Window to include the new information and decided what they needed to change in order to have a positive impact on their effectiveness as a team member.

Step 4: Analysis and results

The team gained many insights into the way they communicated based on their assumptions and projections. Their level of trust increased as they developed a structure for making irritations and conflicts visible and dealing with them.

They also came to understand that the reason they were unable to feel engaged with their objectives was because those objectives were not aligned to the team's mission, and that this uncertainty was creating fear. They gained clarity on how gossiping and laying blame on one member of the team had created unnecessary conflict and pain.

The team went on to complete their outcomes and exceeded expectations. They were able to have open, honest interactions and achieved a genuine, shared vision.

Step 5: Follow-up

Six months later the difference was tangible. Members were collaborating and the team performing to the MD's expectations. He had now settled in and was growing into his role.

The team had designed a structure for dealing with differences and conflict, which brought things into the open as soon as they occurred rather than letting them fester. The trust that they had developed with each other was being generated into the wider organization, particularly with their stakeholders.

Team meetings were now effective, with open, honest communication and a willingness to make sure that it was the team rather than the individual which afforded the focus for success. The group had become a highly performing team which held collaboration and communication at its heart. Although its members had found the two days challenging and at times scary, everyone agreed that benefits were being reaped.

More team role models

52

SUMMARY

- Belbin's Team Role Inventory
- FIRO-B (Fundamental Interpersonal Relations Orientation)
- Nigel Risner's animal types
- The case against learning styles

Belbin's Team Role Inventory

Dr Meredith Belbin's inventory divides people into nine classifications:

Plant	Resource Investigator	Coordinator
Shaper	Monitor Evaluator	Teamworker
Implementer	Completer Finisher	Specialist

Belbin insisted that his classifications represent not fixed personality types but measures of behaviour, and that behaviour can change.

The nature/nurture debate has raged for some decades now. Is our behaviour dictated mostly by our genes or by cultural and family influences? Belbin, and others like Kolb in Chapter 49, would have it that much of our behaviour is learned and that habits can be changed, a view which concurs with the philosophy of coaching.

FIRO-B (Fundamental Interpersonal Relations Orientation)

This model was introduced by William Schutz in 1958. There has been much speculation of what the 'B' stands for ('behaviour' perhaps?) but Sir John Whitmore, who once worked with Schutz, informs me that it was simply the designation of the hut in which the relevant workshops took place.

The divisions are based on the ancient medical definitions of four 'humours' – sanguine, phlegmatic, melancholic and choleric – which were identified by Hippocrates and were developed by a series of philosophers through the ages, including Galen (d. 200 AD), Avicenna (d.1037), Maimonides (d.1204), Nicholas Culpeper (d.1654), Immanuel Kant (d.1804), Ivan Pavlov (d.1936) and Alfred Adler (d.1937). Personalities were thought to arise solely from chemical balances in the body, and Hans Eysenck (d.1997) was one of the first thinkers to bring psychology to bear in the analysis. In common with Belbin, Schultz was emphatic that the results of a FIRO-B exploration did not define the person; they simply reflected learned behaviour which can change. He divided behaviour into three categories:

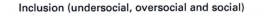

| Inclusion (undersocial, oversocial and social) |
| Control (abdicrat, autocrat and democrat) |
| Affection types (underpersonal, overpersonal and personal) |

Nigel Risner's animal types

This system divides people into lions, monkeys, elephants and dolphins (Risner, 2003). According to Risner:

- lions are strong, silent thought leaders (eg CEOs, inventors, philosophers);
- monkeys are sociable and inventive (eg sales and marketing managers, entrepreneurs, media workers);
- elephants love process and detail (eg compliance officers, lawyers, accountants);
- dolphins like to please (eg administrative assistants).

On face value these categories appear to be too simplistic to be of any real use, and yet they have endowed this particular monkey, who struggles to read an e-mail to its end, with greater tolerance towards the elephants who send three pagers.

Conclusion about team models

From a coaching point of view, I believe that that all of the personality and behaviour type tools function at their maximum usefulness when employed to enhance self-awareness in an individual, rather than to typecast the person. The tests should be undertaken in order to provide participants with knowledge about themselves, not for sponsors to learn about their staff, nor indeed for coaches to make assumptions about their coachees.

When coaching a client through the results of such a test, it is crucial for the coach to ensure that people do not become limited by their labels. It may be that someone veers away from a particular element not because of an inherent tendency, but, say, because of an unfortunate early life experience. Take the analogy of a child who almost drowns and grows up with a fear of water. If this fear could be removed, the adult may discover that swimming is a pleasure, or even a latent talent. If we apply this principle to learning and work areas, we may find that the manager who has always 'kept his head down', and disliked any kind of public platform, may have been thwarted by a one-off experience which knocked his confidence, and if that confidence is restored he may blossom into an effective speaker and leader.

I have had experiences where the boundaries blur between one set of expectations and another. For example, in the Middle East I demonstrated coaching with an Emirati woman in front of her peers. Any of the personality type indicators might have defined her type as open, confident and willing to help. However, I soon realized that, possibly due to her cultural mores, she was not prepared to reveal anything less than a 'blue sky' with the others present. When demonstrating coaching, I always ask for 'real plays' not 'role plays', because coaching is about the emotional shift which comes from new self-knowledge, and which is signalled by a rise in energy and change in body language. If the coachee is inventing the situation, no emotional shift will occur. With my volunteer coachee in the Emirates, I was able to demonstrate the process but not the usual emotional shift. These cross-cultural differences are explored in more depth in Chapter 7, 'Developing a coaching culture'.

The case against learning styles

Baroness Susan Greenfield is quoted from an article in the *Times Education Supplement* that: 'From a neuroscientific point of view [the learning styles approach to teaching] is nonsense.'

It is worth bearing in mind that probably out of all the tools and models covered in this book, probably none has been put to the test in a way that would satisfy scientific academics. Yet practitioners and clients who have benefited from the tools claim to see useful results. This is particularly so in the field of education, where many teachers claim to have experienced improved academic results through paying attention to their pupils' learning styles. To confuse matters, there have been scientific experiments which proved this to be true, and others which have demonstrated the opposite.

Thinking back to the effective teachers at my own school, it was their teaching style that won the day, rather than my learning style, and the popular teachers achieved results across the board, with all types of pupils. It did not seem that some pupils fared better with one teacher and others with another, rather that all pupils fared better with the most effective teachers. Was it possible that the 'good' teachers were able to incorporate a variety of learning styles so that everyone's interest was engaged? That was not part of the teaching methodology at the time. Or were they simply more encouraging, better at giving clear explanations, and more ready to involve the pupils on an interactive level? It is difficult to say from this distance in time.

Dr Paul Howard-Jones, Senior Lecturer in Education at the University of Bristol, said at recent seminar:

> 'A big study by Coffield et al. examined 121 different learning style inventories. However, no independent research has found learning benefit for any of them. I emphasise "independent", because nearly every page of the materials that you pay for says that research has of course shown them to be wonderful, but when you look at who did the research you find that it is published by the same organisation that is selling the product.'

However, although the theories may be doubtful, learning styles practices are probably beneficial, simply because bringing any new perspectives or activity into a coaching session, meeting or classroom is likely to raise energy and release new insights.

So it seems the jury is out on this one, and it may simply be that the scientific proof is not there yet. For me, as I have said several times in this book, the biggest pitfall in any kind of typecasting is that people may become limited by their label. For example, if a woman is told that she is, say, an Abstract Conceptualiser (Kolb, Chapter 49), or an Introvert (MBTI, Chapter 47), at a young enough age, she may modify her behaviour to live up to that description.

Steve Higgins, Professor of Education at Durham University relates an alarming story of this type of conditioning:

'An eight-year old child in Enfield made a comment that was thoroughly depressing. He said: "I'm no good at writing, I'm a kinaesthetic learner." So at that age the child had already decided that there were things that he could not do, of which writing was one, and he had a nice excuse based on his perceived need for kinaesthetic learning activity.'

A common pitfall for coaches to look out for is that a good deal of energy and focus may be diverted into attempts to identify and match their clients' learning styles, and this may be better used in listening to what the clients are saying. This is particularly likely if a particular client's preferences do not align with the coach's own, and the same may be said for a manager in a team-leading situation.

I have noticed that where people show a preponderance towards, say, *auditory* communication, as described in VAK Submodalities (Chapter 31), they often reply in auditory terms no matter how the question was phrased, and that the coach's phraseology does not seem to make any difference to them. Therefore, the effort expended on the coach's part in identifying the client's preference may be better spent in understanding what the client has said and choosing which question will be most helpful to ask next.

Barry Rogers, the Insights consultant and coach whose cross-cultural coaching experiences are described in Chapter 11, recommends caution in the use of psychometric profiling. He says that he noticed he was becoming increasingly dependent on the Insights profile, in which he is an expert, when preparing for client sessions based on psychological preferences. He thought he was 'getting to know' his client when, in reality, he came to realize that he was being influenced through his understanding of the preferences. This awareness prompted Barry to take a fresh approach to initial client coaching sessions and he began to conduct two or three before considering the use of a profile. With the opportunity of working today in a more culturally diverse environment, many coaches use psychometric profiling to support their coaching sessions and at times caution needs to be exercised.

Clearly there are some questions to be addressed in the use of learning styles and psychometric profiles. One benefit I have found in using these techniques is that they enable clients to turn their focus inward, to ask themselves productive questions, and gain some new self-knowledge – which is what I would say coaching is all about.

For the international coach and facilitator, I believe that it is important to uphold the coaching principle of self-directed learning – not only refraining from imposing our own assumptions and expectations, but assisting our clients in recognizing and setting aside their own, whether relating to themselves or their colleagues.

CONCLUSION

In the workplace a coaching approach is becoming commonplace compared to the turn of the millennium, when I was asked by an exhibitor at an HR exhibition whether my organization managed bus drivers after sharing that I had a coaching company. Nowadays, most managers who attend our programmes have a fairly good idea of what coaching means in a leadership context and may even have had some training elsewhere.

Coaching in management is a viable and valuable option for today's global businesses and by no means a soft option. It enables leaders to optimize teamwork and maximize whatever talents exist within their workforces. It reflects today's cultural move towards 'responsibilities as well as rights', aligns with the principles of corporate social responsibility described in Chapter 14 and is the solution to the quest for a replacement of the dictatorial workplaces of the '70s and the 'dog eat dog' power approach of the '80s and '90s.

One of the reasons for its explosive success is that a coach enables individuals to identify what they would like to change in themselves and to help them effect that change in a positive way. Such personal change often triggers a transformation in the person's organization as well: a 'happy virus' in action.

Back in the days when I worked at Virgin, the term 'coach' meant 'teacher', was usually associated with sport, and no word existed to describe someone who encouraged people to teach themselves. Yet the practice has existed for as long as civilization, as evidenced by the questioning approach of Socrates. I think this is why even people who have a naturally directive style do not find it hard to coach after a short period of training and practice. The attitude is inherent in everyone and requires no more than a change in habits.

Coaching can also be beneficial on a personal level, freeing us from self-imposed limitations, enabling us to tap into our personal potential and empowering us to live the lives to which we aspire. Generally our culture has become more relaxed over the last 40 years, is more inclusive and our choices are greater than ever. Coaching principles accommodate all of this, which goes some way towards explaining their effectiveness and popularity.

A further advantage in today's multicultural society is that a coaching way of talking cuts across social differences, whether arising from nationality or intellectual preference, such as IT managers who tend to communicate in a different way from say HR or sales executives, which I described in Chapter 11. I have likened the language of coaching to the Esperanto of communication.

Coaching skills are being adopted by parents raising their children, charities which support disadvantaged young people (as described in Chapter 15) teachers who are responsible for developing their students (Chapter 12), and by organizations in every part of the world. We are seeing a strong and rising demand for coach training in organizations in the Middle East, China, Eastern Europe and Russia, to counteract the dictatorial and hierarchical traditions of these countries, and in all of these places the coaching approach is enthusiastically seized upon. We may be looking at a future where world leaders have grown up with role models who consciously adopt a coaching style and will consequently be capable of listening to and understanding one another at levels rarely seen today.

REFERENCES

Assagioli, R, Girelli, ML and Bartoli, S (2008) *Transpersonal Development: The dimension beyond psychosynthesis* Inner Way Productions/Smiling Wisdom, Forres

Avital, M, Boland, R and Cooperrider, DL (2007) *Designing Information and Organizations with a Positive Lens*, vol 2, Elsevier Science, Oxford

Baer, RA (2005) *Mindfulness-Based Treatment Approaches: Clinician's guide to evidence base and applications*, Academic Press, New York

Bandler, R and Grinder, J (1990) *Frogs into Princes: Introduction to neurolinguistic programming*, Eden Grove Editions, Enfield

Barabasi, A-L (2003) *How Everything Is Connected to Everything Else and What It Means for Business and Everyday Life* Plume Books, New York

Barrett, R (1998) *Liberating the Corporate Soul: Building a visionary organisation* Butterworth-Heinemann, Boston

Barrett, R (2006) *Building a Values-Driven Organization: A whole-system approach to cultural transformation*, Butterworth-Heinemann, Boston

Belbin, RM (2010) *Team Roles at Work*, Butterworth-Heinemann, Oxford

Berens, Linda V (2008) *Understanding Yourself and Others*®: *An introduction to interaction styles 20*, Telos Publications, Huntington Beach, California

Berne, E (2010) *Games People Play: The psychology of human relationships*, Penguin, London

Blanchard (2000) *The One Minute Manager*, Harper Collins Business, London

Blanchard, K, Zigarmi, K and Zigarmi, P (1996) *Leadership and the One Minute Manager: Increasing Effectiveness through Situational Leadership*, Jossey Bass, New York

Branson, Sir R (2006) *Screw It Let's Do It*, Virgin, London

Branson, Sir R (2009) *Business Stripped Bare*, Virgin, London

Buchanan, M (2003) *Small World: Uncovering nature's hidden networks*, Phoenix, London

Carnegie, D (1995) *The Leader in You: How to win friends, influence people and succeed*, Simon & Schuster, New York

Cavanagh, M (2006) Coaching from a systemic perspective, in *The Evidence Based Coaching Handbook: Putting best practices to work for your clients*, ed DR Stober and AM Grant, Chapter 11, John Wiley & Sons

Cooper, C (2010) Hard times call for resilient leaders [article comment], *Director Magazine*, Director Publications, London

Cooperrider, DL, Whitney, D and Stavros, JM (2008) *Appreciative Inquiry Handbook For Leaders of Change*, OH Crown, Brunswick

Crowder, RG (1976) *Principles of Learning and Memory*, Lawrence Erlbaum, Oxford

Doidge, N (2007) *The Brain That Changes Itself*, Penguin, London

Erickson, M and Rosen, S (1991) *My Voice Will Go with You: Teaching tales of Milton H Erikson*, W W Norton & Co, London

Fallon, J (2012) available at www.youtubecom/watch?v=43Mv5Hw4Geg&feature=bf_prev&list=SP4B8EC020E34E22F [accessed 2012]

Ferrucci, P (2009a) *What We May Be: Techniques for psychological and spiritual growth through psychosynthesis*, Jeremy P Tarcher, New York

Ferrucci, P (2009b) *Inevitable Grace: Breakthroughs in the lives of great men and women:*

Gallwey, T (1986) *The Inner Game of Tennis*, Random House, London

Goleman D (1996) *Emotional Intelligence*, Bloomsbury, London

Goleman, D, Boyatzis, RE and McKee, A (2003) *The New Leaders: Transforming the art of leadership into the science of results*, Sphere, London

Gordon, E *et al* (2008) An 'integrative Neuroscience' platform: application to profiles of negativity and positivity bias, *Journal of Integrative Neuroscience*, 7, pp 345–66

Grove, D, Wilson, C and Dunbar, A, www.cleancoaching.com

Grove, D and Panzer, B (1989) *Resolving Traumatic Memories: Metaphors and symbols in psychotherapy*, Irvington, New York

Hall, L (2013) *Mindful Coaching: How mindfulness can transform coaching practice*, Kogan Page, London

Harris, T and Harris, A (1995) *I'm OK You're OK*, Arrow, London

Hay, J, (2009) *Transactional Analysis For Trainers*, Sherwood Publishing, Watford

Hirsh, SK, and Kummerow, JM (1990) *Introduction to Type in Organisations*, Oxford Psychologists Press, Oxford

Johnson, S (2002) *Emergence: The connected lives of ants, brains, cities, and software*, Penguin, London

Jung, CG (1921) *Psychological Types*, Rascher, Zürich

Jung, CG (1961) *Memories, Dreams, Reflections*, Pantheon Books, New York

Jung, CG (1964) *Man and his Symbols*, Aldus Books Ltd, London

Kabat-Zinn, J (2001) *Full Catastrophe Living: How to cope with stress, pain and illness using mindfulness meditation*, Piatkus Books, London

Kabat-Zinn, J (2005) *Coming to Our Senses: Healing ourselves and the world through mindfulness*, Piatkus Books, London

Kline, N (1999) *Time to Think: Listening to ignite the human mind*, Cassell, London

Kline, N (2009) *More Time to Think: A way of being in the world*, Fisher King, London

Knight, S (2009) *NLP At Work: The difference that makes a difference in business*, Nicholas Brealey Publishing, London

Kohlrieser, G (2006) *Hostage at the table: How leaders can overcome conflict, influence others and praise performance*, Wiley, London

Kolb, DA (1982) *The Manual of Learning Styles*, P Honey, London

Kolb, DA (1983) *Using your Learning Styles*, P Honey, London

Kolb, DA (1984) *Experiential Learning: Experience as the source of learning and development*, P Honey, London

Kouzes, J and Posner, B (2002) *The Leadership Challenge*, Jossey Bass, San Francisco

Lakoff, G and Johnson, M (1980) *Metaphors We Live By*, University of Chicago Press, Chicago

Law, A (1999) *Creative Company: How St Luke's became 'the ad agency to end all ad agencies'*, Wiley, London

Lawley, J and Tompkins, P (2000) *Metaphors in Mind*, The Developing Company Press, London

Linden, DE, Bittner, RA, Muckli, L, Waltz, JA, Kriegeskorte, N, Goebel, R, Singer, W, and Munk, MH (2003) Cortical Capacity constraints for visual working memory: Dissociation of fMRI load effects in frontoparietal network, *Neuroimage*, 20, 1518–30

Luft, J (1969) *Of Human Interaction: Johari model*, Mayfield PubCo, Houston, Texas

Marston, W (1979) *The Emotions of Normal People*, Persona Press Inc, Minneapolis

Maslow, AH (1998) *Toward a Psychology of Being*, John Wiley, London

McDermott, I and O'Connor, J (1997) *Practical NLP for Managers*, Gower Publishing Company, Aldershot

Mindell, AA (www.aamindell.net)

Myers, IB, (2000) *Introduction to Type*, Oxford Psychologists Press, Oxford

Nelson, B (2005) *1001 Ways to Reward Employees*, Workman Publishing Company, New York

Newman, M (2008) *Emotional Capitalists, the New Leaders*, John Wiley, London

Ohman, A, Flykt, A and Lundquist, D (2000) Unconscious emotion: Evolutionary perspectives, pychophysiological data and neuropsychological mechanisms, in *Cognitive Neuroscience of Emotion*, eds Richard DR Lane, L Nadel and GL Ahern, Oxford University Press, Oxford

Perls, F (1989) *The Gestalt Approach and Eye Witness to Therapy*, Science & Behaviour Books, Los Altos

Piderit, S, Fry, R, Cooperrider, DL (2007) *Handbook of Transformative Cooperation*, Stanford University Press, Stanford

Porter M and Kramer M (Jan–Feb 2011) Creating Share Value: How to reinvent capitalism – and unleash a wave of innovation and growth, *Harvard Business Review Reprint R1101C*, Harvard Business Publishing

Ready, R and Burton, K (2004) *Neuro Linguistic Programming for Dummies* John Wiley & Sons, London

Rheingold, H (2003) *Smart Mobs: The next social revolution*, Perseus Books, Cambridge, MA

Risner, N (2003) *It's a Zoo Around Here*, Limitless Publications

Riso, D and Hudson, R (2000) *Understanding the Enneagram*, Enneagram Institute: wwwenneagraminstitutecom/

Roche, R and Commins, S (ed) *Pioneering Studies in Cognitive Neuroscience* (Maidenhead, 2009), Chapter 2: 'The Malleable Brain: Neuroplasticity in the motor system', 19–32

Rohm, R (1993) *Positive Personality Profiles*, Personality Insights Inc

Rosenberg, MB (2003) *Nonviolent Communication: A language of life*, Puddle Dancer Press, California

Santorelli, S (2000) *Heal Thy Self*, Crown Publications, New York

Schultz, W (1997) Dopamine neurons and their role in reward mechanisms, *Curr Opin Neurobiol*, 7, 191–97

Schutz, W (1997) *FIRO-B*, Consulting Psychologists Press

Seeger, C (2012) *Investing in Meaning: An alternative approach to leveraging your portfolio*, Completely Novel, London

Semler, R (2001) *Maverick*, Random House, London

Shazer, S de (1988) *More Than Miracles: The state of the art of solution-focused brief therapy* (Haworth Brief Therapy), Routledge, London

Stayer, R (Nov–Dec 1990) How I learned to let workers lead, *Harvard Business Review Reprint 90610*, Harvard Business Publishing

Stein, SJ and Book HE (2011) *The EQ Edge, Emotional Intelligence and your Success*, John Wiley

Steiner, C (1990) *Scripts People Live: Transactional analysis of life scripts*, Grove Press, New York

Stewart, I and Joines, V (2012) *TA Today: A New Introduction to Transactional Analysis*, Lifespace Publishing, Nottingham

Strogatz, S (2004) *Sync: The Emerging Science of Spontaneous Order*, Penguin, New York

Subramaniam, Karuna, Kounios, John, Parrish, Todd B, Jung-Beeman, Mark (1 March 2009) A brain mechanism for facilitation of insight by positive affect, *Journal of Cognitive Neuroscience*, 21 (3), 415–32 Doi: 101162/jocn200921057

Tarcher, Jp

Thomas K and Kilmann, R, online, available at: www.kilmann.com [accessed 2012]

Wagner, A (1996) *The Transactional Manager: How to solve people problems with Transactional Analysis*, The Industrial Society, London

Watts, DJ (2003) *Small Worlds: The dynamics of networks between order and randomness (Princeton Studies in Complexity)*, Princeton University Press, Princeton

Watts, DJ (2004) *Six Degrees: The Science of a Connected Age*, Vintage, London

Whitmore, D (2004) *Psychosynthesis in Action*, Sage, London

Whitmore, Sir J (2009) *Coaching for Performance*, Brealey, London

Wildflower, L (2013) *The Hidden History of Coaching*, Open University Press, Maidenhead

Wilson, C (forthcoming) *The Life and Work of David Grove: Clean Language and Emergent Knowledge in coaching and business*

Woollams, S and Brown, M (1979) *The Total Handbook Of Transactional Analysis*, Prentice Hall, Englewood Cliffs, NJ

Zaltman, G (2008) *Marketing Metaphoria*, Harvard Business School Press, Harvard

Websites

www.cleancoaching.com
www.cleanlanguage.co.uk
www.coachingcultureatwork.com
www.kilmann.com
www.interstrength.com
www.beingmindful.net
www.truepotential.co.uk (mindfulness based training for coaches)
www.bangor.ac.uk (professional training for mindfulness instructors)
www.myersbriggs.org
www.performancecoachtraining.com
www.timetothink.com

INDEX

NB: page numbers in *italic* indicate figures or tables

360-degree feedback 253–57, *254*
   alternatives to 257
   pitfalls of 255
   process of 253–55
   results, managing the 255–57

'action' 8
actions 178–83
   and the GROW model *178*, 178–79
   reviewing 181–83, *182*
   setting *179*, 179–81
active listening 131
anchoring 235, 239
animal types 364–65
Appreciative Enquiry 310–17
   case studies 314–17
   Design 312
   Destiny 313
   Discovery 311
   Dream 312
   origins of 310–11
archetypes 332
Art of War, The 316
Assagioli, Robert 216
Association for Coaching (AC) 16, 115,
            122, 173
attentive listening 130–31
'awareness' 4, 6

Bachini, Christina 358–62
Bandler, Richard 228, *see also* neuro-
          linguistic programming (NLP)
Bar-On EQ-i assessment 100, 258–63
   case study 261–63
   elements of 259
   history of 258–59
   validity indicators 259–60
Bar-On, Reuven 258, *see also* Bar-On EQ-i
      assessment
Barratt, Richard 286, 287, 290, *see also*
      Cultural Transformation Tools
      (CTT)
Barron, William 18

BBC
   Clean Language 197–98, 209–13
   coach training at 54–55
   Emergent Knowledge 209–13
'befriending meditation' 324
Belbin, Meredith 363
   Belbin's team role inventory 363
Berne, Eric 248–49, 250, *see also*
          Transactional Analysis
'blame free' 7, 39–40
Blanchard, Ken 163, 275, 278, *see also*
          Situational Leadership
Body Shop 89
Bostic St Clair, Carmen 228
Bouch, Amanda 344–46
Branson, Richard 19, 21, 41, 164, 284,
          see also Virgin
Bresser, Frank 23
Buffet, Warren 40
bullying 95–102
   case studies 97, 99–100
   coping with being bullied 100–02
   overt vs covert bullying 98–99
   'psychopathic brains' study 96–97
Burt, Stephen 22

calibration 231
Carnegie, Dale 5, 129
Carroll, Lewis 162
Casson, John 247
Castellino, Mariette 237
'challenge' 8
Change Curve model 325–26, *326*
Citigroup 88
clarifying 136
Clean Language 133, 141, 187–200,
          237, 239
   case study 197–98, 209–13
   clean conversations 193–94
   history and principles 187, 193
   metaphor 188–89
   questions in 190
   research into 200

traumatic experiences 189–90
using in coaching 194–97
Clean Space 193, 202–03
CLM 2012 Olympic Delivery Partner
        60–61
coach training 52–56
    case studies 54–56
'coachable moments' 50–51
coaching 11–12
    clean coaching 17
    client, satisfying the 18–23
    coaching-mentoring-management
        continuum 23, 23–24
    origins of term 4–7
    principles of 6–8, 7
        action 8
        awareness 4, 6
        blame free 7
        challenge 8
        responsibility 4, 7
        self-belief 7
        self-directed learning 8
        solution focus 7–8
        trust 8
    vs consultancy 14
    vs counselling 13
    vs mentoring 13, 14–15, 17
    vs therapy 12–13
coaching contract, the 173–74
'coaching culture' 35–46
    blame free 39–40
    creating a 41, 42–45
        buy-in 43
        case study 46
        evaluation 45
        measurement 44–45
        momentum 45
        organizational health check 42
        pilot programme 45
        roll-out 45
        stakeholders 42–43, 44
        starting 43
        vision and purpose 42
    natural coaching leaders 40–41
    responsibility 38
    self-belief 38–39
    at Virgin 35–37
Coaching for Performance 6, 150
coaching sessions 174–77
    final sessions 175, 177
    first session 175–77
    transitional sessions 175, 177
coaching supervision 108–16
    benefits of 113
    defining 'supervision' 108–09

qualifications needed 116
sessions
    content of 113–15
    frequency of 116
    type of 115–16
in the workplace 110, 110–13
'coaching up' 48, 101
consultancy 14
Cooper, Lynne 235–38
Cooperrider, David 310, see also
            Appreciative Inquiry
corporate social responsibility (CSR)
        86–94
    business benefits 88–89
    defining 86–87
    shared value 89–91
    social enterprises 91–94
counselling 13
Crisis at Christmas 82, 83–85
cultural differences 65–73
    case studies 69–73
    within teams 67–68
Cultural Leadership Programme (CLP)
        61–63
Cultural Transformation Tools 120, 257,
        286–93
    case study 291–93
    'Seven Levels of Consciousness' model
        286–87, 287
    values, identifying 287–90, 289, 290

Dalai Lama 5
Daly, Michael 314–17
de Jong, Allard 63–64
DeLozier, Judith 228
de Shazer, Steve 4, 313
Dilts, Robert 228, 239
'directionality' 5
DISC 347–53
    case study 350–53
    conscientiousness 349
    dominance 348
    influence 348
    steadiness 348
    vs archetypes and MBTI 349, 349

Emergent Knowledge 22, 193, 201–15, 239
    case studies 209–15
    Clean Space 193, 202–03
    'Emergence' 204–05
    principles of 203, 203–04
    processes 206–09, 208–09
    small world networks 205–06
emotional intelligence 59, 104
Emotional Intelligence 258

Emotions of Normal People 347
English Schools Foundation (ESF) 79,
     80–81
Enneagram 338–41, *339, 340*
     history of 338
     primary and lesser types 341
     values vs traits 339
EQ-360 260
EQ-i:YV 260
Erickson, Milton 4, 313
Ernst, Franklyn 250–52
Esalen Institute 6
EXACT model 155–62, *156*, 176
     case study 159–61
     goal setting 158–61
     vs SMART 156–58, *157*
*Experiential Learning: Experience as
     the Source of Learning and
     Development* 342
Experiential Learning Theory (ELT) 342

Fallon, James 26, 96–97
feedback models 163–72
     feedback guidelines 169–72, *170*
          appropriate 172
          invited 172
          personal 171
          positive 171–72
          self-directed 172
          specific 170–71
     feedback 'sandwich' 164
     and the GROW model 165–69
     praise, using 163–64
     self-feedback 164–65
FEEL model 322, *323*
Female Eunuch, The 5
Finney, David 17
FIRO-B 364
'forming, storming, norming and
          performing' model 327–31, *328*
     adjourning 328, 331
     dorming 328
     forming 329
     mourning 328
     norming 330
     performing 331
     storming 330
Freud, Sigmund 3
functional magnetic resonance imaging
          (fMRI) 30

Gallwey, Tim 5–6, 74, 151, 292, 294–96,
          297, *see also* Inner Game, the
Games People Play 5, 248
Gandhi, Mohandas 283

Gestalt therapy 4, 232
Goleman, Daniel 59, 258
Gordon, Tony 83
Gould, Jenny 17
Greenfield, Susan 366
Grinder, John 228, *see also* neuro-linguistic
          programming (NLP)
Grove, David 22, 133, 141, 237, *see also*
          Clean Language; Emergent
          Knowledge
GROW model 48, 114, *118*, 118–19, *149*,
          149–54
     flexibility of 154
     goal 150
     history of 149–50
     options 152–53
     reality 151–52
     will 153
Gutsell, Mandy 245–47

Häagen-Dazs 88
Hall, Liz 321–24
Harris, Thomas 250
Hawkins, Peter and Shohet, Robin 110
Hersey, Paul 275, 278, *see also* Situational
          Leadership
Higgins, Steve 367
How to Win Friends and Influence People 5
Howard-Jones, Paul 366

I'm OK, You're OK 250
IKEA 55–56
Incisive Question 305–06
Inner Game of Tennis, The 296
Inner Game of Work, The 296, 301
Inner Game, the 294–301
     case studies 296, 298–301
     critical variables 299
     inner opponent, the 294–95
     non-judgemental awareness 323
     self-directed learning 323
     Work Triangle 296, *296–97*
Insights Discovery model 72
Investing in Meaning 30

Jay, Anthony 257
Jiang, Niran and Feher, Alex 291–93
Johari Window 354–62
     BLIND 355
     case study 358–62
     HIDDEN 355
     negative feedback, managing 355–56
     OPEN 355
     proportions of quadrants 356–57, *357*
     UNKNOWN 355

Johnson and Johnson 91
judgemental questions 139–40
Jung, Carl 3, 189, 194–95, 332, *see also*
    Myers-Briggs Type Indicator
    (MBTI)
Jung-Beeman, Mark 30

Kerr, Fiona 350–53
Kline, Nancy 48, 109, 115, 133, 142, 295,
    302, *see also* Thinking Environ-
    ment
Kolb, David 342–43, 363, *see also* Kolb's
    learning styles
Kolb's learning styles 114–15, 342–46
    case study 344–46
    preferences 343–44
    quadrants 342–43
Kouzes, Jim and Posner, Barry 282, *see also*
    Leadership Challenge model
Kubler Ross, Elizabeth 325, *see also* Change
    Curve model

Law, Andy 5, 41
Lawley, James 201
Leaders Quest 91–92
Leadership Challenge model 282–85, *283*
    challenging 284
    enabling 284
    encouraging 284–85
    inspiring 284
    modelling 283–84
leadership coaching 57–64
    case studies 60–64
    leadership traits 57–58
    skills vs attitudes 59, 59–60
leading questions 140–42
'life coaching', use of term 8
listening 129–33, 306–07
    active listening 131
    advising 130
    attentive listening 130–31
    hijacking 130
    interrupting 129
    non-verbal signals 132–33
logical levels 239
'loving kindness meditation' 324
Luft, Joseph and Ingham, Harry 354,
    see also Johari Window
Lyall, Deni 239–40

Macann, Liz 54, 55, 111, 198, 210
Marks & Spencer 87
Marston, William Moulton 347,
    see also DISC
Maslow, Abraham 3, *4*, 216, 286, 310

McCarthy, Ruth 307–09
Men are from Mars, Women are from
    Venus 5
mentoring 13, 14–15, 17
mindfulness 318–24
    case study 321–24
    in conflict 320
    FEEL model 322, *323*
    history of 318
    questions 320–21
    relaxation and meditation 319
    in yoga 319–20
Ministry of Entrepreneurship (MOE)
    Foundation 81, 82, 91,
    92–94, 117
multitasking 31–32
Murdoch, Edna 22
Myers, Isabel and Briggs, Katherine 333,
    see also Myers-Briggs Type
    Indicator (MBTI)
Myers-Briggs Type Indicator (MBTI)
    332–37
    16 personality types 333–34, *334*
    archetypes 332
    case study 336–37
    Extraversion-Introversion (E-I) 333,
        334–35
    Judging-Perceiving (J-P) 333
    and self-limitation 335
    Sensing-Intuition (S-N) 333
    Thinking-Feeling (T-F) 333
    vs DISC 349, *349*

Nelson, Bob 163, 285
Nestlé 91
neuro-linguistic programming (NLP)
    228–40
    anchoring 235, 239
    calibration 231
    logical levels 239
    meta model 229, *229*
    mirroring and matching 230
    New Code NLP 228
    origins of term 228–29
    perceptual positions 232–35
        case studies 235–38
    submodalities 232
    timeline 239
    visual, auditory and kinaesthetic (VAK)
        230–31
neuroscience 28–32
    and bullying 28, 95–98
    and goal-setting 28–29
    and insights 30–31
    and learning 30

neuroscience (*continued*)
    and multitasking 31–32
    'neuroplasticity' 98
    and positivity 29–30
New Code NLP 228
non-verbal signals 132–33
Non-Violent Communication 272–74, *273*
    compromise 273–74
    conflict 272–73

OFGEM 122–26
OK Corral *250*, 250–52, *251*
One Minute Manager, The 163, 278
open and closed questions 139

Perls, Fritz 3, 4, 228, 232, 310, *see also*
        Gestalt therapy
permission, asking 144–48
    and control 147–48, *148*
    permission as a tool 144–45
    protocol *145*, 145–47
Pickin, Carolyn 336–37
Plato 11
Porter, Michael and Kramer, Mark 89–90
psychiatry 12
psychology 13
'psychopathic brains' study 96–97
Psychosynthesis 216
psychotherapy 13

questioning 138–43
    judgemental questions 139–40
    leading questions 140–42
    multiple questions 142
    open and closed questions 139
    silence, using 142–43

reflecting 135
resilience 103–07
    defining 103–04
    developing 106–07
    in leaders 104–05
    in organizations 105–06, *106*
'responsibility' 4, 7, 38
Risner, Nigel 364–65
Robson, Darren 261–63
Roddick, Anita 89
Rogers, Barry 72–73, 367
ROI of coaching, measuring the 117–26
    case study 122–26
    feedback *121*, 121–22
    planning measurement 118–19
    research *122*, 122
    surveys 119–20, *120*
Rosenberg, Marshall 272, *see also*
        Non-Violent Communication

Salesforce.com 87
schools, coaching in 74–82
    case studies 76–82
Schutz, William 364
Seeger, Clare 30
'self-actualization' 3
'self-belief' 7, 38–39
'self-directed learning' 8
self-limiting beliefs 25–27
    challenging 26–27
Semler, Ricardo 5, 40–41
Seven Eyed Model 110, *111*
'Seven Levels of Consciousness' model
        286–87, *287*
shared value 89–91
silence, using 142–43
Silverthorne, Graham 75–79, 82
Situational Leadership 275–81
    case study 278–81
    and coaching 277–78
    history of 275–76, *276*
    revised quadrants 276–77
SMART goals 156–58, *157*, 176
social enterprises 91–94
Socrates 1, 12
'solution focus' 7–8
solution focused brief therapy
        (SFBT) 4
Somers, Matt 298–301
Sony 88
South East Coaching and Mentoring
        Network 46
speed coaching 51
Stayer, Ralph 41
submodalities 232
Sugar, Alan 20
Sugawara, Paula 278–81
summarizing 135–36
Supervision Steering Group 109
Systemic Coaching 241–47
    case study 245–47
    childhood behaviour, impact of
        242–43
    in organizations 243–44
    patterns and change 241–42
    and systems theory 244

Taylor, Denise 269–71
therapy 12–13
Thinking Environment 302–09
    case study 307–09
    components of *303*, 303–04
    Incisive Question 305–06
    listening, importance of 306–07
    origins of 302
    Thinking Session, the 304–05

Thomas, Kenneth and Kilmann, Ralph
    264, *see also* Thomas-Kilmann
    Conflict Mode Instrument (TKI)
Thomas-Kilmann Conflict Mode Instrument
    (TKI) 264–71
  accommodating 265
  avoiding 265
  case study 269–71
  collaborating 265–66
  competing 264–65
  compromising 266
  healthy vs unhealthy conflict 268–69
  pitfalls of 267–68
  process of 266–67
Timberland 87
Time to Think 48
Tompkins, Penny 201
Transactional Analysis 248–52
  and change 249–50
  defining 'transactions' 248
  OK Corral *250*, 250–52, *251*
  parent, child and adult states
    248–49
Transpersonal Coaching 216–27
  case study 217–27
  sub-personalities 216–17
Treanor, Benita 112
'trust' 8

Tuckman, Bruce 328, *see also* 'forming,
    storming, norming and
    performing' model
Tzu, Sun 316

Virgin 34, 35–39, 164, 268, 284
visual, auditory and kinaesthetic (VAK)
    230–31
von Bertalanffy, Ludwig 244

Walker, Caitlin 198–200
Whitmore, John 4, 6, 83, 150, 216, 217–27,
    291, 296, 364
Work Triangle 296, 296–97
workplace coaching 47–56
  coach training 52–56
    case studies 54–56
  'coachable moments' 50–51
  'coaching up' 48, 101
  internal vs external coaching 49–50
  speed coaching 51

You Get What You Reward 163
'Youth at Risk' 83

*Zen and the Art of Motorcycle
    Maintenance* 5

CPSIA information can be obtained at www.ICGtesting.com
Printed in the USA
LVOW10s2241050514

384571LV00004B/30/P